T0330298

Africa-centred Knowledges

Africa-centred Knowledges
Crossing Fields
& Worlds

Edited by
Brenda Cooper
& Robert Morrell

Foreword by Crain Soudien

JAMES CURREY

James Currey
an imprint of
Boydell & Brewer Ltd
PO Box 9, Woodbridge,
Suffolk IP12 3DF (GB)
www.jamescurrey.com

and of

Boydell & Brewer Inc.
668 Mt Hope Avenue
Rochester, NY 14620-2731 (US)
www.boydellandbrewer.com

British Library Cataloguing in Publication Data
A catalogue record for this book is available on request

ISBN 978-1-84701-095-7 James Currey (Cloth)

This publication is printed on acid-free paper

Typeset in 11/13 pt Photina MT by Kate Kirkwood

Contents

List of Figures

Notes on Contributors

Akosua Adomako Ampofo is Professor of African and Gender Studies, and Director of the Institute of African Studies at the University of Ghana. Her research, teaching and civil interests address African knowledge systems; race and identity politics; gender-based expressions of violence; constructions of masculinities; women and work; and representations of women in popular music. She was awarded the 2010 Sociologists for Women in Society Feminist Activism award, and was a Fulbright New Century Scholar from 2004 to 2005. Adomako Ampofo's recent publications include: 'Changing representations of women in Ghanaian popular music: Marrying research and advocacy' *Current Sociology* (2012, with Awo Asiedu); 'Phallic competence: Fatherhood and the making of men in Ghana' in *Culture, Societies and Masculinities* (2009, 1 (1): 59-78) with Michael PK Okyerefo and Michael Pervarah). She co-edited with Signe Arnfred the book *African Feminist Politics of Knowledge: Tensions, Challenges, Possibilities* (Uppsala: Nordic Africa Institute, 2010). Adomako Ampofo is co-editor of *Ghana Studies* with Stephan Miescher (from the University of California, Santa Barbara).

Signe Arnfred is Associate Professor in the Department of Society and Globalization and Centre for Gender, Power and Diversity at Roskilde University in Denmark. She is an anthropologist with a particular interest in Africa, and especially in Mozambique where she has researched for 30 years. She is the author of *Sexuality and Gender Politics in Mozambique: Rethinking Gender in Africa* (2011), editor of *Re-thinking Sexualities in Africa* (2004), and co-editor, with Akosua Adomako Ampofo, of *African Feminist Politics of Knowledge: Tensions, Challenges, Possibilities* (2010). All these titles are from the Nordic Africa Institue, in Uppsala, Sweden, of which she was programme coordinator from 2000 to 2009.

Bill Ashcroft is Professorial Fellow in the School of English, Media and Performing Arts, at the University of New South Wales in Australia. He was a founding exponent of post-colonial theory, and co-author with Gareth Griffiths and Helen Tiffin of *The Empire Writes Back*, (1989, 2002) the first text to examine the field of post-colonial studies systematically. He is the author or co-author of 16 books, variously translated into five languages, Including *Post-Colonial Transformation* (2001), *Post-Colonial Futures* (2001), *Caliban's Voice* (2008) and *Intimate Horizons* (2009; all published by Routledge). He has written over 150 chapters in books and papers in journals, and he is on the editorial board of ten international journals.

Edwin Blake is Professor of Computer Science at the University of Cape Town. He obtained his PhD in 1989 at Queen Mary University of London. His research has almost always covered human-computer inter-action, and related fields such as computer graphics, visualization and virtual reality, ICT policy, the use of information technology for socio-economic development, and (what is known as) socially-aware software engineering. He is currently working collaboratively with researchers in Namibia.

Brenda Cooper was for many years the Director of the Centre for African Studies and a Professor in the English department at the University of Cape Town, where she is now an Emeritus Professor. In 2009, she moved to Salford, where she is an Honorary Research Associate at the University of Manchester and runs *Burnish*, a company which organizes workshops on academic-research productivity. She has published widely on African fiction and postcolonial literary theory. Her book of memoir, art and literature, *Floating in an Antibubble from South Africa to Salford*, is forthcoming from Africa World Press.

Linda Cooper is Associate Professor in the School of Education at the University of Cape Town. She teaches in the field of adult education, and is involved in initiatives to broaden access to university education for adult learners. She has published on the history and contemporary practice of worker education in South Africa; the impact of globalization on work and learning, particularly in the geopolitical South; the recognition of prior learning; and on the relationship between knowledge and power across different institutional contexts. Her recent publications include a book co-edited with Shirley Walters, *Learning/Work: Turning Work and Lifelong Learning Inside Out* (Cape Town: HRSC Press, 2009), and an article entitled 'Activists within the academy: The role of prior experience in adult learners' acquisition of postgraduate literacies in a post-apartheid South African university' in *Adult Education Quarterly*, (2011, 61 (1): 40-56).

Ariane de Lannoy is a Senior Researcher at the Children's Institute, and a Lecturer at the Department of Sociology at the University of Cape Town. Most of her work is aimed at the understanding of young adults' lives, choices and interactions with both their local and global environments. Her PhD focused on educational decision-making among youth in the context of the dramatic levels of HIV and AIDS prevalence in South Africa. She currently manages a longitudinal ethnographic study with young adults that involves collaboration with Dean Newman of the Krieger School of Arts and Sciences at Johns Hopkins University. The project is known as 'Twenty Years of Freedom', and it examines the views of young people on the opportunities available to them in post-apartheid South Africa.

Robert V. H. Dover is Associate Professor of Anthropology at the Universidad de Antioquia in Medellín, Colombia. Most of his research has been conducted among indigenous communities in Canada and Colombia. More recently, he has focused his work on the coexistence of state and alternative jurisprudences, the politics and mechanisms of community participation, as well as stakeholders' rights in the Colombian health care system. This research has resulted in the co-authored book, *El Derecho a la Salud: Participación en el Régimen Subsidiado de Salud* (The Right to Health Care: Participation in the Subsidized Health-care Sector), which proposes a methodology for stakeholder empowerment in the context of the differentiated citizenships imposed on vulnerable populations.

Lesley Green is Associate Professor of Anthropology in the School of African and Gender Studies, Anthropology and Linguistics at the University of Cape Town, where she heads the Environmental Humanities Initiative. She is the editor of *Contested Ecologies: Dialogues in the South on Nature and Knowledge* (Cape Town: HSRC Press, 2013) and the author, with David Green, of *Knowing the Day, Knowing the World: Engaging Amerindian Thought in Public Archaeology* (Tucson AZ: University of Arizona Press, 2013).

Astrid Jarre is a marine-systems ecologist, and holds the position of South African Research Chair in Marine Ecology and Fisheries at University of Cape Town's Marine Research Institute. Her keen interest in fisheries management opened up research positions at the International Center for Living Aquatic Resources Management in Manila, Philippines (now World Fish Center, Penang, Malaysia) and the Danish government's laboratory for fisheries. From here, she moved to South Africa. Professor Jarre has served on the Scientific Steering Committee of the Global Oceans Ecosystems Dynamics Programme (GLOBEC) and was a member of its Working Group on Human Dimensions. Inspired by multidisciplinary research into fisheries management in Denmark, and the interdisciplinary Canadian 'Coasts under Stress' programme, she works with colleagues in the humanities and social sciences to further interdisciplinary research into marine social-ecological systems undergoing global change, and focuses particularly on the Benguela Current.

Lansana Keita has taught philosophy and economics at institutions such as the University of Ibadan in Nigeria, Fourah Bay College in Sierra Leone, and the University of the Gambia, where he is Professor of Economics and Philosophy. He has published numerous articles in the areas of economic theory, philosophy of science, evolutionary anthropology, and general epistemology. He is also the author of *Science, Rationality, and Neoclassical Economics* (1992), *The Human Project and the Temptations of Science* (1998), and editor of *Philosophy and African Development: Theory and Practice* (2011) (all from African Books Collective).

Leadus Madzima is a postdoctoral fellow at Rhodes University in Grahamstown, South Africa, researching indigenous knowledge practices and African identities. She is a Zimbabwean by birth and holds a Doctor of Philosophy in Education obtained at the University of Cape Town (2010). She also has a Master's Degree in Education Psychology (London), a Post Graduate Certificate in Education (London) and an Honours Degree in English (London) all obtained through the University of Zimbabwe. She was the principal of two girls' High Schools in Harare, Zimbabwe for ten years before entering the world of regional and international management consultancy in developing contexts. She is concerned to facilitate the production and equitable distribution of relevant knowledge especially to diverse and marginalized communities.

Gary Marsden was Professor of Computer Science at the University of Cape Town, and Director of the university's ICT4D research centre and the UCT–Hasso Plattner Research School. His research interest was in mobile-interaction design and information and communication technology for development. He won the 2007 ACM SIGCHI Social Responsiveness award for his research on using mobile technology in the developing world. In 2006 he co-authored with Matt Jones *Mobile Interaction Design* (Hoboken NJ: Wiley). Shortly after Christmas in 2013, Gary Marsden tragically died of a heart attack. He is survived by his wife and two children.

Robert Morrell is Co-ordinator of the Programme for the Enhancement of Research Capacity at the University of Cape Town. Since the early 1990s, he has been researching gender in Africa and Southern Africa, focusing specifically on men and masculinities. His edited works include *Changing Men in Southern Africa* (Pietermartizburg: University of Natal Press/London: Zed Press, 2001), with Lahoucine Ouzgane: *African Masculinities* (London: Palgrave Macmillan, 2005), and with Linda Richter: *Baba: Men and Fatherhood in South Africa* (Cape Town: HSRC Press, 2006). Robert Morrell is currently working with Rachel Jewkes of the Medical Research Council on issues of gender, poverty, AIDS and violence.

Marieke Norton is currently a PhD candidate in Social Anthropology at the University of Cape Town, doing interdisciplinary work on marine resource law enforcement in the fisheries of the Western Cape, South Africa. Her project seeks to investigate marine compliance inspectors at the interface between the State and public fishing rights. She has been working in the field of marine fisheries for a number of years, having done her Master's research on the implementation process of marine resource regulations on small-scale fishers in Arniston on the Cape South Coast.

Michael PK Okyerefo is a Catholic priest who holds a BA Hons from the University of Ghana, an M.Phil. and D.Phil. from the University of Vienna, and a PGCE from the University of Cambridge. He is a Senior Lecturer in the Department of Sociology, University of Ghana. His core research is on two general areas of sociological enquiry: cultural sociology and sociology of religion. He was a Visiting Fellow at the University of Cambridge, Centre of African Studies, in 2007 and 2008. Currently, he is Principal Investigator in a research project on the religious and health beliefs and practices of prayer-group members in Achimota Forest. His recent published work includes 'Pentecostalism in the City of Accra: A blossom on functional appeal and urban fecundity' *American Journal of Sociological Research* (2011, (1): 27-34), and 'Christianising Africa: A Portrait by two African novelists' *Studies in World Christianity*, (2010, 16 (1): 63-81).

Barbara Paterson grew up in Germany, obtaining a Masters degree in Linguistics, Philosophy and Computer Science from Aachen University in 1995. She now lives in Namibia. Her doctoral research at the Animal Demography Unit of the University of Cape Town explored the interstices between information technology, nature conservation and ethics, against the background of a post-colonial society in which the deficits of the past constrain the impact of technological interventions. After obtaining her PhD in 2005, Barbara Paterson worked as a postdoctoral fellow of the University of Cape Town and of Memorial University of Newfoundland and Labrador. She is currently a research associate of the University of Cape Town's Marine Research Institute, where she examines the ethical and epistemological implications of mathematical approaches to social-ecological contexts, and is helping to develop interdisciplinary methodologies to support an ecosystem-approach to fisheries management in Namibia and South Africa.

Ulrike Rivett is an Associate Professor in the Department of Civil Engineering at the University of Cape Town, South Africa. She leads the iCOMMS Research Team (www.icomms.org), which focuses on developing mobile infrastructure with the aim of improving service delivery in rural and under-resourced communities in relation to fields such as e-health and water-quality monitoring. To date, the team has contributed to theories of data collection, and has improved understandings of the impact of local contexts on the success of information systems.

Warren Smit is a Researcher and Co-ordinator of the Healthy Cities CityLab research programme at the African Centre for Cities, which is an interdisciplinary urban-research institute at the University of Cape Town. He has been engaged in research on urban issues in South Africa since 1993, mainly for non-governmental organizations. His background is in urban planning, and one of his areas of interest is the intersection between urban planning and human health, in relation to how healthier urban environments can be created. Warren Smit was the lead writer for the urban planning/design working group of the Global Research Network on Urban Health Equity.

Lucia Thesen is a Senior Lecturer in the Centre for Higher Education Development at the University of Cape Town. Since the 1980s, she has been working at the intersection of the politics of writing and access for students on the margins of the university. From her position as coordinator of postgraduate writing development, she is committed to debating and interrogating the current forms in which research is communicated in writing in the English language. She has published widely and co-edited two books, the first with Ermien van Pletzen, *Academic Literacy and the Languages of Change* (London and New York: Continuum, 2006) and *Postgraduate Writing, Risk and the Making of New Knowledge* (Bristol: Multilingual Matters, 2013).

Mbugua wa Mungai is Senior Lecturer and Chair of the Literature Department at Kenyatta University in Nairobi, Kenya. He completed his PhD at the Hebrew University of Jerusalem on *matatu* (taxi) culture in Nairobi. His research interests are popular culture, Kenyan urban folklore and disability in culture. He has written book chapters and journal articles on various aspects of Kenyan popular culture, especially on signification in material culture. Within these research interests, he has recently focused on the nature and place of masculinity in the same context. To this end, he was a Fulbright scholar at the Center for Folklore Studies, Ohio State University in 2008 and 2009.

Vanessa Watson is Professor in the School of Architecture, Planning and Geomatics at the University of Cape Town in South Africa. She is also Deputy Dean of the Faculty of Engineering and the Built Environment, and a founder of the African Centre for Cities. Her research is focussed on planning in a global context, and on developing these ideas from the perspective of the global South. She is an editor for *Planning Theory* and on the editorial boards of *Planning Practice and Research*, *Progress in Planning* and the *Journal of Planning Education and Research*. She is co-ordinator of the Association of African Planning Schools, and represents them on the Global Planning Education Association Network, which she has also chaired and co-chaired.

Foreword
The Power of Knowing
Crain Soudien

There are many deeply evocative contributions in this collection of readings brought together by my colleagues Robert Morrell and Brenda Cooper. One that struck me intensely was Cooper's reference to Haraway's injunction that we have 'to design classification systems that do not foreclose on rearrangements suggested by new forms of social and natural knowledge' (quoted in Chapter 5, this volume). How we do this, given the grip that our epistemic orders have on our political, social and cultural imaginations, is a fundamentally ethical question. It is so for those of us who presume to have achieved, through our epistemes, the power to place, analyse and evaluate all that we have known, know now, and will need to know in the future. It is so for those of us who argue that we never have to explain the innermost articulations of how things work in the close confines of our own immediate universe. Reflected in the first instance is the conceit of method – of 'powerful knowledge' structured around procedures capable of the most sophisticated forms of deconstruction now known. Evident in the second instance is the conceit of ineffability – of communication of the *sacred* being reserved only for the chosen few.

What makes the challenge this book presents to us so intensely ethical is the fact of our co-existence and co-dependence. What we know, and how we give practical expression to it in the decisions we make, is no longer a question which affects just us – *our* people, however the idea of *our* people is constituted. The likelihood now is that most decisions we make, including those that we imagine concern only ourselves, will in one form or another and to one degree or another, have repercussions outside of the intimacy of our immediate selves.

The significance of this epistemic challenge is that we have to come to a sense of what the obligations of our knowledge are to each other. This is, at one level, a matter of sharing what we know, or the democratization of knowledge. But, at another level, and this is always going to be contro-versial, it is the development of an awareness of how much our stores of understanding are no longer being put out and received on their own ethno-, religio-, class-, or cultural-centric terms, anywhere. We are in a situation *now*, and this is important to understand, where we can no longer present ourselves to each other without explanation. We need civilizational procedures for how to deal with ourselves in each other's presence. Given how badly we have managed this challenge of being alongside of and in relation to each other in the past, our utter failure to appreciate our complex capacities, and our inability to see beyond our skins, the task before us is great. But, and this is the incredible learning opportunity before us, nothing can be taken for granted, so we are going to have to come to a much deeper appreciation of each other and of what we know. Hopefully, what comes out of this is both self-affirmation and humility, the affirmation that we bring something different, and the sense that we always have much to learn. In this volume, these important readings grapple with this challenge. That this text emanates primarily from South Africa, that complex child of modernity, with its often unacknowledged and therefore unexamined racialized scientific epistemes, is an extraordinary moment in the sociology of knowledge.

Acknowledgements

Brenda Cooper would like acknowledge her colleagues in the Centre for African Studies at the University of Cape Town in South Africa. In 2005, the Trilateral Reconnection Project was established to foster cooperative intellectual exchange, research and learning, involving the Africana Studies Department at Brown University in the United States; the Centre for Caribbean Thought at the University of the West Indies at Mona; and the Centre for African Studies at the University of Cape Town. Brenda Cooper, with Nick Shepherd, Harry Garuba, Tony Bogues, Geri Augusto and others from these institutions, developed the 'Knowledge Project' as the intellectual focus for cross disciplinary, tri-continental conversations within the teaching and researching of Africa and elsewhere. Without their contributions, the Africa Knowledge Project, which in 2009 became an integral part of the Programme for the Enhancement of Research Capacity (PERC) in the Research Office of the University of Cape Town, would not have been possible.

The Africa Knowledge Project in PERC was strongly supported by the Carnegie Corporation of New York, which, in 2009, awarded the University of Cape Town a grant to contribute to the transformation of knowledge at the institution. Some of these funds were made available to the Africa Knowledge Project and we gratefully acknowledge this support.

Since 2010, Robert Morrell has coordinated PERC, and in this position partnered Brenda Cooper in compiling this collection. The production process included hosting a workshop in 2011 near Cape Town, where potential contributors gathered to brainstorm ideas and refine themes. It is in the nature of putting a collection together that some people are put to labour that is ultimately invisible in the final published volume. We would like to thank those whose ideas contributed to this collection even though they do not appear among the list of contributors: Afe Adogame, Lillian Artz, Mignonne Breier, Carlos Cardoso, Raewyn Connell, Jeanne Flavin, Gabriela Glattstein-Young, Yonina Hoffman-

Wanderer, Leslie London, Elísio Macamo, Charles Masango, Selvan Naidoo and Maria Stuttaford.

We would also like to thank commissioning editor at James Currey, Jaqueline Mitchell, for her patience and support. Before publication, the manuscript was blind reviewed twice – a process that generated a demand for extensive revisions and resulted in a slimmed down and tighter volume.

We would like to thank the South African National Research Foundation and the Research Office at the University of Cape Town for their contribution to the funding of this project. The staff of the Research Office, as well as the University of Cape Town's Deputy Vice Chancellors, Crain Soudien and Danie Visser, and Executive Director (Research), Marilet Sienaert, were unflinching supporters of the project throughout. Mary Ralphs was a wonderfully diligent copy-editor. Paul Weinberg helped with the cover photograph.

Robert would like to remember his father, Richard Frost Morrell, for the gift of his insatiable curiosity, and his gracious wife, Monica Fairall, who grew up speaking isiZulu and loving people. For their constant presence, he would like to thank his mother, Bridget Kathleen Forsyth Thompson whose African roots began in Kampala; his siblings, Christopher and Penny, who together trod the path through childhood that stretched from Cape Town to Swaziland; and his daughters, Tamarin and Ashleigh, whose mere existence is a daily joy.

Brenda would like to acknowledge Martin and her children with boundless respect, gratitude and love.

List of Frequently used Acronyms

PCC   Pentecostal and charismatic church
PfA   Beijing Platform for Action
ICT   Information Communication Technologies
ICT4D Information and Communications Technology for
      Development
ICPD International Conference on Population and Development
      (Cairo)
UN   United Nations

Introduction
The Possibility of Africa-centred Knowledges
Brenda Cooper & Robert Morrell

The knowledge focus

In this book we question how knowledge is made in African contexts, as a way of exploring the nature of what we term Africa-centred knowledges. Africa-centred knowledges are predicated on the recognition that Africa is highly diverse but, at the same time, there is a geopolitical and historical unity that continues to underpin it. This requires that we acknowledge the multiplicity of understandings on the continent, which come forward as forms of knowledge, needs and questions. Moving away then from the idea of universal truths and realities, we focus instead on the process by which knowledge is made. In so doing, it becomes clear that we need to understand 'knowledge' as plural. Instead of one knowledge, there are knowledges, and this is a necessary complement to the recognition that Africa is not homogenous or monolithic. Our contexts are political, historical and ontological; our starting point is knowledge itself, and the epistemological question of how we know what we know. In this collection, we aim to raise different aspects of this complex question, rather than bring it to closure with definitive answers.

This brings us to what it is that unifies a book that includes chapters by, among other contributors, literary critics, marine biologists and city planners. It is the focus on knowledge production that enables us to scrutinize concepts, such as those of indigenous knowledge and modernity, alongside issues such as the success rates of pupils living in poverty in a Zimbabwean high school and the fiction of Ben Okri or Helen Oyeyemi. Our authors consciously contribute to what Raewyn Connell has called 'Southern theory', which emphasizes 'relations – authority, exclusion, inclusion, hegemony, partnership, sponsorship, appropriation – between intellectuals and institutions in the metropole and those in the world periphery' (Connell 2007: viii–ix).

All of the chapters are organized around the question of the nature of the knowledge that is produced about their chosen angle on Africa. We say 'chosen angle' advisedly as the book works within a familiar paradox: we cannot generalize about Africa, and yet we must do so. Albeit that African knowledge cannot be generalized, it has been filtered predominantly through the lens of its colonial and postcolonial (including apartheid) pasts, and this makes some continental unities real. Generalization is, moreover, appropriate within the particular terms of this book because the specificity and differences of each of the chapter's concerns are united by their shared scrutiny of codes of meaning-making that lie behind their particular research fields. This guides the outcomes. This is what working at the *meta* level, at the level of epistemology, entails. All of the contributors problematize the assumptions, hypotheses and benchmarks that silently mediate the knowledge outcomes with which they engage. In other words, each chapter demonstrates its own particular struggle over meaning. The substance of the struggle in each chapter is unique, but the battleground in each case is familiar. And within these struggles, the possibility of Africa-centred knowledges emerges. Neither Euro- nor Afrocentric, what are these Africa-centred knowledges?

The meaning of 'Africa-centred': between a bad place and an immoveable rock

This collection is poised in a creative and productive third space between the polarization of the bad place of Eurocentrism and the immoveable rock of Afrocentrism. Africa-centredness is premised on an understanding of the African continent as multiple, global and dynamic. It is a concept that assumes that knowledge, wherever and by whomsoever it is produced, is available for transgressive, emancipatory and counter-hegemonic use, even as it will necessarily be contradictory, contested and fluid. Africa-centredness insists that unless we are aware of our tools and concepts and the politics to which they are linked, we will invariably reproduce old forms of oppressive power and new orthodoxies.

V. Y. Mudimbe deplores the 'dichotomizing system' that is built on 'paradigmatic oppositions' such as 'traditional versus modern; oral versus written and printed; agrarian and customary communities versus urban and industrialized civilization; subsistence economies versus highly productive economies' and so on and on (1988: 4). In opposition to these binaries, Mudimbe evokes 'an intermediate, a diffused space' between these extremes (1988: 4). This is a space, which is hard to pin down; precariously pertinent and dangerously important (1988: 5). It is a 'locus of paradoxes' revealing as it does the fault-lines 'between a modernity that often is an illusion of development, and a tradition that sometimes reflects a poor image of a mythical past' (1988: 5).

We locate Africa-centred knowledges in such an intermediate space, and focus on the processes that give rise to it. We understand the dangers and precariousness of this space. Whereas rocks and hard places are fixed in place and time, this tricky intermediate space is a maelstrom, or, as Achille Mbembe characterizes processes of transition and change in Africa, they do not move 'in a closed orbit'. For Mbembe, these processes

> are neither smooth nor unilinear, but point in several directions at once. Further, they are occurring at different speeds and on different time scales, and take the form of fluctuations and destabilizations (sometimes very sharp ones), periods of inertia and spurts that appear quite random but actually combine several regimes of change: stationary, dynamic, chaotic, even catastrophic. (2001: 66)

Mbembe sums this up in one word, '*entanglement*' (2001: 66). 'Entanglement' is the diametric opposite of binary oppositions. In Mbembe's writing, this everyday word thickens into a theoretical concept designed to capture the complexities, variations within, and unruliness of, knowledges in what he calls the postcolony. 'Entanglement' captures the subjective locked into the objective (2001: 6), time as historical and simultaneously not linear (2001: 66), and it embodies a visceral understanding of privilege and poverty (2001: 106). Africa-centred knowledges are entangled, contextual and contingent.

At the same time, we acknowledge the stubborn and continuing dominance of theory, methodology and research practice originating from Europe and North America. This dominance is what could be termed a bad place. It is a bad place because it perpetuates the legacies of colonialism and of racism; it buttresses privilege, and presents obstacles to education for emancipation and local relevance (Fiske and Ladd 2004; Mamdani 1993; Samoff and Stromquist 2001; Soudien and Corneilse 2000; Wolpe 1995). This is the place in which Mudimbe declares that both Western and African scholars use 'categories and conceptual systems which depend on a Western epistemological order' (Mudimbe 1988: x). He questions, 'what does this mean for the field of African studies?' and in attempting to transform this field, he is (like us) 'directly concerned with the processes of transformation of types of knowledge' (1988: x).

At the same time, it is important not to conflate the use of Northern theory with Eurocentrism. What this collection suggests is that knowledges can become Africa-centred regardless of where they originate. But they do so only when they get entangled in African realities, lexicons and matrices and are shaped by these contexts. This particularly includes conceptions of identity, agency and subjectivity, which emphasize relatedness rather than individuality (Nyamnjoh 2002). Mudimbe himself later defends the fact that 'the idea of Africa' may seem 'too dependent upon Western texts' (1994: 213). What he realizes, however, is that given the world capitalist system of which Africa is obviously a part, it is impossible not to consider Western writing (1994: 213). Going further, those striving to achieve the Millennium Development Goals, for example, are attempting to give priority to development and the problems afflicting millions of people on the planet. Advances in knowledge have, at times, undoubtedly been used to benefit poor and marginal people. The question remains, how to decide which advances best serve the interests of the planet and its people, rather than just a small percentage of those who can afford to pay? Put differently, what forms of knowledge are appropriate to the multiplicity of issues, needs, questions and dilemmas of researchers on Africa – and, more broadly, those working in resource-poor, historically disadvantaged and politically marginal countries?

This optimizing and global view of knowledge sits apart from the immoveable rock that dreams up the notion of a pure, pre-colonial gold mine of African knowledge, and suggests that only nuggets mined from this source may be categorized as African knowledge. For those adopting this approach, being African provides privileged access to a precolonial past (Ntuli). This view makes knowledge an effect of history, location (geographical or racial) and origin, and results in static and essentializing versions of reality, which we term Afrocentric. Our preference for the term Africa-centred suggests the more fluid formulation that Irene Gedalof captures in the title of her book, *Against Purity*. She argues for an approach which acknowledges that identities and knowledge are fluid, and that all social categories are 'impure' (Gedalof: 16). Along the same lines, Mudimbe believes that 'it would be illusionary to look for pure originary and definitively fixed African traditions, even in the precolonial period' (1994: 206). Mudimbe insists on the existence of 'historical and intellectual discontinuities, social ruptures, and political negotiations of African traditions' and concludes that 'discursive formations in Africa ... offer tables of intellectual and epistemological dissensions witnessing to fabulous acculturations (1994: 207).

'Fabulous acculturations' is an evocative phrase. It resonates with ruptures, compromises and negotiations that are not exclusive to, and pre-date, European drives and interests; it insists that tradition, as a source of unmoving and solid indigeneity, is a fabrication. Tradition, as fabulously acculturated, challenges what Mbembe, also critically, calls 'nativism'. 'Nativist currents of thought' claim 'that Africans have an authentic culture that confers on them a peculiar self irreducible to that of any other group' (Mbembe 2002: 254). This results in an emphasis on producing 'endogenous knowledge' which demands 'an "African science" an "African democracy," an "African language"' (2002: 255).

While there are obvious differences between them, the immoveable rock and the bad place are also the same; they are flip sides of each other. In other words, Afrocentric and Eurocentric knowledges may appear to be at loggerheads but, in fact, they are structurally very similar. They both have a single, monolithic benchmark by which to judge and value the world; they share a view of history that denies change and multiplicity, as well as the movement of people and things in more than one direction. Eurocentrism deludes itself that 'the West' has lit a path to a universal state of advanced humanity, technology and religion, under the umbrella of so-called modernity. Afrocentrism peddles the myth that Africa cradles the origins of all knowledge, and that, although denied by colonialism, these knowledge sources may be unearthed and reused in their original forms.

A degree of caution is called for in making this point, however. The positioning of the immoveable rock and the bad place within similar knowledge paradigms is only one arm of a many-tentacled history and politics; it is also necessary to recognize the differences in power between Europe and Africa, both in the past and in the present. Africa and Europe do not play on the proverbial level field. And the struggle over knowledge is no game. The 'third' Africa-centred space, which refuses both Afro- and Eurocentricity, is a political one that opens up new forms of policy and practice.

In other words, knowledge is not made in an egalitarian way; not all voices make the same (or equal) contributions or have the same authority. Some voices are louder, some marginalized and others inaudible. The balance of authorial voices in knowledge-production processes depends, in part, on their respective epistemological powers, which in turn, reflect histories of inequality. This the German anthropologist, Richard Rotten-burg, understands all too well in his book, *Far-Fetched Facts: A Parable of Development Aid* (2009). He demonstrates that in order to capture the visible and invisible workings of power in a concrete development context, scholars need to use different tools of writing from conventional academic modes of expression. He evokes fiction, writes a parable, and creates a narrative of multiple players whose inheritances and interests negotiate a complex web with sometimes unforeseen outcomes.

The framework of Rottenburg's research rests on the hypothesis that knowledge production involves agreement about both what knowledge is and the codes by which it is negotiated. He examines the roles of various actors in a process of knowledge production in a development setting in Africa using a water-supply project in a fictional country where the actors include representatives of a Western development bank, a foreign consultant, an anthropologist (who is a different kind of 'expert'), and local expertise vested in waterworks engineers in the project. All the power appears to lie with the foreign funder and his consultant, and be vested in a knowledge consensus that Rottenburg calls the '*metacode*' (Rottenburg 2009: xxix). Locals and foreigners alike buy into this knowledge as universal truth – its claim to universality being that it is 'scientific' and neutrally technical. In reality, the metacode is steeped in the rhetoric of a burgeoning capitalist modernity that purports to benefit everyone. Without the terms of reference offered by Rottenburg's metacode, there can be no common ground for co-operation in the development projects that characterize African economic and political life.

The metacode contrasts with what Rottenburg ambiguously calls the 'cultural code', which is a mix of construction and context, of local knowledge, tradition and belief. The foreign expert packages this mix together, and identifies it as a problem of the Africans not understanding what needs to be done. The cultural code contrasts, in the foreign expert's mind, with the universal wisdom of the metacode.

But are things this simple? Rottenburg shows how listener and speaker are connected by their shared use of the metacode, even if they have other understandings that do not fit it. In fact, conversations proceed by way of code switching between the consensus of the metacode and the rhetoric of the cultural code. In this process, knowledge is contested, broken down and recreated. Since the balance of power is uneven, local and other stakeholders engage in struggles over knowledge and the interests that it carries. Neither code provides the answer to meaning-making in development contexts as the codes are in constant tension. One way to deal with the tension is for those who participate in the process of knowledge production to be reflexive, and to reflect critically on their own knowledge codes.

In the language of this volume, the metacode of Eurocentrism (for all its universal posturing, and the tendency among local players to buy into it) is at odds with the cultural code of Afrocentrism. In negotiating between these two codes, the reflective meaning-maker has the opportunity (we would say 'the duty') to unpack the mechanisms by which the codes and their switching operate. Taking this opportunity is a choice that prevents one from 'being trapped by one's own blind spots' (Rottenburg 2009: 200). When knowledge-makers review and reflect upon their own frames of reference, the possibility of Africa-centred knowledges emerges. And this is so despite all the maelstrom, mobilities and multiplicities that accompany such knowledges.

All the contributors to this book seek to transcend the immoveable-rock-and-bad-place binary. Creating space is a constitutive act, not simply an act of occupying what already exists and is mapped out. Given the imbalance of world power, as reflected in its knowledge assumptions, those who choose to occupy this creative, suggestive third space struggle to enlarge its archives, its case histories, and its theoretical concepts. For us, it is important that the space is expanded, and that methodological tools are developed for this work.

Concepts and cases

A cursory reading of the book reveals the artificiality of the division between theoretical concepts and cases. All of the chapters are simultaneously theoretical and context driven. We have been interrogating binary thinking, and it would be a big mistake to wheel the distinction between local and global knowledges, or between theory and practice, into the organisation of this book. Rather, as Clifford Geertz puts it, there is 'a shifting focus of particularity' (2000: 134). All knowledge is local and the shift is rather 'between one sort of local knowledge ... and another' (2000: 134).

Yet the distinction offers us a useful organizing device for the book. Thus, key conceptual themes are raised and treated in some depth in the first part of the book, and are used and tested in the second part. More or less. More importantly, what this division foregrounds is how the basis on which knowledge is produced soaks into the fabric of everyday lives. Questions of how meaning making happens (through the lenses of Eurocentrism, of modernity, or of indigenous knowledge) are scrutinized in the opening chapters. Then, in the second part of the book, one chapter after the other substantiates the urgency and concreteness of these daily contestations over (and translations to create) meaning.

At the same time, epistemological foundations are laid in Part One through questions of gender, literature, popular music, and the South African HIV and AIDS debate. And the everyday issues of Part Two are embedded in the tools and concepts raised in earlier chapters. The everyday predominates in Part Two, however, and shows itself in a new light when it is viewed alongside the silent codes that drive and motivate it. This includes the pressures on doctoral students in a South

African university; the crisis in knowledge about declining marine fish populations; perplexities around why certain ICT provisions fail; or how some Zimbabwean students, despite being beset by the impediments of poverty, succeed. The light thrown on the mechanics of how knowledge comes into being, and in whose interests, illuminates the popularity of charismatic religions, as well as the spiritual and physical ill-health of many citizens of modern African cities who are subjected to inappropriate European city-planning models.

Part One: Epistemology – struggles over meaning-making

In Chapter 1, Lansana Keita provides a historical overview of how a template of European knowledge, embedded in technological domi-nance, became the benchmark of truth in all spheres. From the vantage point of this bad place, however, Keita insists that knowledge is not entirely relative, and that the search for Africa-centred meaning entails the asserting of historical truths and accuracies that have been distorted in European power struggles. Keita's insistence is timely. The language of this collection is that of codes, hypotheses and lenses, through which the world is viewed differently. However, if the emphasis of these chapters is simultaneously on forging new meanings that drive different policies and practices, then surely they must be based on a belief that some meanings, interpretations and analyses are more accurate, more true, than others. The language of truth is difficult for us, given that war and intolerance have often been forged in the name of one big truth and moral high ground. This is one of many unresolved tensions that the book holds in play.

Chapter 2 begins with Lesley Green's apt adaptation of one of Aesop's fables, which could stand for the spirit of this collection as a whole. The traveller, Herakles, finds himself between two great walls of rock – or between an immoveable rock and a bad place. Instead of negotiating a better, different route, man that he is, he does violent battle with what he perceives as the obstacles in his path. Green likens Herakles's stand to the hard, warlike lines of polarization that have bedevilled the indigenous-knowledge debate. She calls instead for intellectual hospitality, and a widening of the rigid canon of scholarly acceptability. This involves venturing into the new territory of the post-humanities, which 'offers resources for rich engagements with different knowledges and ways of knowing' (Green, this collection).

Concepts may be right, wrong, or grey, but they are never innocent, as Signe Arnfred reminds us in Chapter 3, which focuses on conceptions of gender. The struggles she charts are discursive ones; the power she unpicks is both epistemic and economic – it is the power to draw up the template that drives policy. Her question is whether gender paradigms, or these epistemic templates, have shifted as a result of world conferences, such as the series of United Nations meetings held in the early 1990s, which led to the Platform for Action being adopted at the Fourth World Conference on Women in Beijing in 1995. A paradox and a problem frame this chapter. The paradox is that while Southern feminists have become more visible and influential, little progress has been made on the ground. This is partly because powerful donor organizations, of which the World Bank is exemplary, were able to appropriate new terms in the language for their own interests, and partly because Southern feminists, themselves, often share the metacodes that frame discussions of gender at global events. This meant that, even as Southern feminists became more visible, and able to influence gender discourses, their respective geopolitical positionings continued to constitute a fault line between Northern and Southern feminist ways of understanding.

There is a critique of the assumptions that accompany the concept of modernity in all three of the chapters described above, and this critique becomes an organizing principle in the next two chapters, which focus on the genre of African and diasporic fiction. Given the maelstrom surrounding the definition of *modernity*, it seems useful at this point to indicate the particular significance of the term in relation to African knowledge production. The difficulty of definition arises because, as Comaroff and Comaroff put it, the concept is 'a shifter' (2012: 119) that metamorphoses in different contexts. In its most positive sense, modernity stands for the ability of a society to be part of the ever-changing global order, with whatever technological and material benefits this brings. To be modern is to be future-looking rather than clinging to the past; it is to be dynamic rather than closed; it is to be open rather than defended and cut off from the world. Or, according to Anthony Giddens, modernity is 'a certain set of attitudes towards the world, the idea of the world as open to transformation by human intervention' (1998: 94). Thus, modernity involves 'a general break with all sorts of pasts ... a theory of rupture' within the context of 'the postelectronic world' (Appadurai 1996: 3, 5).

Unfortunately, however, modernity has often been defined in terms of the particular routes followed by Western countries – 'the Euro-centric myth that there is only one authentic, patented instance of it' (Comaroff and Comaroff 2012: 120). In other words, many chapters pose questions about whether *the content* of European transformation has been erroneously defined as *the form* of modernity. That is, Western capitalist forms of the industrial nation state, a market economy and, most especially, positivistic scientific methods, have come to define the substance of modernity itself. Modernity may be considered 'marked and defined by an obsession with "evidence"', with visuality and visibility (Leppert 2004: 19). And here comes the crunch for Africa-centred knowledges: when 'scientific evidence' becomes the gatekeeper, other sources and forms of making meaning are barred from entering the citadel of knowledge.

Modernity may constantly metamorphose, be a 'shifter', in Comaroff and Comaroff's terms, but one function it serves quite consistently is as a sorter, 'serving to put people ... on the near-or-far-side of the great divide between self and other, the present and prehistory' (Comaroff and Comaroff 2012: 119). Europe is the present and the future; Africa is the archaic past; progress involves bringing Africa into the European future. Although crudely put, this is the command control that silently governs much of the reportage on African wars, shortages, droughts and elections.

In Chapter 4, Bill Ashcroft thickens this interrogation of modernity by scrutinizing 'the fallacy of time as linear', drawing on evidence from African fiction. Ashcroft understands 'Afro-modernity' as the 'transformed and transformative modernity created by Africans'. He embeds Afro-modernity in a concept of time in which the past and the present are entwined, destroying the binary between archaic pasts and progressive presents. He demolishes the 'teleology', the evolutionary map that 'has been the means by which European concepts of time have been naturalised for post-colonial societies' (Ashcroft, this collection). He demonstrates all this in the fiction of three very different writers – Chinua Achebe, Ben Okri and Dambudzo Marechera.

Brenda Cooper, in Chapter 5, examines the sorting principles of classification systems, which, like Arnfred's concepts, are not innocent. It is no coincidence that the European Enlightenment, which stamped the desirability of modernity on the definition of progress, sought to name and cluster species of birds, animals and plants. This it did in the name of 'Science', which was itself classified as existing in opposition to a cluster which included 'superstition' and 'savagery'. Cooper (this volume) suggests that the coded, organizing principles of classification are buried in what Bruno Latour calls 'the black box'. And, of course, 'one of the most powerful and stubborn binaries buried in the black box, is the polarization between modernity and the indigenous, or between pre-scientific/pre-industrial societies and their post-opposites' (Cooper, this volume). Cooper focuses on the language experiments of diasporic writer, Helen Oyeyemi, who is aware of the perniciousness of European forms of literary and linguistic classification, and who attempts to wrest her use of the English language from these pigeonholes.

When Ashcroft tells us that '*how* we know determines *what* we know', (this volume, his emphasis), and when Cooper highlights the nature of the knowledge embedded in the form and nature of language itself, they gesture towards the final chapter in this section. In Chapter 6, Mbugua wa Mungai investigates the nature of the knowledge that is produced in Kenyan popular music – and by Nairobi's rappers in particular. His key point is that radical, transformative knowledge is embedded in the 'rhetorical flavour, rather than the ideological content' of this art form (Mbugwa wa Mungai, this collection). In fact, the ideological content is contradictory and ambivalent as the musicians' lyrics veer between opposing and colluding with state power.

Mbugua wa Mungai's chapter sits on the bridge between the two parts of the book. He theorizes and interrogates the political costs and benefits of local popular culture, by way of a concrete and detailed analysis of the lyrics of a range of musicians, and, in particular, of Baba Otonglo and his song, 'High Budget'. Mbugua wa Mungai conceptualizes what Nairobi's urban youth nation might look like, and reads its characteristics through the lens of a popular musician in a time of structural adjustment that wrought economic havoc on the nation as a whole.

Part Two: Policy and practice – applying the knowledge

Part Two gets to the nub of the interface between research and transformation, with its guiding question: research for what? To paraphrase Marx's famous statement from his 'Theses on Feuerbach', (1888) is the point of research to understand the world or to change it? The purpose to which research is put has a profound influence, not just on how it is conducted but also on the very knowledge economy that currently entrenches Northern dominance. Clifford Geertz sums up this point when he asks:

> Who knows the river better ... the hydrologist or the swimmer? Put that way, it clearly depends on what you mean by 'knows', and ... what it is you hope to accomplish. Put as which sort of knowledge we most need, want, and might to some degree conceivably get, in the human sciences anyway, the local variety – the sort the swimmer has, or, swimming might develop – can at the very least hold its own against the general variety – the sort the hydrologist has, or claims method will one day soon provide. It is not ... a matter of the shape of our thought, but of its vocation. (2000: 140)

The vocation of our thought, the profound consequences of our knowledges, drives policy decisions and influences everyday lives. While the contributors to both sections anticipate changes in practice arising out of Africa-centred knowledges, in Part Two these changes are the focus of each contribution. Each chapter examines a particular case where rival meanings are presented, contrasted, merge, and then throw up something different, distinctive, new and potentially transcendental.

In Chapter 7, Barbara Paterson, Marieke Norton, Astrid Jarre and Lesley Green critique the reliance of fishery managers on the statistical-knowledge approach to counting fish that dominates marine science. The problem is that this approach excludes the perspectives of the people who actually do the fishing, and who have a different kind of knowledge about the seas and about fish. This divide works against the development of policies and practices that could help to both conserve fish stocks, and sustain the livelihoods of fishers. The authors of this chapter suggest combining the large-scale overview of the one grouping with the detailed local knowledge of the other, and argue that this 'has the potential to provide a more complete understanding of the ecology of fishing' (Paterson et al., this collection).

The contributors to this book understand heritage and dispossession to be political issues that are deeply implicated in the link between power and knowledge. They also recognize that the threat to local, 'small' knowledges embodied in ways of trapping fish, has dire consequences for our hopes of a diverse, 'new' South Africa. This is a good moment to comment the image on our cover: the photograph is by South African photographer, Paul Weinberg, and his caption reads as follows: 'An elder fisherman of the Kosi Bay fishing community makes a traditional fish trap at a time when the community was threatened with removal and the loss of their ancestral land and heritage, 1992, Kosi Bay, KwaZuluNatal, South Africa'. The camera does not objectify the man whose lines of concentration indicate that he is too engrossed in his task to smile for the viewer. Small is big and we simultaneously see the intricate detail of the weaving, and how the fish trap becomes a tunnel of vision onto a hazy, grassy future.

In Chapter 8, Ulrike Rivett, Gary Marsden and Edwin Blake insist that a conversation between the users and makers of information technology systems is necessary for the fashioning of appropriate tools for development. They base this insistence on the astonishingly high failure rate of ICT projects in Africa. What the chapter demonstrates is that a new theoretical framework is necessary if we wish to understand the adoption of digitally based systems in the developing-world – a framework based on interrogating cherished notions of development and transformation. That is, tools for monitoring and evaluating ICT provision and take-up in Africa cannot be based on what has been termed the 'techno-economic rationality of western modernity' (Rivett et al., this collection). These authors interrogate the foundation of some of the basic assumptions that drive their discipline; while they acknowledge that the language for this conversation does not yet exist, they see the devising of means of communication between technology, technicians and communities in a co-design process as imperative.

Similarly in Chapter 9, a multidisciplinary group of authors question the dominant body of knowledge in the field of urban planning. Warren Smit, Ariane de Lannoy, Robert Dover, Estelle Lambert, Naomi Levitt and Vanessa Watson suggest that the relationship of urban space to health needs to be rethought. Most research into the relationship between the built environment and public health has taken place in cities of the industrial North. These authors illustrate how the unquestioned hypotheses of Northern urban theorists leads planners to overlook the emotional wellbeing of, and the physical dangers experienced by, inhabitants of Khayelitsha, a Cape Town township. Smit et al. (this volume) call for a co-design framework, along the lines of those suggested in the previous two chapters. To establish this new system, they draw on the innovative methodology of body mapping (where individuals make images of their bodies in relation to their felt environment: some examples are included in the chapter). The use of such methods, argue the authors, may help city planners in the South develop a deeper awareness of local conceptions of the urban environment as well as local understandings of the relationship between human health and wellbeing.

In Chapter 10, Akosua Adomako Ampofo and Michael Okyerefo delve into the phenomenon of the enormously popular movement of Pentecostal and charismatic (independent) churches. Like wa Mungai in Chapter 6, they recognize the importance of local knowledge, this time produced by preachers, those 'men of God' mentioned in their title. They focus on three preachers who have captured the media, and whose churches 'produce television and radio programmes, as well as video, audio and printed materials, which reach a wide audience, well beyond the congregations that attend Sunday services'. These preachers are actively engaged in producing new knowledge, and their words carry particular weight in the context of the 'material poverty and social exclusion' of many in their ambit (Adomako Ampofo and Okyerefo, this collection). What these authors are particularly focused upon is the nature of this knowledge, especially as it pertains to issues of gender. And, like that of Nairobi's rappers, the message is mixed. In addition to providing genuine support and strength in adversity, this new Pentecostal knowledge also perpetuates older and well-entrenched gender stereotypes. This places these churches, and the substance of their message, in a liminal position – perched between the old and the new.

Linda Cooper and Lucia Thesen grapple with knowledge production from an intriguing angle in Chapter 11. They enter into the institution of the university, an exemplary knowledge producing machine, and examine how novice researchers – postgraduate students – are inducted into the accepted, and also unacceptable, codes and conventions mediating this knowledge production. In 2013, the two contributors co-edited a collection by various authors that examined how dominant codes within academic-writing practices either enable or constrain postgraduate students' abilities to write up their research (Thesen and Cooper). This concern is particularly justified in a situation where universities, such as the University of Cape Town where they both work, operate within 'a global academic terrain that is dominated by "Northern theory"' (Cooper and Thesen, this collection). Where does this leave PhD students, who may be the first in their family to reach university, and whose language and experience appear to be at odds with the demands and traditions of the institution?

Cooper and Thesen take seriously the imperative of self-reflection and they foreground the process of sharpening their own theoretical tools for their book, in order rigorously to assess, critique, and provide alternatives to the codes that govern academic writing. They do not throw out the dominant archive, but recognize the existence of the traces of transgression against it, which are closer to the experience, language and politics of some postgraduates. Instead of deleting these traces, they, like many of the other contributors to this volume, call for a conversation and a debate between these dimensions.

Finally, in Chapter 12, Leadus Madzima overturns the predictable question and obvious answer about the relationship between poverty and failure at school by returning us to the nature of indigenous knowledge. Her interest is in how some pupils in situations of extreme deprivation succeed at school in general, and at a Zimbabwean secondary school in particular. She looks critically at the work of three prominent European scholars, Pierre Bourdieu, Anthony Giddens and Judith Butler, who explore the relationship between agency and structures of power and domination. However, none of these theorists provide the missing piece in Madzima's puzzle regarding those students who overcome barriers. She finds that Bourdieu focuses most on the constraints, Giddens less so, and Butler least of all in offering mechanisms that describe the confrontation of power through, for example, performativity. However, without including knowledge of local Shona culture, Madzima notes that none of these mechanisms account for the phenomenon she is exploring. Again, Northern templates of description and explanation skew local African complexities and realities. Madzima argues that the Shona philosophy of *hunhuism*, or personhood, provides people with the drive, the community support and the incentive to make something of themselves, and then shows how powerfully this value system operates among some Zimbabwean school pupils.

Connections, segues and hauntings: cutting across

Africa-centred knowledges are made and situated in the creative space between the bad place and the immovable rock, and are open to *collaborations* and strategic alliances across the divide. This is what Green means when she calls for a different kind of intellectual hospitality, and when she asks what conditions within the humanities would support the emergence of new conversations, that would be both forms of new knowledge and processes that lead to Africa-centred knowledges? This is why Cooper calls for the fluidity of articulation in place of the rigidities of classification. In the same spirit, Paterson et al.(this collection) call for the collaboration of scientists and fishers, and Rivett et al. (this collection) for the co-design of technology by technicians and communities. Similarly, Cooper and Thesen (2013) are aware that both the mainstream, dominant archive, as well as the traces of alternative traditions in its underbelly, are crucial if practice is going to be transformed by new knowledge. Madzima (this collection) gleans what she can from some Western knowledge makers, and melds their insights with others from indigenous knowledge sources.

What is clear from this is that *knowledge sources* are more varied and available than the gatekeepers of the dominant-knowledge-producing systems would have us believe. The key questions are: what counts as evidence and what counts as a source? In order to disturb Northern theory, it is necessary to include a range of sources ordinarily discounted as being non-scientific or anecdotal, including works drawn from imagination, such as novels, stories and music (Nyamnjoh 2011). Keita, Ashcroft and Cooper (this collection) offer fiction as a source, and wa Mungai recognizes that the lyrics and music of Kenyan rap are a form of local knowledge that reward being taken seriously, as do the writings and preachings of Adomako Ampofo and Okyerefo's Pentecostal church leaders. Cooper and Thesen explore the excluded sources in postgraduate student writing.

Embodied knowledge is another source that often finds itself on the wrong side of a one-way turnstile. Green defines this form of knowing as understandings of the 'relationship between bodiliness, food, and the kinds of care or enmity that bring it to the body' (Green, this collection). This is what Ashcroft means when he questions if there is, 'a form of knowledge that is accessible beyond meaning', and links this to 'the materiality of the form rather than the narrated subject matter' (Ashcroft, this collection). Cooper, too, demonstrates this in the way that a diasporic writer returns words to their literal sound and feel, in opposition to the inheritance of colonially infused symbolic meanings, such as Africa being the world's dark heart. Smit et al. (this collection) derive a visceral sense of the relationship between people and the cities they inhabit, by inviting them to map their bodies onto their living spaces. While it is certainly the case that the translation from story or feeling, rhythm or rap is a challenging topic on its own, these questions are seldom asked because the knowledge they contain is unrecognized within the metacodes shared by policymakers and planners alike.

Gatekeeping is a subtle, silent and unconscious process, deeply embedded and inherited in knowledge-making institutions. Arnfred (this collection) shows that gatekeeping can also occur in policy settings, where ostensibly all opinions are canvassed but some are heard more than others. And it is the weightier opinions that prevail and are transformed into policy documents, while dissenting voices are ignored even as the policy documents are held to proclaim a universal truth or political commitment. Green recognizes the exclusions existent in the academy in canons of curriculae that dictate what is able to pass for knowledge, as do Cooper and Thesen when they examine the constraints on student writing. When Ashcroft refers to embodied knowledge that never makes its way into epistemology, he is defining the epistemological as the dominant form of understanding the world, which has made its way into the Western archive, leaving other knowledges 'to wander outside the city walls of modernity, rejected by the guardians of knowledge' (Ashcroft, this collection). Or as Green puts it, indigenous forms of knowledge are classified as belief, and admitted through the gates of knowledge only via the tests of the science. 'Thus, anything outside of science must either be proven by scientific methods, and incorporated into the canon of knowledge ... or remain ... alongside superstition, charlatanism, snake-oil and hocus-pocus (Green, this collection).

A miniaturization of these fortified city walls is to be found in Cooper's use of Bruno Latour's notion of a black box. This box is exemplary of the dominant archive, replete with invisible codes and consequences, which conceal themselves as 'common sense'. All too often, haunting traces are all that remain of forms of knowledge that are locked out of the dominant archive, its boundaries fiercely guarded by turnpikes and gatekeepers. These ghost traces may assemble outside the gates, or be incarcerated within the citadels and prisons; they may be in the lyrics of Mbugua wa Mungai's rappers, which sing out their 'philosophy *sedi*' (seditious philosophy) – a view of life balanced on the periphery of the urban mainstream. Rappers risk incarceration, given the ruling view that they are 'mad people who should be locked away in psychiatric institutions', as lamented by Ukoo Flani's 'Dandora L.O.V.E' (quoted in wa Mungai, this collection).

The question of gatekeeping, and the basis on which knowledge is admitted or excluded, brings us back to the *false binary* between 'tradition' and 'modernity', outlined at the outset of this introduction, and which is so potent in African studies. Smit et al. (this collection) contest the polarity between modernity and backwardness, and insist that the African city does not need to emulate the forms that modernity as manifest in the ideal Northern city, with its orderly linear grid. This undermining of linear space is partnered by the fallacy that Ashcroft exposes of the necessity for linear time. This questioning of the desirability of linear spatial and temporal grids in rethinking routes to modernity takes us to Leadus Madzima's chapter, where schoolchildren find a way of excelling in their studies of maths and science by drawing on their Shona beliefs and values.

Modernity versus tradition is linked to the false divide between local – as backward –and global – as progressive and forward-looking. In this volume, Paterson et al., Rivett et al., and Smit et al. argue that *local knowledge* (understood as emanating from a locale, as well as from individuals) can contribute to the sustainability of an environment and of local cultures. Local knowledge can contribute to improving the quality of life (including health and educational performance), as shown by Madzima, Smit et al., and Cooper and Thesen. In this process of imbibing local, embodied knowledge, lies the possibility of liberating individual agency and enhancing empowerment.

Local knowledge takes us to the theme of *language*, which is integral to the project of making Africa-centred knowledges. Our inherited words, and their metaphorical associations, construct barriers and open vistas. Old and new words, applied in other places, times and contexts, are used to make new theory. And with theory comes the production of knowledge, recognized as such in the injection into the chapters of this book of the following ideas – 'epistemicide', 'curricular justice', 'post-humanities', 'risk', 'canons of knowledge', 'embodied knowledge', 'personhood', 'rhetorical reason', 'mosaic epistemology', and 'ecologies of knowledge'. These provocative and challenging concepts light a way through this apparently diverse collection. And all along the path are signposts to collaborations, and invitations to conversations, rather than polarisations and false options. Not Afro- or Euro-, but Africa-centred knowledges that are driven by and reflect a politics that acknowledges global inequities.

This is not to proclaim some newly captured moral high ground, on its way to setting yet another knowledge orthodoxy in concrete. Many of the chapters describe the *messiness*, nuance, and Janus-faced nature of the Africa-centred knowledges that they are negotiating and making. Mbugua wa Mungai confronts the sad possibility that local knowledge – the popular outpourings of talented musicians – may not set themselves or their audiences free. In the context of global feminist politics, Arnfred concedes that 'third-world' feminists have failed to translate their goals and successes, at forums such as the 1995 Beijing conference, into concrete actions. Southern women have had to confront the reality of global agencies, such as the World Bank, which have agendas and use language in ways that differ from their own, and which are in a more powerful position to give effect to their visions. Arnfred warns of the possibility that 'first-world' feminists will pursue their own interests, even as they seem to stand together with their African sisters. The danger that wa Mungai's and Arnfred's chapters alert us to is of collusion and co-option. Similarly, Adomako Ampofo and Okyerefo are less than sanguine about the gender implications of the local knowledge produced by their 'men of God'. Ambivalence, forked tongues, paradoxes and contradictions attend this complex web of old and new, local and global, knowledge production.

This said, there are hints that, alongside the hospitality towards all ideas, which we argue is constitutive of Africa-centred knowledges, *person-hood* may emerge in place of the liberal humanism that benchmarked the western-European version of our supposedly shared humanity and desirable human values (Nyamnjoh 2012). Personhood raises the possibility of an enlarged and accommodating conceptualisation of our shared humanity, our responsibilities and of the consequences of our actions. Green opens this collection with this not-small dream: 'understandings of what it is to be a person', which 'encompass an understanding of person-in-relationship' (Green, this collection), and Madzima ends the book by concretizing the dream via her description of *hunhuism*, a Shona belief in *personhood* as based on community.

Ultimately, the key word with which we would like to open this book is the imperative to *listen* to that which is not always loud enough or easy enough to hear. Listen to the narratives of fishers. Listen to postgraduates whose life experiences should not be erased before they have an opportunity to transform them into tools and knowledge in their academic writing. Listen to the city dwellers whose stories of their forms of recreation, exercise, shopping, and commuting could transform city planning in a place like Cape Town, where wealth and poverty co-exist across an abyss of difference. Listen to the 'men of God' as they amass support within independent churches that answer the desires and pains of communities and individuals in ways that simultaneously oppress and liberate them, and who are perhaps maximizing their agency in unpredictable ways. Listen to the woman whose mobile phone has become her new way of doing business, but who ignores your calls, and the supposed added benefits you offer, when these do not suit her needs. Listen to the writers whose novels are structured around narratives that follow unexpected paths, and whose protagonists sing and dance and speak in new tongues. Listen to the beat of rap, to verses in song that decry power and dictatorship. Listen to poor women in Nigeria, for whom finding a means of livelihood is more urgent than winning a legal right to abortion.

Throughout this collection are whisperings and hauntings; spirits and ghosts lurk between the sections and dip in and out of many of the chapters. There are traces of the unspoken and the misheard. Africa-centred knowledges emerge in conversations that are sometimes difficult to follow as they carry the echo of history and cultural context. And yet, such conversations occur, and they carry the prospect of new imaginings and understandings that, in themselves, unsettle Eurocentric and Afrocentric modalities, and may help to create Africa-centred knowledges.

References

Appadurai, Arjun (1996) *Modernity at Large*, Minneapolis: University of Minnesota Press.

Comaroff, John and Jean Comaroff (2012) 'Theory from the South: Or, how Euro-America is evolving toward Africa' *Anthropological Forum: A Journal of Social Anthropology and Comparative Sociology*, 22 (2): 113-131.

Connell, Raewyn (2007) *Southern Theory: The Global Dynamics of Knowledge in Social Science*, Sydney: Allen & Unwin.

Fiske, Edward B and Helen F Ladd (2004) *Elusive Equity: Education Reform in Post-apartheid South Africa*, Cape Town and Washington: HSRC Press and Brookings Institution Press.

Geertz, Clifford (2000) *Available Light: Anthropological Reflections on Philosophical Topics*, Princeton NJ: Princeton University Press.

Gedalof, Irene (1999) *Against Purity*, London and New York: Routledge.

Giddens, Anthony (1998) *Conversations With Anthony Giddens: Making Sense of Modernity*, Stanford CA: Stanford University Press.

Leppert, Richard (2004) 'The Social Discipline of Listening' in Jim Drobnick, ed., *Aural Cultures*, Toronto: YYZ Books.

Mamdani, Mahmoud (1993) 'University crisis and reform: A reflection on the African experience', *Review of African Political Economy*, 20 (58): 7-19.

Mbembe, Achille (2001) *On the Postcolony*, Berkeley and Los Angeles; London: University of California Press.

Mbembe, Achille (2002) 'African modes of self-writing', *Public Culture*, 14 (1): 239-273.

Mudimbe, V.Y. (1988) *The Invention of Africa: Gnosis, Philosophy, and the Order of Knowledge*, London: James Currey.

Mudimbe, V.Y. (1994) *The Idea of Africa*, London: James Currey.

Ntuli, Pitika P. (1999) 'The missing link between culture and education: Are we still chasing Gods that are not our own?', in Malegapuru W. Makgoba, ed., *African Renaissance*, Cape Town: Tafelberg/Mafube.

Nyamnjoh, Francis (2002) '"A child is one person's only in the womb": Domestication, agency and subjectivity in the Cameroonian grassfields', in Richard Werbner, ed., *Postcolonial Subjectivities in Africa*, London: Zed.

Nyamnjoh, Francis (2011) 'Cameroonian bushfalling: Negotiation of identity and belonging in fiction and ethnography', *American Ethnologist*, 38 (4): 701-713.

Nyamnjoh, Francis (2012) 'Blinded by sight: Divining the future of anthropology in Africa', *Africa Spectrum*, 47 (2-3): 63-92.

Rottenburg, Richard (2009) *Far-fetched Facts: A Parable of Development Aid*, Cambridge MA: MIT Press.

Samoff, Joel and Nelly P. Stromquist (2001) 'Managing knowledge and storing wisdom? New forms of foreign aid?' *Development and Change*, 32 (4): 631-656.

Soudien, Crain and Carol Corneilse (2000) 'South African higher education in transition: Global discourses and national priorities', in Nelly P. Stromquist and Karen Monkman, eds, *Globalization and Education: Integration and Contestation Across Cultures*, Lanham MD: Rowman & Littlefield.

Thesen, Lucia and Linda Cooper, eds, (2013) *Postgraduate Writing, Risk and the Making of New Knowledge*, Bristol: Multilingual Matters.

Wolpe, Harold (1995) 'The debate on university transformation in South Africa: The case of the University of the Western Cape', *Comparative Education*, 31 (2): 275-292.

Part I

EPISTEMOLOGY
– STRUGGLES OVER MEANING

1 Validated Knowledge
Confronting Myths about Africa

Lansana Keita

Knowledge about Africa is still constructed under the cloud of colonialism. European colonizers denied the existence of African civilization, history and culture while simultaneously casting the continent and its people as noble and awe-inspiring. Knowledge production about, and in, Africa still is afflicted by confusions over race and geography – the effects of Eurocentric schemas that rest on hierarchical understandings of humanity. While there is a postmodern dispute about what can be known, this chapter makes the case for the possibility of a validated knowledge that will help to dispel the many myths that surround the continent.

From archaeological times to the present, the world has had a long history in which a kind of telos of humankind has made itself evident. Humankind, as a species within the animal kingdom, has been variously described as 'the rational animal' or, according to Aristotle, as 'a political animal'. But on the basis of the empirical history of humankind, one can argue that our species can just as easily be described as 'the technological animal'. After all, according to standard evolutionary biology, humankind has been in an evolutionary stasis over the last 180,000 years. Thus, the great differences that are observable between human social arrangements, beliefs, and practices are essentially attributable to advances in our understanding of the structures of the natural world, and its practical representation in forms of tool-making, commonly known as technological knowledge.

I argue that it is technological knowledge that serves as the main explanatory variable for the vagaries and paths of human history. It is this variable that explains the migratory movements of peoples over time, the wars and conflicts that arise, and the various aspects of cultural diffusion that accompany these events. Using this lens, one can find rational explanations for the expansion of Western Europe into the four corners of the globe over the last 500 years, including into the vast land mass now known as Africa.

The evident qualitative distinctions between forms of technologies

23

and their accompanying cultures best explain the irruption of the Western European nations into Africa. In the initial stages, the compass, the printing press, long-haul galleons and their cannons afforded maximal technological advantages over the extant technologies of the Americas, Africa, and parts of Asia. This differential was crucial for the European successes in settling in the Americas and parts of Africa (Angola, Mozambique and the Southern Cape). Later, the Gatling gun and other weaponry facilitated European technological dominance. Along with its embedded modes of knowing, this was used to effect and justify cultural dominance.

The technological knowledge that facilitated the European conquest or control of most of Africa became a kind of template for a claim to a general superiority in all spheres. Thus European technological advantage – promoted as technological superiority – was extrapolated not only as a cultural advantage but also – crucially – as a qualitative superiority. The simple logic behind this extrapolation was that superior humans produce superior (more advanced) technologies and, by further inference, superior cultures. As a result, hierarchies of humankind were established according to which the world's populations were graded, not only in terms of the evolutionary worth of their cultures, but also in terms of the evolutionary status of their bearers. The modern idea of 'race' then developed to classify human groups along evolutionary lines, and thereby explain technological and cultural differentials.

One of the by-products of Europe's irruption into Africa was cultural diffusion. Thus, traditional modes of knowing and acting in various African cultures were much impacted by the diffused technologies and modes of knowing that emanated from Europe. The most pervasive examples were European forms of religion and language. Thus, the traditional metaphysical lives of Africans as much as their traditional technological practices, were thrown into conflict with those of European origin. Various versions of Christianity made much headway in Africa, disseminated as they were by missionaries. The various languages of Western Europe also spread in areas where economic interests meant that their use was necessary. This was the basis for the dissemination of Western modes of knowing in Africa – whether religious (metaphysical) or technological (empirical). But cultural dissemination did not stop there. It impacted on most aspects of African life, thereby creating diverse forms of psychological and intellectual conflict.

The general impact of Europe's cultural diffusion into Africa was to impose forms of knowledge that were decidedly Eurocentric in material and normative terms. It is important to note, however, that there was some reciprocal diffusion from Africa to Europe in the form of abstract motifs in representational art – particularly in the more recent cultural products of artists such as Picasso, Mondrian, and so on. A similar kind of diffusion was evident in the musical forms transported to the West by way of West African human transplants into the Americas: much modern popular music, dance and jazz are cases in point.

But in general, cultural diffusion from Europe to Africa was far more influential in material and psychological terms. Consider for example the exogenous creation of the nation states of Africa with no clear input from the populations involved. Consider, too, the languages imposed on the colonized territories that were increasingly structured to include terms and meanings that normatively devalued the lifeworlds of the peoples involved. In brief, colonial languages were structured and employed to establish, as fact, both the biological and cultural superiority of the colonizer. This assumption of general superiority was then used to justify the idea that indigenous technological practices and metaphysical beliefs should be replaced by those of European origin.

But in this encounter between Europe and Africa, a dialectic was established in which the thesis of European irruption produced an antithesis of African opposition. The result was a variegated synthesis. For example, take the case of Ghana, which at independence rejected the imposed colonial name of Gold Coast in favour of Ghana, thereby revivifying the medieval African empire bearing that name. The same held for the southern African nation of Zimbabwe, which rejected the name Rhodesia and replaced it with a name that reflects the indigenous archaeological history of that region. This was significant because Eurocentric archaeology had made the claim that the old stone structures of Great Zimbabwe could not have been developed by the area's indigenous peoples, so that the structures were variously attributed to Persians, Arabs, and others. Similarly, the various bronze and terracotta artworks of the pre-modern Benin culture were deemed too sophisticated and realist to be produced by indigenous artists. The African reactive antithesis to the prevailing Euro-centred thesis that eventually led to a problematisation of the Eurocentric project itself.

But one of the most significant forms of African reaction to Europe's one-sided impositions was realized in the world of literature. From the twilight of the colonial era to the dawn of formal independence, Europe's languages were used to express the cultural and psychological ambiguities engendered by the Europe–Africa encounter. Novels such as *Things Fall Apart* by Chinua Achebe and *Ambiguous Adventure (L'aventure ambiguë)* by Cheikh Hamidou Kane are internationally recognized for their portrayal of the African psychological response to the European presence in Africa, engendered by the initial clash of cultures. Also notable in this regard was the Negritude movement, whose major exponents included Aimé Césaire, Léopold Sédhar Senghor and Léon Damas. This reactive movement began in the 1930s and continued until formal independence was achieved by most African nations in the 1960s. It sought to enhance Africa's past in racial, cultural and moral terms: Césaire's *Discourse on Colonialism* is well known in this regard. Senghor's poetry extolled the aesthetic allure of Africa's peoples and cultures.

In the social sciences, noteworthy responses came from Samir Amin (*Eurocentrism*, 1999), Cheikh Anta Diop (*Nations nègres et culture*, 1973, *The Cultural Unity of Black* Africa,1959, and *Civilization or Barbarism*, 1991), and Frantz Fanon (*Wretched of the Earth*, 1991, and *Black Skin, White Masks*, 1952). But even so, Euro-centred forms of control still manifest themselves in the area of the human imagination, thereby reflecting the continuing psychological function of the old Eurocentric colonial stereotypes. I refer here to images portrayed in certain popular films with African themes produced for Western consumption. It is evident that the basis of Eurocentric structuring of knowledge about Africa is complex, but a major consideration is that its foundations are heavily motivated by economic interests. A diminished African economic status inevitably accords increased agency to others in terms of access to and utilization of African resources.

It is within the broad context outlined above that this chapter aims to expose various manifestations of the ways in which Eurocentric knowledge is presented as objective fact. It should be recognized that Eurocentric knowledge does not limit itself to just one area, but presents itself as a paradigm or *weltanschauung* through which the world of the past and the present is viewed and understood. Thus, there is a Eurocentric approach to structuring the facts of the empirical world, in both the natural and the social sciences. A critique of Eurocentric knowledge in its universalizing mode with regard to Africa should, therefore, provide corrective mechanisms for a more accurate account.

What follows is a condensed discussion of what constitutes knowledge in the empirical sciences. I argue for a 'unity of science model' – which holds that it is possible to obtain genuine knowledge in both the natural and social spheres – but with the caveat that the social sciences produce objective knowledge less readily, given that human interests are involved at all levels. Thus the epistemological goal would be to unpack the ideological content of Eurocentric knowledge in all its dimensions as a prelude to replacing it, where possible, with a more objective account. The counter-argument in favour of epistemological relativism cannot be supported because accepting such a thesis would lead to an experiential world of epistemological anarchy. Although all empirical claims are subject to revision, some, such as Newton's Second Law or the Second Law of Thermodynamics, cannot be falsified. Similarly, the anthropological claim that humankind began in what is now known as Africa is accepted scientifically because no countervailing theory stands up to scrutiny.

Epistemology and the foundations of knowledge

Contrary to those who argue for a relativistic approach to knowledge, it is indeed possible to establish empirically certifiable knowledge, even though all knowledge exists in a social context. There is a reasonably large body of literature on this topic, and authors such as Barnes, Bloor, Feyerabend and Hacking, as well as Popper, all have interesting things to say about the sociology of knowledge. The general thesis is that knowledge in any social context is necessarily a kind of meta-knowledge that is constructed and filtered through reified but socially constructed lenses. This approach has its modernist epistemological roots in Kant's *Critique of Pure Knowledge* (1781). Marx argued for a social science committed to the transformation of society, based on an objective analysis of economic and sociological facts, or what is known as 'the materialist conception of history'. Mannheim (*Ideology and Utopia*) queried this approach, arguing that all social knowledge is relative. The idea that supposedly 'objective' scientific knowledge is framed according to theoretical constructs was pursued by Kuhn in his ground-breaking work, *The Structure of Scientific Revolutions.*

The question of the existence of 'truth' goes to the heart of the question of 'knowledge' production. It is the central question for empirical science, both natural and social. There is a firm assumption within the natural sciences that an existent empirical world is knowable if the correct epistemological research criteria are followed. On this basis, the findings of natural science research are deemed to be universally valid for all sociological locations. Thus, there is no such thing as scientific research in, for example, China reporting different but equally valid findings from Germany; researchers cannot argue that theory X on topic Y, although valid in China, is not valid for Germany. Critics of Kuhn point to eventually disproven theories that were once universally accepted, such as the 'ether theory', 'Lamarckian theory', and 'Lysenkoism'.

However, in the social sciences (sometimes referred to as the 'human sciences') matters are rather different. Human subjectivism, reinforced by a myopic epistemology, has fuelled the debate as to whether an objective social science could fit the 'unity of science' model. This question goes all the way back to the pioneering and purportedly objectivist work of Emile Durkheim and Marcel Mauss, who both wrote during the post-Comtian period of the late-nineteenth century. In later years, the work of Alfred Schutz et al., as well as that of Peter Berger and Thomas Luckmann (1966) became known, alongside that of Barnes (1977) and Bloor (1976), for promoting the phenomenological approach to the social sciences. This debate continues, as is evidenced by the more recent work of McCarthy, (1966), Camic et al., (2011), and Hostettler (2012).

Nevertheless, I remain committed to the idea of 'objectivism', not only for the natural sciences but also for the human and social sciences. It is just that, in the case of the human and social sciences, a more critical epistemological analysis is needed. Thus, it should be possible to produce satisfying explanatory studies of the Russian and French revolutions, although some may be palpably better than others in terms of testability: one can speak of an objective social science that measures up epistemologically to all counterclaims.

Thus, an Africa-centred knowledge paradigm need not repeat the errors and misrepresentations that have often marred the constructions of knowledge about Africa promulgated by European theorists. Such theorists were often epistemologically compromised by the orthodox Eurocentric paradigm, which arbitrarily ascribed a universal superiority to all European modes of knowing, simply on the basis of technological primacy. What follows, therefore, are critical analyses of structures of knowledge developed in the social sciences and that are assumed to be conventionally factual but which, when probed epistemologically, are seen to be heavily compromised in terms of Eurocentric content and orientation. The decision to examine the social sciences in general rather than just a single discipline is because the Eurocentric ideological paradigm, often under the colour of objectivity, presents itself in universalist terms across all disciplinary forms of knowledge.

Eurocentric human biology and anthropology

The rise of modern science was accompanied by the classification of the constituents of the animal kingdom, including humans, as demonstrated in the works of Linnaeus and Cuvier. In the case of humans, classifications were based purely on phenotype, which were associated with particular temperaments. With the advent of Darwinian theory the idea developed that humans could be classified not only according to phenotype and temperament but also in terms of evolutionary status. The idea of 'race' as representing different human categories assumed centrality. On account of the technological advantages of western European societies, the Eurocentric thesis developed which ranked non-Europeans as biologically less evolved than Europeans. Hume, Kant and others pursued this line of argument. The crucial implication of this thesis was that those human groups deemed biologically less evolved were subject to the supposedly Darwinian principle of 'natural selection'. Thus the populations of Africa, described by the patently non-scientific and Eurocentric term 'negro', were assumed to be not only biologically less evolved, but also slated for extinction. Under this ideology, Tasmanians and Australian indigenes were subjected to much abuse, eventually leading to the extinction of the former and the near extinction of the latter. The inhabitants of Africa were subjected to similar strictures of Eurocentric evolutionary biology, both those transported to the Americas for forced slave labour, and those later colonized and virtually enslaved on the African continent, especially in those areas marked out for European settlement such as southern Africa.

To offer justificatory support for the theory of evolutionary gradation, Eurocentric ideology, under the guise of empirical science, resorted to the physical measurements of the crania and other physical aspects of the African phenotype. It was on this basis that the Tutsis of Rwanda and Burundi were rated higher up the evolutionary scale than their Hutu kinsmen. A popular approach was to appeal to the pseudoscience of phrenology to make the dubious claims that prognathism and nasal indices afforded proof of African evolutionary retardation.

This argument was easily belied by the fact that the facial structures of East Asians approximated those found in Africa, yet the thesis of evolutionary retardation was not applied in this instance. The biologist, Stephen Gould pointed out in *The Mismeasure of Man* (1981), that the data of a significant number of these supposedly scientific studies on race and biology were manipulated. One proof that could have been used to counter the Eurocentric claim of the evolutionary retardation of African populations was how easily colonized Africans learned to communicate in the European languages. Another was the impressive achievements of various individuals, such as philosopher Anthony Amo, who lectured at the German universities of Halle and Jena during the first half of the eighteenth century, or Olaudah Equiano (also known as Gustavus Vassa), a victim of slavery, whose autobiographical work and political activism was highly influential in the movement to abolish the Atlantic slave trade.

A further erosion of the Eurocentric thesis occurred when scientific evidence demonstrated that humankind has its origins in East and southern Africa some 160,000 to 200,000 years ago, and that migration from the continent took place only around 50,000 to 60,000 years ago. Thus, the period of time for evolutionary differentials to have occurred is just too short to be of any real significance. The 'Out of Africa' hypothesis has, however, been opposed by the multi-regional hypothesis, which claims that the three major human populations, designated as African, European and Asian, evolved separately, not at the *Homo sapiens* level but at that of *Homo erectus* (Wolpoff and Caspari 1997). Another argument in opposition to African origins, put forward by Klein (1989), states that *Homo sapiens*, although anatomically modern since approximately 165,000 years ago, evolved further at the cognitive level to become 'behaviourally modern' only some 40,000 to 50,000 years ago. This cognitive evolution did not occur in Africa, as the migration of *Homo sapiens* to other parts of the globe had already been concluded by then. McBrearty and Brooks (2000) responded to Klein by arguing that the transition to the cognitive status of being 'behaviourally modern' did take place in Africa and was, therefore, social rather than biological. The purpose of both theories was to offer continuing support to the orthodox Eurocentric model under challenge on the evolutionary stages of the world's geographically different populations (Wolpoff and Caspari 1997). Yet the 'Out of Africa' hypothesis stands firm on the basis of continuing research (Stringer and McKie 1997), providing an example of an Africa-centred knowledge being empirically and objectively confirmed.

Biological theories of human evolution, first established in Eurocentric discourse to chart the course of human development, were eventually used as the template on which modern physical and cultural anthropology was structured. The discipline of anthropology began, therefore, as the cultural and biological study of the non-European other. This enterprise required, above all, a specialised vocabulary with specific references. Non-European humans from Africa and pre-Columbian America were seen as inhabitants of the woods and forests, hence the coining of terms such as 'savage' (from the Latin 'silva'), 'primitive' (signifying 'early stages of humanity'), and 'tribe' as opposed to 'people' and 'ethnic group', which were terms that were reserved for the 'civilized' people of Europe. Thus, for example, conflict between different non-European groups was inevitably described as 'tribal warfare' between groups that were implicitly understood to be 'uncivilized'.

In the case of Africa, anthropology as a research enterprise met with no opposition as its peoples were classified into 'tribes', with peculiar cultures that were doomed to be replaced by the superior cultures of

Europe. But to reinforce the antipodal idea of the natural superiority of the European over the African – and other non-Europeans – the sub-discipline of physical anthropology was developed. Thus, based on physical phenotypical observation – mostly founded on frivolous considerations of a dubious scientific nature – Africans were variously described as 'negroes', 'true negroes', 'negroid but not negro', 'Hamitic', 'Bantu' (often mistakenly used as a racial term), 'Semitic' (a linguistic term often used erroneously as a racial term), 'bushmen', and so on. The racial categories employed were, for the most part, founded on unscientific criteria. The term 'negro', for example, was casually used by Portuguese seamen to describe the people they met on the West African coast during the fifteenth century. The term itself was defined only in very broad terms referring principally to pigmentation. The word was later imported into the other European languages, and used interchangeably with 'black'. It is interesting to note that, in the sixteenth century, preferred terms for Africans in England included 'blackamoor' and 'tawnymoor' (see Shakespeare's *Othello*).

The scientifically dubious classification of Africa's populations into pseudo-racial types eventually became standardized in anthropological literature. In order to explain away what were seen as instances of 'civilization', the term 'caucasoid' was coined in anthropological literature. This conceptual move was coupled with a physical anthropology by gradation. African groups that did not fit the arbitrarily selected ideal-type criteria of the 'negro' seemed to fall more into the Eurocentric phenotypical ideal. Those deemed to have developed cultures of some note were explained as having been positively influenced by 'caucasoid genetics'. This was the basis of the 'Hamitic hypothesis' expounded by Charles Seligman in his classic Eurocentric text on African anthropology, *The Races of Africa* (1930), and the linguistic truncation of Africa into 'negro languages' and 'Hamito-Semitic'. General critiques of such classifications have led to a more objective categorization of 'African languages', and the replacement of the term 'Hamito-Semitic' by 'Afro-Asiatic'.

Scientific advances in the area of genetics have demonstrated that the indigenous populations of Africa are more interrelated than the simplistic theories of orthodox Eurocentric anthropology had claimed (Tishkoff et al. 2009). Genetic studies of the populations of Africa demonstrate that two major haplogroups dominate the African continent: E1b1a and E1b1b. The former is found mainly in West Africa and parts of southern Africa, while the latter has its origins in East Africa (Tanzania and the Horn of Africa), and is dominant in East and North Africa. Thus the anthropological, archaeological, cultural and political classification of the African continent into 'black Africa' (euphemistically referenced as 'sub-Saharan Africa') and North Africa (referenced tendentiously in Eurocentric discourse as 'the Middle East'), is easily exposed as being founded on dubious assumptions.

African archaeology and history reconfigured

The research area of African archaeology has been a major area in which Eurocentric ideology has exercised much academic influence over the years but it has witnessed a number of challenges in recent times. Popular ideology had it that African tool technology had not progressed beyond the level of the Neolithic until more advanced metal technologies such as copper and iron were introduced from outside the continent. The most egregious example of such misconceptions is iron smelting. Research data now confirms that not only was iron smelting in almost universal usage in Africa by the tenth century, but also that its origins were mainly indigenous (Miller 1997).

More important in the ongoing research debates is the assumption that the archaeology of Africa includes only the so-called 'sub-Saharan' areas. This is an exemplary instance of Eurocentric ideology. This arbitrary truncation of the continent in terms of its archaeological history reinforces pseudo-racial notions concerning the concepts of race and 'civilization'. The archaeological history of Ancient Egypt and Kush (Nubia) has been deemed to be so impressive that Eurocentric archaeology cannot conceive of including these research areas in the matrix of African archaeology. The standard thesis of early Egyptologists such as James Breasted was that the archaeological structures and the relatively advanced level of the civilization of Ancient Egypt, were due to some 'dynastic race' that invaded Egypt from West Asia, bringing with it the ingredients of civilization. But scientific research has since shown that the archaeology of ancient Egypt, Nubia, Axum, among others, are all properly designated as sites for African anthropological research (Diop 1991). The same principle applies to Eurocentric appraisals of other aspects of Africa's material cultures and civilizations, and in areas such as urbanization and pre-colonial architecture, outside ancient Egypt and Kush.

All this leads us to the issue of African history, which has been debated contentiously in some quarters. The history of Africa has been a central research area where Eurocentric thought has held sway for many years. Its cornerstone hypothesis was that human rationality should not be invoked in any attempt to explain past events on the African continent. Certainly, events took place on the continent, but these were seen as unstructured and not susceptible to explanation in terms of human behavioural cause and effect. A prototypical statement in this regard was made by Hegel in his *Philosophy of History* (1902), where he discounts the idea of rational history as applicable to Africa. In Hegel's conception of world history, a 'universal spirit' (*Geist*) moves from the East to the West, imbuing civilizations with a rational historical destiny, the telos of which is to increase human freedom at each temporal juncture. But, for Hegel, this rational dialectical movement completely bypasses Africa – apart from ancient Egypt, which he described as a puzzling phenomenon.

Hegel's view of an ahistorical Africa was supported by European historians throughout the colonial era. The basic assumption was that Africa's history did not really begin until the encounter between Africa and Europe from the fifteenth century onwards. The argument advanced in support of this was that a necessary condition for historical movement and explanation is that events be understood as resulting from rational and purposive behaviour. In addition, they had to be recorded in writing and stored for posterity. The British historian, Hugh Trevor-Roper for example, advanced precisely this thesis with respect to African history.

One post-colonial counter-argument has been that oral histories should be recognized. Whatever the merits of this argument, it is a fact that there were written histories in parts of Africa before colonialism. Furthermore, historical movement in terms of cause and effect, can be seen in the rise and fall of the medieval nations of Ghana, Mali and Songhay, as documented in historical works such as *Tariq es-Soudan* by by Abderrahman es-Sa'di (1900) and *Tariq al-Fettach* by Mahmoûd Kati (1913). It was Kati who so movingly described the fall of Songhay at the Battle of Tondibi in 1591 at the hands of Moroccan mercenaries. Many written historical records concerning Ghana, Mali and Songhay have been found in old family libraries in Mali. Written records of the history of the Hausa peoples of northern Nigeria also exist. Thus the Eurocentric model of African history has been exposed as false. This explains the revisions that well-known historians such as Oliver and Fage have had to make to more recent editions of their longstanding histories of Africa. Definitive refutations of the Eurocentric model of African history are to be found in Cheikh Anta Diop's *L'Afrique noire précoloniale* (1960) and *L'unité culturelle de l'Afrique noire* (1960). UNESCO and Cambridge University Press's voluminous publications on African history, that also demonstrate that the argument that African history was unstructured, and that none of it had ever been written down, can be easily refuted. Well-argued histories of West Africa by the duo, Jacob Ajayi and Michael Crowder as well as Joseph Ki-Zerbo were published as far back as 1972. Further developments have seen the linking of the post-fifteenth-century history of West Africa with that of the transatlantic truck in humans, and the peopling of southern Africa in post-archaeological times.

Conclusion

One of the most stubborn surviving distortions is the geopolitical compartmentalization of the physically continuous African continent into sub-Saharan Africa and the Middle East. The basis for this lies in Eurocentric anthropology's racial classification of the peoples of Africa into diverse racial groups such as 'negroes', Hamites, Semites, Bantus, and so on. Thus the idea of 'negro Africa' was concocted with its interchangeable cognate 'black Africa'. The Northern part of Africa was excised from the rest of Africa and linked with West Asia under the rubric of the so-called 'Middle East'. African political theorists had no say in these configurations. The result is that, over time, this distortion became embedded in linguistic and official discourse. It has been reified to the extent that it is now a standard classification in journals and other texts, and has become embedded in the policy and practice of international institutions such as the IMF and the World Bank.

Throughout this chapter, I have attempted to show that there are valid epistemological grounds for a critique of the cognitive impositions that a technologically dominant Europe imposed on the world, including Africa, from the sixteenth century onwards. Such impositions are of dubious content. Yet, at the cognitive level, such Eurocentric impositions have become the normal discourse of diverse forms of knowledge found in all research areas, and especially in the social sciences. In this chapter, I have examined different modes of knowledge as they have been ideologically configured according the dictates of Eurocentric discourse on Africa, but more than this, I have offered alternative analyses, statements and correctives. This should constitute a basis for the development of models of Africa-centred knowledge. The goal here is not to replace the ideological instrumentalism of Eurocentric discourse with some kind of African alternative; rather, it is to promote objectivist discourse on all forms of knowledge as these relate to Africa and the rest of the world.

References

Ajayi, Jacob and Michael Crowder, eds. (1970) *History of West Africa*, (Vol. 1). New York: Columbia University Press.

Ajayi, Jacob and Michael Crowder (1974) *History of West Africa*, (Vol. 2). London: Longman.

Amin, Samir (1989) *Eurocentrism*, New York: Monthly Review Press.

Barnes, Barry (1977) *Interests and the Growth of Knowledge*, London: Routledge.

Berger, Peter and Thomas Luckmann (1966) *The Social Construction of Reality: A Treatise in the Sociology of Knowledge*, Garden City, NY: Anchor.

Bloor, David (1976) *Knowledge and Social Imagery*, London: Routledge & Kegan Paul.

Breasted, James H (1905/1964) *A History of Egypt*, New York: Bantam.

Camic, Charles, Neil Gross, and Michele Lamont (2011) *Social Knowledge in the Making*, Chicago: University of Chicago Press.

Césaire, Aimé (1955/2000) *Discourse on Colonialism*, New York: Monthly Review Press.

Diop, Cheikh A (1973) *Nations nègres et culture*, Paris: Presence Africaine.

Diop, Cheikh A (1987) *Precolonial Black Africa*, New York: Lawrence Hill.

Diop, Cheikh A (1991) *Civilization or Barbarism*, NewYork: Lawrence Hill.

Durkheim, Emile (1982) *The Rules of Sociological Method*, New York: Free Press.

Fanon, Frantz (1963) *The Wretched of the Earth*, New York: Grove.

Fanon, Frantz (1967) *Black Skin, White Masks*, New York: Grove.

Feyerabend, Paul and Ian Hacking (1988) *Against Method*, London: Verso.

Gould, Stephen J (1981) *The Mismeasure of Man*, New York: W.W. Norton.

Hegel, Georg W (1902) *The Philosophy of History*, George Bell & Sons.

Hostettler, Nick (2012) *Eurocentrism: A Marxian Critical Realist Critique*, New York: Routledge.

Kati, Mahmoûd (1913) *Tariq el-Fettach*, (trans. Octave Houdas and Maurice Delafosse). Paris: Ernest Leroux.

Klein, Richard (1989) *The Human Career: Human Biological and Cultural Origins*, Chicago: University of Chicago Press.

Kuhn, Thomas (1962) *The Structure of Scientific Revolutions*, Chicago: University of Chicago Press.

Mannheim, Karl (1936) *Ideology and Utopia*, London: Routledge and Kegan Paul.

Mauss, Marcel (2005) *The Nature of Sociology*, New York: Berghahn.

McBrearty, Sally and Alison Brooks (2000) 'The revolution that wasn't: A new interpretation of the origin of modern human behavior', *Journal of Human Evolution*, 39 (5), p. 453-63.

McCarthy, E Doyle (1996) *Knowledge as Culture: The New Sociology of Knowledge*, New York: Routledge.

Miller, Duncan (1997) 'Ironworking technology', in Joseph Vogel, ed., *Encyclopedia of Precolonial Africa*, Walnut Creek, CA: Altamira.

Oliver, Roland and John Fage (1986) *Cambridge History of Africa*, (8 vols). Cambridge: Cambridge University Press.

Popper, Karl (1963) *Conjectures and Refutations*, London: Routledge.

es-Sa'di, Abderrahman (1900) *Tariq es-Soudan*, (translated by Octave Houdas). Paris: Leroux.

Schutz, Alfred, Thomas Luckmann, Richard M. Zaner and J. Tristam Engelhardt Jr (1973) *The Structures of the Life World*, (translated by Richard M. Zaner and H. Tristram Engelhardt). Evanston, IL: Northwestern University Press.

Seligman, Charles G (1930) *The Races of Africa*, London: Butterworth.

Senghor, Leopold S (1991) *Leopold Sedar Senghor: The Collected Poetry*, Charlottesville, VA: University of Virginia Press.

Tishkoff, Sarah, Floyd A. Reed, Francoise R. Friedlaender, et al. (2009) 'The genetic structure and history of Africans and African Americans' *Science*, 324 (5930), 1035-44.

Trevor-Roper, Hugh (1964) *Rise of Christian Europe*, London: Thames and Hudson.

Stringer, Christopher and Robin McKie (1997) *African Exodus: The Origins of Modern Humanity*, New York: Henry Holt.

Wolpoff, Milford and Rachel Caspari (1997) *Race and Human Evolution*, New York: Simon and Schuster.

2 Re-theorizing the Indigenous Knowledge Debate

Lesley Green

Introduction

One of Aesop's fables tells the story of Herakles whose journey took him over a distant mountain pass. At the point where the road narrowed between two great walls of rock, he came across an object in his path that looked like an apple. Why Herakles thought the object was an apple, or why an apple should have been quite so offensive to him, Aesop does not say. Perhaps, as the son of Zeus and the champion of the Olympian order over underworld monsters, he thought that it was the apple from Hades, who had given Persephone a fruit to keep her a prisoner. Perhaps the apple was the harbinger of another Mediterranean story with shades of the serpent of Eden. Perhaps Herakles just developed a blind road rage, or suffered the low oxygen of the moral high ground. Whatever the reason, our hero stamped on the hapless apple, to crush it. Instead it doubled in size. So he stamped on it again, and hammered it with his club for good measure. The apple swelled up so much that it blocked the road. At that moment Athena appeared. "Stop!" she called, "this is the thing about disputes and quarrels. If you fight, do you see how it blows up?" Herakles dropped his club and stepped back, agape. His way was blocked. All he could do was to turn around and go back home.[1]

Like Herakles, our scholarly pathways take us on long journeys in search of many things: fresh perspectives on familiar landscapes, and the fellowship of new ideas. One of many such journeys in our time is scholarship that seeks a route away from familiar intellectual regimes, a journey that looks for ways to question the dominance of the modernist vision, and the legacy of coloniality in scholarship of all kinds, in the fields of science, engineering, health, law, the humanities and the social sciences.

In South African critical scholarship, the journey toward the terrain

---

[1] Adapted from 'Fable 129, Herakles and Athena' in Aesop. See also the discussion on *The Root* on whether Aesop himself was African, as depicted in an eighteenth-century statue. http://www.theroot.com/views/aesop-black-fabled.

of indigenous knowledge has been overwhelmingly focused on former president Thabo Mbeki's view that HIV and AIDS would one day be cured by a locally-made pharmaceutical – ideally one home-grown from a traditional medicine, and patentable so that it could be a source of (rather than a drain on) state revenues (Fassin 2007; Green 2012; Levine 2012; Nattrass 2007). The consequences have been devastating. Millions of graves have been dug earlier than they should have been, and the science war that ensued has been shattering. So determined were scholars to stamp out the post-apartheid state's traditionalist ideas that anything that looked as if it might be linked to 'AIDS denialism' had to be struck from academic debates. Like the apple that defeated Herakles, any topic that looked even vaguely like a questioning of science caused many a scholar to retreat. Such questions, went prevailing scholarly wisdom, had no right to be on the scholarly road.

Like Herakles, South African scholars who were grappling with AIDS denialism were left with little option but to retreat into the fold of scientific objectivity, and into public debates that returned to the grand old South African narrative about defeating the alleged anarchy of traditionalism. In this chapter, I question that retreat, asking whether a scholarly engagement with debates in the indigenous knowledge movement necessarily has to hammer all things that smack of apples. Could we heed the counsel of Athena, the goddess of war, who brings to difficult situations the ability to reflect before acting, and find the courage to walk past a debate that, notwithstanding its importance, tends so quickly to engulf further discussion? Might it be possible to hold on to the importance of truth and evidence, as well as the accountability of publically funded scholars, yet hold back on hammering out home truths, thereby enabling us to find path home from a different direction?

Paradigm shifts and the idea of 'IK'

The language of objective modernist scholarship, as it appears in various forms across the globe, is deeply invested in the idea that in order to know, 'one' must be objective rather than subjective. In other words, 'one' must distance 'oneself' from what 'one' knows. Such a theory of knowing is based on the absence, rather than the presence, of the 'person who knows'.

Post-modern scholars take the contrary view. Demythologizing illusions of objectivity, they ask scholars to recognize and theorize their presence. Post-modern anthropology asks questions such as: How am I looking? Whose perspective do I occupy? How am I representing reality?

What histories allow me to be a researcher? What is the relationship between my research and colonial projects?

The scholarly approach that can broadly be termed the 'post-humanities' builds on the theory of the presence of the knower, but it takes a different view of the world, nature, and reality. The writings of Bruno Latour, Donna Haraway, John Law and Tim Ingold (among others) break with the modernist concern about the accuracy of representing things, and with the post-modern preoccupation over who has the power to represent things in particular ways. For 'post-humanists', the problem with both modernist and post-modernist approaches is that they rest on the Enlightenment assumption that there is a single nature or reality that can be known, either in itself or via a critical view of the social conditions that have influenced its representation.

For the post-humanities, what is of interest is the network of mutually dependent relationships through which objects of study emerge as things. Such an approach does not take as given the idea that reality is 'out there', and that it can be accessed and represented by experts. Rather, it proposes that reality is constantly being produced, enacted or brought into being between actors – both human and non-human. According to this view, the 'nature' that scholars know and represent is the product of a series of activities that produce particular versions of nature. It is argued that these versions can be produced in many different ways – hence the idea that the object of study is neither 'nature' nor 'culture' but natures-cultures (Latour 1999; Law and Lien 2010). Crucially, the reduction that enables one to know is seen as an effect of the relationships between actors; that is, it is in relationships that things and objects come to be defined.

This chapter explores the ways in which debates about indigenous knowledge proceed in relation to these different approaches to knowledge. My contention is threefold. First, I suggest that these views offer very different ways of thinking about indigenous knowledge, such that the very concepts ' indigenous' and 'knowledge' mean different things. Second, I aim to make the case that some of the major arguments around the idea of indigenous knowledge derive from problems within the modernist and post-modernist paradigms themselves. In other words, the ways in which each of these approaches produces the idea of 'indigenous', and the idea of 'knowledge' sets up the great irremediables in the various stand-offs between the categories 'indigenous knowledge' or 'traditional knowledge' and 'science' or 'scholarship'. Third, I propose that the post-humanities offer an opportunity to reframe scholarly engagements with knowledge and ways of knowing that currently lie outside of the formally recognized canons of knowledge.

My argument opens with an account of modern and post-modern framings of the debate on indigenous knowledge. I outline these framings briefly (since they are, by and large, readily recognizable), and suggest why and how they contribute to the defence of a canon of scholarship that is narrow, and largely Euro-American. Thereafter, I provide an account of the post-humanities in some detail, and argue that it offers resources for rich engagements with different knowledges and ways of knowing. However, while the post-humanities gives knowledge researchers the opportunity to engage different intellectual heritages within the halls of scholarship, the challenge is for us to do so without once again privileging the newest innovations in Euro-American philosophy.

Modernist scholarship

Modernist scholarship has the potential to move in at least two directions. For defenders of the concept of indigenous knowledge, this knowledge is a product of bounded cultures: there is Zulu indigenous knowledge in South Africa, Cree in Canada, Xavante in Brazil, Yolnngu in Australia, and so on, and these are tied together by the assumption that they share their opposition to Western knowledge and science. Among those who hold this view, indigenous knowledge tends to be represented as an unchanging product of 'culture' and 'tradition', passed down from ancestors, and often tied to a specific place. Consonant with this view, such 'indigenous knowledge' is a 'reality' that is often patentable because its ownership is defensible by law, it is recognized by international organizations, it can be mapped, and so on.

Within the same modernist, objectivist approach, detractors of indigenous knowledge argue that it passes no tests of knowledge. 'Prove it', they say, 'using scientific methods.' Such a 'show us that your gods exist' approach is premised on the idea that the methods of science are universal, and can reveal all of 'reality'. Thus, anything outside of science must either be proven by scientific methods, and incorporated into the canon of knowledge ('justified true belief'), or remain as 'unjustified, untrue beliefs' alongside superstition, charlatanism, snake-oil and hocus-pocus.

The debate inevitably breaks down. The arguments back and forth tend to trade accusations and counter-accusations in a moral argument, in which the 'good' and 'bad' – as conventionally associated with 'the West' and 'the rest' – are transposed. African or indigenous knowledges are seen as 'worthy' and science as 'unworthy', 'racist' and 'colonial'.

Alternatively, some take the position that both science and indigenous knowledge are equivalent in that they are both belief systems. This is a position of radical relativism, in which knowing depends on who you are. However, this identity politics of knowledge collapses within its own paradigm. Given that a modernist theory of knowledge assumes that observers can know the real regardless of their socially constrained perspectives, it is undone by the assertion that the observer's perspective is shaped by the politics of knowledge.

Post-modernist approaches

This school of thought would have us read knowledge claims in relation to politics, political economy, social construction or ideological invention. This argument, too, is wielded to contrasting ends.

In South Africa, where former president Thabo Mbeki's Aids denialists cast virus science as a construction of something that did not exist, their opponents in the humanities and sciences cast 'traditional medicine' and indigenous knowledge as a construction of realities that did not exist. That debate, and its relation to postcolonial knowledge, sets up an extraordinary responsibility for scholars anywhere who seek to pursue the value of alternative intellectual heritages (Green 2009). In the words of Judith Farquhar, a medical anthropologist whose work engages contemporary Chinese medicine, asks 'On what philosophical basis can heterogeneous networks of global medicine be responsibly built?' Her question underscores the difficulty of finding agreements about knowledge. We are quick to be tolerant in matters of belief, she points out, but are as quick to become dogmatic about what constitutes knowledge.

Much of Farquhar's thinking builds on Latour's critique of post-modernism, and it is helpful to consider why Latour finds post-modern critiques of knowledge – and particularly the sciences – quite so unpalatable. In a paper titled, 'Why has critique run out of steam?' Latour writes:

> entire PhD programs are still running to make sure that good ... kids are learning the hard way that facts are made up, that there is no such thing as natural, unmediated, unbiased access to truth, that we are always prisoners of language, that we always speak from a particular standpoint, and so on, while dangerous extremists are using the very same argument of social construction to destroy hard-won evidence that could save our lives. (2004b: 229)

Central to his argument is the assertion that post-modern thought confuses criticism with anti-fetishism. To illustrate his argument, Latour holds up to scrutiny the post-modernists' twin projects of demolishing idols and exposing interests. For Latour, demolishing idols involves the rejection of belief, since, in this view, belief in gods or idols is what makes people do things. However, those beliefs are merely reflections of the power of belief and imagination to project their own power onto an object, or to invent a Being.

The second project of post-modernist methodology is the deconstruction of free will; this involves a reading of will in relation to the determinism of genes, interests, drives, etc. With characteristic wit, Latour observes the condition of the post-modern scholar or the 'never sleeping critic':

> Better equipped than Zeus himself you rule alone, striking from above with the salvo of antifetishism in one hand and the solid causality of objectivity in the other. The only loser is the naive believer, the great unwashed, always caught off balance. (2004b: 239)

For Latour, social explanations cannot account for scientific objects, be they viruses or climate change. That is, discussions of power, interests, social forces, social construction, and so on, cannot account for verifiable science. This reality is excruciatingly evident to scholars in South Africa who have grappled with the appropriation of post-modern arguments by AIDS denialists. Latour's ideas serve to make the case that the contradictions at the core of post-modernism cause 'indigenous knowledge' to be treated either as a product of social forces – class interests, ethno-nationalism, discourses of genetics, etc., or as a resurgence of naive belief in superstition. In my view, this traps the debate in a binary of 'knowledge' versus 'belief' or 'fact' versus 'fetish'.

The post-humanities

For Latour, the issue is not to swear off post-modern constructivism, but to rethink its target. Thus, instead of directing attention to the conditions that make facts possible – an approach that leaves 'facts' and 'reality' intact, while problematizing thought about them – the issue is to cultivate a radical empiricism, and attempt to move closer to reality (2004b: 231). In other words, what we are encouraged to do is focus on the ways in which a concept becomes real through agreements, actions, linkages and investments. Indigenous knowledge would be one such concept. What is needed, Latour argues, is for scholars to move beyond the social determinists' position on 'fact' and the antifetishists' position on what Latour calls 'fairy'. Such an intellectual programme begins with a rethinking of the division between objects and subjects; objectivities and subjectivities; knowledge and belief. From this perspective, many of the debates about indigenous knowledge derive more from the philosophical approach of the discussants than they do from the knowledges and ways of knowing that are apparently under discussion.

Perhaps most seriously, the debate, then, is confined to a terrain called 'Culture', and the political programme that emanates from this. In other words, where knowledge diversity is translated as 'indigenous knowledge' and 'culture', the task of the humanities becomes one of promoting tolerance. But, as distinguished philosopher of science Isabelle Stengers asks, 'Who wants to be tolerated?' (2011) Her argument is that accepting a division between nature and culture generates a profoundly compromised, and indeed patronizing, politics. Her commentary offers an interesting moment of convergence with the arguments put forward by indigenous movements: surely it might be possible to work with versions of nature that assemble the world differently, which speak with a wisdom regarding relationships, and which do not just collect data on isolated objects?

To be sure, plenty of overlaps and partial connections have been demonstrated between the sciences and ways of knowing the world that fall outside the terms of the sciences. But the approach that takes scientific nature as the only true given, asks 'indigenous knowledge' merely to fill in the gaps. Thus ideas presented as 'indigenous knowledge' are 'mined', and any that might prove lucrative are extracted for use in the knowledge economy – something like pharmacologically active ingredients from a plant, for example. In effect, 'indigenous knowledge' is split into aspects that concur with scientific nature, and those that do not, leaving the nature–culture divide and the belief–knowledge duality intact.

Re-evaluating the project of modern thought initiated by Descartes, post-humanist thought resists the idea that only humans are capable of actions and responses in systems that are otherwise governed by laws and rules. The argument, therefore, rejects the founding dualism – the division between subjects and objects – that undergirds the divides between nature and culture, mind and body, tradition and modernity. In what follows, I sketch briefly some of the kinds of conversations that are possible between the post-humanities and what I would call 'non-canonical' ways of knowing. I do so under three themes: Nature | Culture; Mind | Body, and Traditional | Modern.

Nature | Culture

Even things as apparently universal as the ocean or the human body mean very different things to different people. Many fishers, for example, relate to the ocean as a partner to whom they listen and with whom they have a relationship. Many scientists, on the other hand, tend to see the sea as a collection of water molecules of a certain temperature that sustain an ecosystem. In other words, for a great many fishers, Nature is not an object (or a thing) but an actor. It is worth noting that such an approach is very different from that offered by ecosystem services assessment, for example. The relationship between people and nature is a resource that, for conservationists, has no price tag. It is an approach that is profoundly political, as is apparent in contexts such as Ecuador, where nature's rights have been written into the country's constitution (see De la Cadena).

Another example: the deep insights into the consequences of social relationships for health and disease offered by *izangomas* derives from their understanding of the networks – human and non-human – that extend notions of personhood, health and wellbeing beyond the spatial boundaries of the body. Such understandings of what it is to be a person encompass relationships across time, with those who have passed on, and across space, including the relationship between bodiliness, food, and the kinds of care or enmity that bring it to the body. Such ideas generate very specific forms of ethical political actions, which may play out not only in the work of a traditional healer but also in networks of care, in community conflict resolution, parenting and jurisprudence, for example (see Cornell 2009; Mokgoro 1998; Devisch 1993).

My interest in the political projects and protocols attached to these ideas relates to the point that such differences are not 'decorative', cultural, optional extras in a world of politics informed by scientific nature: rather, that scientific nature is profoundly politicized, and has consequences for the ways in which we do politics. 'Cosmopolitics' is the word offered by Isabelle Stengers (2005) to describe how all knowledges rely on ontological moorings that are not, in themselves, part of 'nature'. For Latour, as for Stengers, the word 'cosmopolitics' has come to stand for a way of thinking about the relationship between science and politics that exceeds the possibilities of the cosmopolitan project. In a paper entitled 'Whose Cosmos, Which Cosmopolitics?' (2004a), Latour argues that multiculturalism fails intellectually to offer grounds for world peace. Peace, he argues, will not come through 'pedagogical warfare', which teaches people about the 'universal nature' known by Science (in the singular, and with a capital 'S'). This 'leave your gods at the door' approach to peace negotiations already asserts a profoundly political reality, he argues; it is a questionable reality, which leaves unexplored the fetishes of contemporary modernity.

Latour is no relativist, however. His argument is profoundly in favour of responsible empiricism, which enables contestations over the sciences to enter public debates, rather than remain outside of them. But in order for this to happen, the tools of intellectual life must include a critique of the central tenets of modernity. Contemporary democracies draw matters of culture into parliaments, he asserts, but leave 'nature' to the scientists, where it is, for the most part, outside the frameworks of public accountability. A project that expands the terrain of the real across the sciences, and into an understanding of the ways in which things are brought into being, is what he has in mind. That kind of political project is able to engage the limits of modernist techniques of knowing the world. Rather than proposing that the central challenge for contemporary politics is multiple cultures, the suggestion is that multiple *natures* are at issue; that is, different ways of knowing and assembling information about the world.

The idea of 'multiple natures', however, can easily slip the old idea of multiple cultures into a new language, and the challenge of the post-humanities is to resist dualism altogether. 'Nature' is not necessarily that which is known by science; nature exceeds the specific reductive processes through which the sciences generate agreement on specific facts.

Mind | Body
In his 2007 book, *Lines: A Brief History*, anthropologist Tim Ingold critiques modernist technologies of data collection. He notes that cartography, musical notation, architectural drawing, and so on, remove movement and bodiliness from the notation of information, and argues that the elimination of the body from modern technologies derives from the broader quest to generate apparently 'objective' information. Ingold's project yields many possibilities for re-engagement with the humanities, sciences, technologies, as well as with ways of knowing that have not found their way into curricula. Ingold's work draws attention to the ways in which the practices of scientific knowledge-recording specifically serve to exclude ways of knowing the world that are based on movement, or touch, rather than stasis and image. These scientific practices are meaningful and important in specific contexts, but they become exclusionary where tactile knowledges, embodied knowledges, and movement-based knowledges are disavowed as meaningful ways of knowing the world, and are then relegated to the status of 'culture' or 'intuition'. Fishers' knowledges (see Chapter 7) are very difficult to translate into the languages of the sciences for this reason.

Anthropologies of knowledge are increasingly turning ethnographers' attention towards practice-based knowledges. These are not easily rendered in a form that a court of law might regard as 'justified true belief'; nor do they generate the databases that technologies such as maps or heart-rate monitors do. How do we account for the ways of knowing that exists in the touch of a midwife who reads a birthing belly with her hands? How might we defend what she knows in a court of law where her accusers charge her with 'malpractice' because she did not generate a stream of numbers from the foetal heart-rate monitor that would have tethered the birthing mother to a hospital bed? Under what conditions would her accusers acknowledge that years of experience in obstetric medicine build a very similar set of skills, which many practitioners prize as much as the patterns emitted by heart-rate monitors? At the core of this argument is the recognition that some ways of knowing lie outside the terrain of formally accredited knowledge. This is so often not because these ways of knowing are unjustifiable, but because they synthesize many forms of sensory data, and the technologies that might be used to measure them have not been developed. In addition, knowledge that resists being written down is difficult to fit into a curriculum.

In this scenario, the relationship between law, technology, writing and knowing comes under scrutiny again. The relationship between science and the practices of the state is very close indeed, and is central to the functioning of the judiciary and policing. For the post-humanities, then, what is of interest are the kinds of knowledges that fall outside the formal canon. These include the intellectual heritages that bring certain knowledges to us as legitimate and authorized; the technologies that make these knowledges real; and the entanglements of such knowledges with capital. Ultimately, the post-humanities provoke questions about the ways in which such ideas become practices of governance in the knowledge economy, where rationality and the sciences are often framed by the logics of capital.

Isabelle Stengers (2008) foregrounds ways of knowing that are part of life and care – aspects of knowledge and knowing that are not easily made into objects. These are the qualitative aspects of wellbeing that the 'knowledge economy' is unable to measure using familiar kinds of enumerations, and which it therefore fails to notice. Stengers' emphases provoke many questions for South Africa's debate on 'AR vs ARVs' (African Renaissance versus anti-retrovirals). For example, in what ways does the South African science war, with its stark positions on science and traditional medicine, set up conditions in which discussions of care, nurture and nutrition are seen as 'dissident science'? In what ways does this, in turn, contribute to conditions of thought that allow a diabetic patient to spend a day in a primary health-care clinic and receive four successive drips but no food?[2] The point is not to blame-shift from one side to another, but to recognize that stark polemic makes for stark choices, and that sometimes the polemic itself is caught up in that which undermines nurture, care and wellbeing. Stengers' call is for knowledge-makers in the knowledge economy to stop developing ever cleverer denunciations of those whose views they oppose, but to recognize and engage with efforts to bring vitality, nurture, and wellbeing into the knowledge economy. Her appeal is for a dialogue about a different ecology of knowledge that might offer researchers a line of flight from the destructive fallout of the science wars. Crucially, her work builds upon a profound respect for the possibilities of the sciences, and a deep reading of the social and political conditions that enable or foreclose research. In addition, she has made a careful reading of epistemic practices (how knowledge is produced) in relation to criticism of the ontological frame that the West acquired during the Enlightenment era, when the notions of nature and culture were first separated.

Stengers' work also provokes questions about the entanglement of 'indigenous knowledge' with the knowledge economy in emerging markets such as those of South Africa, India and Brazil. For example, once particular molecules have passed their clinical trials, they are defined as trademarked traditional medicine (TM™). The trademarked product then constitutes a new knowledge object and takes on a very particular life in national wealth-creation and black-empowerment projects, whether in South Asia or South Africa, as well as in global networks that hold pharmaceutical retailers, street vendors, rural museums, biopiracies, and nascent ethno-nationalisms together. Without question, wealth creation is an important part of redressing the historical injustices that are built into the knowledge economy, but I think we need to also be asking whether the TM™ approach has become a new form of 'thingification'? Does it not render unnameable exactly the sorts of vitalities and ways of knowing and being, that constitute indigenous resistance to the global economy elsewhere in the world, whether this be among Ecuadorean mining activists or in a women's housing project in Philippi in Cape Town, South Africa?

Traditional | Modern
Once one can begin to recognize the ways in which regimes of knowledge transform traditional medicine into TM™ , it becomes possible to

---

[2]   This experience was related to me by an elderly black Capetonian after she was treated at one of the day clinics in the greater Cape Town area in October 2010.

recognize that while 'indigenous knowledge' takes its rhetoric from tradition, it operates and stands very firmly within the frameworks of modernity.

South Africa's policy on indigenous knowledge, published in 2004 (Department of Science and Technology), is heavily invested in the neoliberal knowledge economy. The model evinces a trade-off: it gets space in the Department of Science and Technology and in some universities but in a way that all too frequently sets it up as a project of 'African knowledge for wealth creation'. Because of its very separateness – as African knowledge – and its paradoxical marriage to global capital, it has very little capacity to challenge what Latour calls the 'three goddess sisters of reason in the knowledge economy', namely '(technical) Efficiency, (economic) Profitability and (scientific) Objectivity' (2007: 14). And yet it is precisely the different ecologies of knowledge, and different iterations of reason and the reasonable, that inspire much of what the indigenous knowledge movement claims to represent. How might we recover these resources for a critique?

In my view, their recovery begins with recognizing their entanglement with capital in state-led approaches to indigenous knowledge in contemporary South Africa. Once this is on the table, it becomes possible to ask different kinds of questions, and to develop a different intellectual project. Might 'indigenous knowledge' be pursued via investment somewhere other than the stock market? If so, what kinds of dialogues about knowledges might be possible where tools of testing, criticism and innovation are encouraged? How might the capacity to test knowledge and ways of knowing be rethought and rekindled? What aspects of knowledge lie beyond the realm of monetarization? What kinds of practices lie outside laboratory testing? What aspects of knowing resist quantitative research? What kinds of public spaces are opening for criticism of patriarchal elites, and what conditions within the humanities would support the emergence of these new conversations?

For Latour, it is of great fascination that the very word 'things', in early languages, implied a gathering around a shared concern (Latour 2005). He argues that the moment at which a thing is identified as a thing becomes possible through shared understandings, actions, concerns, assemblages, responses. For this reason, Latour argues for a shift of focus away from 'the facts', or 'matters of fact', to the kind of 'expanded reality' spoken of earlier. In this context, the consonances of entire networks of people and things are understood to be part of the social process that generates agreement on the nature of 'a thing'. As the idea of (for example) indigenous knowledge gathers momentum and becomes 'a thing' in itself, more and more research effort is poured into 'it': conferences are held, actions are coordinated, networks are fostered, government sub-departments are established, legitimacies are conferred, professorships are created, and products are patented. Gradually, the idea becomes contracted into its acronym: the indigenous way of knowing the world becomes 'IK', at which point 'IK' itself becomes a sector, an actor alongside others such as the 'gender', 'disability' or 'corporate' sectors.

A post-humanities view on 'IK' then, wholly rethinks the idea of indigenous knowledge. It welcomes different ways of assembling the world, and finds profoundly important resources for thinking in diverse intellectual heritages. This does not just involve mining for ideas (or patents!), but finding different resources for thinking itself, and engaging with different ways of thinking in the world. The post-humanities view is interested in the enactments that bring 'indigenous knowledge' into being as a player in settings as diverse as community groups, academic life, corporate sectors, and parliaments. It is concerned with finding different insights into vitality, systemic relations, philosophy, and causality. Such a view does not take the object known as 'IK' as a given; it is interested in how this concept has meaning, life, reality, and limits in different contexts, in how it can be different things, and play out in different ways. The move from matters of fact to matters of concern shifts attention away from 'IK' as a thing given in nature, to understanding it as an actor that mobilizes resources and actions in different contexts and in various ways.

The insights of the post-humanities bring to the table a robust critique of the ontologies that form the intellectual heritage of modernity and, for that reason, this perspective offers a productive intellectual space for engaging the terrain of knowledge diversity.

Conclusion: expanding the canon?

All of the approaches and questions above make a case for critical engagement with South Africa's current policy on indigenous knowledge. Such an engagement requires rethinking the assertions that are currently enshrined in policy. These include, first, that the notion of 'indigenous knowledge' exists primarily as a static inheritance with potential for wealth creation in the knowledge economy. Second, that formal science and its associated technologies are the only way to measure and define the things we can call knowledge in relation to the indigenous. Much more interesting and productive is to pursue a critical enquiry into intellectual heritages, including the ways in which the project of contemporary scholarship continues to define the particular kind of divide between knowledge and belief that emanates from the battle to separate church and state in Europe so long, long ago. Do we really need to continue to fight that battle in the way that we do?

South Africa's science war has taught many important things. In this chapter, I have focused on one: the urgency of finding fresh, intellectually tenable approaches to the idea of indigenous knowledge. I have sketched three theoretical positions, and explored the ways in which they would treat the object of 'indigenous knowledge'. My aim is to open up an approach that is mindful of the real challenges and responsibilities involved in being a knowledge producer, and that avoids the mistake made by Herakles, when he declared war on an apple, thereby blocking his own path.

References

Aesop (1998) 'Herakles and Athena', Fable 129, in Olivia and Robert Temple, trans. *The Complete Fables*, London: Penguin.

Cornell, Drucilla (2009) 'uBuntu, pluralism and the responsibility of legal academics to the new South Africa', *Law and Critique*, 20 (1): 43-58.

De la Cadena, Marisol (2010). 'Indigenous cosmopolitics in the Andes: Conceptual reflections beyond "politics"', *Cultural Anthropology*, 25 (2): 334-70.

Department of Science and Technology, Republic of South Africa (2004) *Indigenous Knowledge Systems Policy*, Pretoria.

Devisch Rene (1993) *Weaving the Threads of Life: The Khita Gyn-Eco-Logical Healing Cult among the Yaka*, Chicago Ill: University of Chicago Press.

Farquhar, Judith (2012) 'Knowledge in translation: Global science, local things' in Susan Levine, ed., *Medicine and the Politics of Knowledge*, Cape Town: HSRC Press.

Fassin, Didier (2007) *When Bodies Remember: Experiences and Politics of AIDS in South Africa*, Berkeley CA: University of California Press.

Green, Lesley (2009) 'Knowledge contests, South Africa, 2009', *Anthropology Southern Africa*, special issue on Anthropologies of Knowledge, 32: (1&2): 2-7.

Green, Lesley (2012) 'Beyond South Africa's "indigenous knowledge" versus "science" wars', *South African Journal of Science*, 108 (7/8):. 44-54.

Ingold, Tim (2007) *Lines: A Brief History*, London: Routledge.

Latour, Bruno (1999) *Pandora's Hope: Essays on the Reality of Science Studies*, Cambridge, MA: Harvard University Press.

Latour, Bruno (2004a) 'Whose cosmos, which cosmopolitics? Comments on the peace terms of Ulrich Beck', *Common Knowledge*, 10 (3): 450-62.

Latour, Bruno (2004b) 'Why has critique run out of steam? From matters of fact to matters of concern', *Critical Inquiry*, 30 (2): 225-48.

Latour, Bruno (2005) 'Introduction: From realpolitik to dingpolitik – or how to make things public', in Bruno Latour and Peter Weibel, eds, *Making Things Public: Atmospheres of Democracy*, Cambridge MA: MIT Press.

Latour, Bruno (2007) 'The recall of modernity', *Cultural Studies Review*, 13 (1): 11-30.

Law, John and Marianne Lien (2010) Emergent Aliens: Performing Indigeneity and Other Ways of Doing Salmon in Norway. Working paper.

Levine, Susan (2012) 'Testing knowledge: Legitimacy, healing, and medicine in South Africa', in S. Levine, ed., *Medicine and the Politics of Knowledge*, Cape Town: HSRC Press.

Mokgoro, Yvonne (1998) 'Ubuntu and the law in South Africa', *Buffalo Human Rights Law Review*, 4: 15-23.

Nattrass, Nicoli (2007) *Mortal Combat: AIDS Denialism and the Struggle for Antiretrovirals in South Africa*, Durban: University of KwaZulu-Natal Press.

Stengers, Isabelle (2005) 'The cosmopolitical proposal' in Bruno Latour and Peter Weibel eds, *Making Things Public: Atmospheres of Democracy*, Cambridge MA: MIT Press.

Stengers, Isabelle (2008) 'Experimenting with refrains: Subjectivity and the challenge of escaping modern dualism', *Subjectivity*, 22: 38-59.

Stengers, Isabelle (2011) *Cosmopolitics II*, (trans. Robert Bononno). Minneapolis MN: University of Minnesota Press.

3 Battlefields of Knowledge
Conceptions of Gender in Development Discourse

Signe Arnfred

Concepts are not innocent. On the contrary: concepts and categories are hugely important in determining what is seen and understood, as well as what is marginalized and/or made invisible. This is true in any field of knowledge, and very much so in development studies and development discourse – fields in which African cases figure prominently. In this chapter, I look critically at conceptions of gender as produced in and by the development establishment, with a particular focus on the World Bank, which ranks highly on a global level in terms of both the production and dissemination of knowledge.

My intention is to map some important struggles in the discursive field regarding how to think and talk about gender and power in development contexts. Of course, the power differential between an exceptionally well-resourced institution such as the World Bank on one hand, and women's organizations on the other, is clearly unequal. Nevertheless, during the two UN Decades for Women (1975-1985 and 1985-1995), women's organizations succeeded – particularly during the series of UN conferences held in the early 1990s – in influencing development discourse regarding women and gender on a global scale. This resulted in the 1995 Beijing Platform for Action (PfA), which still – almost 20 years later – serves as 'the Bible', or bottom line, for development NGOs working with issues of women and gender. As noted by Annelise Riles in her anthropological study of transnational network processes leading up to the Beijing conference:

> In general these conferences remain low-status events from international lawyers' point of view owing to the 'nonbinding' nature of conference agreements and resolutions. The hope of their proponents, however, is that as 'language' is quoted and repeated from one conference document to the next and as states begin to conform their practices, or at least their discourse, to the norms expressed therein, some of what is agreed upon at global conferences gradually will become rules of 'customary international law'. (2000: 8)

This has indeed happened. Yet, as discussed in this chapter, this very success is problematic on at least two accounts. First, in the process of formulating concepts, problems arose between feminists from the North and the South in terms of ambiguities and divergences. Second, some discursive victories are being co-opted and reused in different contexts by powerful donors.

In writing this chapter, I drew on contributions to *African Feminist Politics of Knowledge: Tensions, Challenges, Possibilities*, (Adomako Ampofo and Arnfred 2010), which I co-edited. I also drew on selected writings, predominantly by feminists from the global South, and on my own analysis of some post-Beijing reports by the World Bank, namely its 2001 report, *Engendering Development Through Gender Equality in Rights, Resources, and Voice* – including the preceding draft that was circulated for consultation (World Bank 2000) – and the *World Development Report 2012: Gender Equality and Development*.

After an introductory section on *struggles in the discursive field*, I take a closer look at the Beijing PfA, investigating some of its conceptions in order to identify their backgrounds and implications, as well as to see how these have been changed when reused in World Bank contexts. I then discuss some of the *ambiguities* and North/South contradictions in the 'discursive struggle' process, before I investigate the process of *co-option* by the World Bank. Finally, I consider feminist critiques of World Bank notions, and Southern (post-colonial) feminist challenges to Western/Northern feminist thinking. As it turns out, the fixed global language on gender that emerged from the UN's conferences on women, was born not only of powerful development institutions but also of Western/Northern (second-wave) feminism.

Struggles in the discursive field

In her positive and optimistic report about struggles relating to concepts of women and gender in development contexts, Gita Sen highlights the discursive battles that took place during some of the UN conferences in the early 1990s. Focusing particularly on the 1993 World Conference on Human Rights in Vienna, and the 1994 International Conference on Population and Development in Cairo, Sen argues that important paradigm shifts were introduced, thanks to concerted action by women's movements and organizations worldwide:

> Women's organizing in preparation for the 1993 International Conference for Human Rights in Vienna set the stage for the broadening of the human rights

framework ... Women's activism brought the issue of women's human rights squarely to the centre of the human rights debate ... This created a climate that made it possible for violence against women to be placed for the first time on the agenda for a major human rights conference. (2006: 133-34)

As noted by Sen, new concepts make it possible to ask new questions, to see other things. This is what discursive struggles are all about: rephrasing and reconceptualizing the field in question. The success of women's organizations at this level to date, has a lot to do with good organizing, and the concerted efforts of women, North and South. It might also, however, reflect the fact that the focus on gender offers a modification rather than a structural challenge to lines of thinking already established in development contexts.

The introduction, at the 1994 Cairo conference, of a conception of women's reproductive rights – later extended to include sexual health and rights – was a paradigm shift according to Sen. Previously, population growth had been portrayed as the single most serious threat to economic development, with population control being the primary policy response. Much of the work behind the paradigm shift was motivated by activists' concerns to challenge the coercion, human-rights abuses and unethical practices inherent in population policies and programmes. As Sen writes: 'The paradigm shift at ICPD [the International Conference on Population and Development] made it possible to begin to ask entirely new questions that were not focused on population control, but on the guaranteeing of rights and the meeting of needs' (2006: 139). In her analysis, Sen emphasizes the joint force of women's organizations in opposing the development establishment and national governments participating in the UN conferences; she does not mention possible North/South divergences. Sen is, however, very well aware that such conceptual victories are not cast in stone:

> The typical trajectory whenever significant changes in discourse occur is that critical research supported by activism first wages a major struggle to change old concepts and frameworks and introduce new ones. In the field of gender and development many such struggles have been waged to gain acceptance and use for concepts such as 'gender', 'empowerment', 'women's human rights', 'reproductive and sexual health' and 'sexual and reproductive rights'. But such a struggle is not a once-and-for-all event ... Winning the struggle over discourse (as happened at Vienna or Cairo) is only the first step. The greater the victory the more the likelihood that others will attempt to take over the discourse and subvert its meaning. *The battle is not over, it has just begun.* (2006: 138-39, emphasis added)

A major achievement of Sen's paper is her framing of the struggles over discourse as a battlefield in itself: a battlefield of knowledge. The elements of this battlefield are many; first and foremost, power and money play a role – even if, as shown at the UN conferences in Vienna, Cairo and Beijing, this power can be circumvented. Development discourse may be challenged, and donor organizations sometimes have to revamp their language, or even – in the rare cases when paradigm shifts take place as described above – be forced to think along new lines. Power relations are, however, less easily shifted. In the daily life of women's organizations (when applying for funding, for instance), donor organizations retain the upper hand. As pointed out by Andrea Cornwall and Karen Brock (2006), donor-funded project reports have to use a certain language to be taken seriously. Thus, donor organizations command not only economic, but also epistemic power.

In gender research in Africa, as elsewhere in the global South, donors set the agenda, either explicitly or implicitly. The World Bank is a major, indeed a decisive, producer of knowledge. Staffed by clever academics, the institution tends to pick up trends, sometimes controversial trends, and reissue these as development blueprints. Such powerful organizations determine what is worth knowing, and, frequently, who is deemed worthy as a knower. What is not worth knowing, in this episteme, tends to be labelled as ignorance. Less powerful donors follow the powerful ones and, in so doing, reveal the implicit and often unrecognized politics of knowledge embedded in funding dilemmas.

On the surface, and in its own self-representation, the World Bank is pursuing 'rightness' and 'goodness' (Cornwall and Brock 2006). At times, the bank almost takes over this role from the UN, speaking the language of rightness and goodness on behalf of everybody. The fact that it is a capitalist bank, which, like all capitalist entities, does what it does for money (which, in real life, means exploitation), is effectively concealed or overlooked. Furthermore, as pointed out by Charmaine Pereira ,'one of the unfortunate consequences of the convergence of epistemic and economic power wielded by funders is that their practice (like that of dictators) is rarely subject to critique' (2010: 101). Those who would be able to provide this critique are all too often the same people who receive the funding – and who bites the hand that feeds her? This is where the comparison with dictatorships becomes relevant. As Pereira asks, 'The willingness to engage with dissenting views is a precondition not only for knowledge building, but also for democratization. Yet, how many agencies, particularly those that champion both knowledge building and democratization, are themselves able to engage with dissent or critique?' (2010: 101).

The Beijing Platform for Action –
a victory for women's movements

The PfA resulting from the UN's Fourth World Conference for Women in Beijing in 1995, is often seen as the pinnacle and culmination of the struggles for discursive change waged by women's movements. And in many ways it was; the language of the World Bank, and other donor agencies, changed after Beijing, as did dominant images of women in development. Before Beijing, the dominant image of women in development was – by and large – 'woman the victim': that is, women as mothers suffering from poverty or malnutrition, or women as workers (mostly in agriculture), working around the clock, while the men of their households sit drinking under a tree. These oppressed and suffering women in need of rescuing by valiant white men[1] are (along with notions of lazy black and brown men) colonial tropes, implicitly and smoothly carried from the colonial era into the age of development.

After Beijing, however, a very different image of women in development emerged: 'woman as hero' is the post-Beijing image of women, the active, enterprising woman in whom it makes sense to invest. This new image adds a progressive, even feminist, touch to gender and development projects and programmes.[2] The 'woman-as-victim' image is, however, still invoked on certain special occasions, such as in contexts of emergency aid, and with regard to Muslim women (who are continually seen as victimized, oppressed, and waiting to be rescued). Later in the chapter, I elaborate on the ways in which the World Bank, in particular, and development discourse more generally, have reinterpreted issues of women and gender.

The Beijing documents clearly emphasize gender equality and rights. The PfA itself reads – at least partly – as a document written by women's movements. It offers a (mild) critique of World Bank structural-adjustment programmes from the points of view of women, and it notes that economic recessions and political instability often lead to poverty, which affects women more than men: women form an overwhelming majority of the world's poor. The PfA mentions the feminization of poverty, and the fact that female-headed households – the numbers of which are increasing worldwide – are often among the poorest of the poor. Women's unpaid household work is discussed in several contexts, e.g. in the following terms:

---

[1]   Here I draw on the image of 'white men saving brown women from brown men' – as famously put by Gayatri Spivak (1988: 296).
[2]   See Arnfred (2011) for an elaboration on images of women in development aid.

...women contribute to development, not only through remunerated work, but also through a great deal of unremunerated work ... This work is often not measured in quantitative terms and is not valued in national accounts. Women's contribution to development is seriously underestimated and thus its social recognition is limited. The full visibility of the type, extent and distribution of this unremunerated work will also contribute to a better sharing of responsibilities. (UN 1995: 70)

Further, it is noted that 'the boundaries of gender division of labour between productive and reproductive roles are gradually being crossed', with women entering into formerly male dominated areas, and men having started to accept greater responsibility for domestic work. It is, however, acknowledged that 'changes in women's roles have been greater and much more rapid than changes in men's roles' (UN 1995: 15). Thus women are left with a greater burden of unpaid and invisible work. The connection between this situation and the feminization of poverty is obvious: women cannot spend all their time earning money; they have other responsibilities as well.

The PfA points to important gender imbalances in how men's and women's work is calculated, while suggesting new approaches, in line with the paradigm shifts initiated in Cairo and Vienna. It was for good reason that having this document endorsed by the world's governments was seen as a victory for women's movements. This is one side of the Beijing story.

Ambiguities: the discursive victories of the Beijing process tempered by Southern views

Another side of the story focuses on North/South differences, and on difficulties and ambiguities embedded within the same series of UN conferences. As pointed out by Amina Mama (1997: 416), it was during the UN decades of women that African feminists first made their voices heard on the international scene. Nevertheless, Mama talks of 'United Nations feminism' as a bureaucratized version of feminism and of the ways in which the donor push for women's projects 'created huge institutional needs for WID [women-in-development] expertise, which in turn generated a bureaucratic discourse on women in development ... [that] had little to do with the everyday concerns of ordinary women' (1997: 417).

Ifi Amadiume also sees the Beijing PfA as a two-sided phenomenon. On the one hand, she noted that it was a unique achievement in terms of pressing governments and policymakers to take action on women's issues; on the other hand, she also sees 'how easy it is for European women to return from Beijing with an illusion of a truly global process and a harmonious global sisterhood, with all women saying the same thing in spite of diversity' (1997: 10). Comparing the UN's third World Conference on Women, held in Nairobi in 1985 with the 1995 Beijing conference, Amadiume notes that 'The intensity of interaction[3] has led to participants almost speaking the same language, as opposed to the creative dissent and tensions of Nairobi 1985' (1997: 10). At Beijing, she notes, the language changed: 'With this shift from a community or grassroots-articulated focus to professional leadership imposed from above, issues and goals have become repetitive in a fixed global language, and discourse is controlled by paid UN and other donor advisers, consultants and workers' (1997: 14).

The problems, as identified by Amadiume and by Mama, are i) the emergence of a fixed global language for talking about gender in development contexts, and ii) the fact that the field is dominated by UN and donor advisors, and professional NGOs. That is, much of the language has not emerged from grassroots struggles – and where it has (as was the case with the word 'empowerment', for example) it has since been appropriated and redefined by donors and professional advisors.

While Sen celebrates the introduction of the concepts of reproductive health and rights to development discourse at the 1994 UN conference in Cairo, Adetoun Ilumoka, who was present at the conference, presents a somewhat different story. In Ilumoka's version (2010), trumpets of victory and success are replaced by painful tales of being silenced by established power. She describes how feminist organizations and the feminist discourses of the global North effectively sidelined Southern feminists. Through her account, Ilumoka makes it possible to follow and feel the clashes, misunderstandings and uneasy moments experienced by African women during the processes and meetings held in preparation for the UN conferences, as they confronted the fixed global language, as well as the professional NGO workers and/or feminists of the North.

In Nigeria, Ilumoka explains, induced abortion is illegal, but this law is rarely enforced. Unsafe abortions are widely practised, but from the points of view of poor women, the problem that should be addressed is not the abortion law so much as the difficulties women face in accessing a decent livelihood, food, clean water, shelter, education and access to health services. The concepts of 'reproductive health and rights', successfully promoted by the women's lobbies at the series

---

[3] By 'intensity of interaction', Amadiume is referring to the series of UN conferences that occurred in the early 1990s, from the 1992 Earth Summit in Rio, to the 1993 Vienna conference on human rights, and the 1994 conference on population and development in Cairo.

of UN conferences held in the 1990s, belong to a language that has little resonance among poor women in Nigeria. For these women, the distinction between 'reproductive health' and health in general does not make sense, Ilumoka says. Furthermore, she notes a certain uneasiness among Nigerian women related to abortion, a feeling of its being wrong, and thus of there being no need to change the law. Nevertheless, according to Ilumoka:

> The discomfort of many of the African women participants at the NGO Forums for the Preparatory Committee meetings and the ICPD [International Conference on Population and Development] itself, with advocacy for abortion rights threatening to dominate discussions, was ignored, glossed over or even labelled as anti-feminist by many Northern colleagues. (2010: 121)

As a result, the language of rights, and more particularly of reproductive rights – or sexual and reproductive health and rights – has come to dominate the entire field, excluding other ways of conceptualizing concerns related to pregnancy and childbirth.

The picture painted by Ilumoka is one of powerful Northern women, lobbies which perceive themselves as acting for the benefit of women worldwide, but which in fact promote a certain language that connects to particular state constructions (namely, Western liberal democratic states and conceptions of positive law) and specific economic interests. The economic aspects of this fixed global language impact on the lives of Nigerian women in various ways; for example, in order to access donor money, you have to speak the language of the donors. As noted by Ilumoka:

> The magic words 'reproductive rights' brought forth donor funding for projects professing to be focused on promoting women's rights, whilst any critique or reservation was met with suspicion. When some women raised the issue of developing a Nigerian Women's Agenda to feed into post-Beijing processes, rather than a post-Beijing agenda that took the Beijing conference PfA as the starting point and point of reference, this was resisted on the grounds that it might alienate funders of post-Beijing activities. This fear of not fitting into funding priorities or of losing funding by articulating an alternative emphasis or process is rife among Nigerian and African NGOs. (2010: 130)

Co-option: change and recontextualization of PfA language in World Bank contexts

'Gender inequalities are costly to development.' This phrase is repeated several times in the May 2000 'consultation draft' that was distributed prior to the publication of the 2001 World Bank Policy Research Report,

Engendering Development Through Gender Equality in Rights, Resources, and Voice. Evidently, the World Bank report takes the Beijing PfA as its starting point, but interesting twists and turns of context, language and focal points take place in the World Bank's process as it moves from the 1995 PfA, to the 'consultation draft' of 2000, to the 2001 report, and eventually to the *World Development Report 2012: Gender Equality and Development*. The *World Development Report* is the World Bank's annual flagship report, and of course its focus on gender equality in 2012 is significant. According to Ananya Roy (2010: 550), from 2000 onwards, the bank has adopted a softer tone, and 'a more compassionate rendering of capitalism, one that must demonstrate the "double bottom line" of financial and social performance'. In this context, a focus on gender and gender equality works very well.

The consultation draft (May 2000) takes up the Beijing PfA's language of equality and rights, but the context has changed. In the Beijing PfA, gender equality was understood as an outcome of women's struggles, including a critique of prevailing economic trends, whereas, in the World Bank context, gender equality is seen as an automatic result of development and economic growth. The implicit timeline from a dark past, replete with gender inequalities, to a bright future of equality is indicated in the very first sentences of the document: 'Despite considerable progress in recent decades, gender inequalities are *still* pervasive ... Gender gaps *remain* widespread in access to and control of resources, in economic participation, in power and political voice' (World Bank 2001: 1, emphasis added). The PfA talked about increasing gender gaps, and the feminization of poverty but in the World Bank's view this is not the case. Instead, it asserts that 'Income growth and economic development promote gender equality in the long run' (2001: 1). No evidence is provided for this statement, but this is how the ideological world of donors is constructed.

The 2001 document *Engendering Development*, was thoroughly rewritten after the consultation draft. Here the process is taken yet another (decisive) step further. From being seen as a *result* of economic growth, gender equality is now also positioned as a *means* to achieve the three top priorities of development at that point in time: economic growth, poverty reduction and good governance. The 2001 report states: 'Gender equality is a core development issue – a development objective in its own right. It strengthens countries' ability to grow, to reduce poverty and to govern efficiently' (2001: 1).

This new World Bank line, in which gender equality has become as a tool of (soft) governance, is developed and consolidated in the 2012 *World Development Report*. In the supplementary *Main Messages* document, which reduces the 400+-page report to four pages for busy readers, the bank states that 'Gender equality is a core development objective in its own right. It is also smart economics. Greater gender equality can enhance productivity, improve development outcomes for the next generation, and make institutions more representative' (World Bank, 2012b: 1). The first sentence is a gesture to the women's movements, and also – importantly – an element in the Bank's legitimation and branding of itself as an institution working for rightness and goodness (see Cornwall and Brock 2006). The second sentence is a gesture towards transnational companies and other potential investors: 'Don't worry. It pays off!' The third sentence reveals the new trend – gender as governance; that is, gender as a means to higher productivity (economic growth), long-term general improvements (the social dimension) and representativity (democracy, politics).

From being an issue reluctantly taken up under pressure from global women's movements after Beijing 1995, the gender equality theme has become central to the World Bank's new and 'softer' image, as a tool of legitimation and (soft) governance. And all in the name of *smart economics* and economic growth as the ultimate goal of development.[4]

The *World Development Report 2012* uses the same basic modality as the previous reports: gender equality is portrayed as a development objective in its own right – but also as smart economics. The arguments with which the report tries to convince world governments and 'international partners' (donor agencies) are all economic: gender equality is an instrument for development; gender *in*equalities are costly, and even more so in a world of open trade; gender inequalities diminish a country's ability to compete; and, conversely, 'In a globalized world, countries that reduce gender-based inequalities will have a clear advantage.' (World Bank 2012a: 5). As before, the basic assumption is that economic growth promotes gender equality – which in return promotes economic growth. Economic growth and gender equality are perceived as mutually reinforcing – in principle, that is.

Later in the report, it does become clear that things may be more complex, and that certain aspects of gender inequality do not seem to change with economic growth, such as the gender division of unpaid care and housework.[5] It is noteworthy that such work is discussed, and the uneven gender division of unpaid care and housework is shown in a full-page illustration (Fig. 10), which reveals systematic and very similar

---

[4]   See Arnfred (2012) for a more developed critique of gender equality in World Bank politics.
[5]   Other aspects that according to the report do not seem to change with economic growth are domestic violence and the gender balance of cabinet positions (globally, fewer than 20 per cent of such positions are held by women) (World Bank 2012a: 20).

gender disparities in market activities, housework and child care across the world, from Sweden, Bulgaria and Italy to Pakistan, Cambodia and South Africa. However, current trends in global inequalities, particularly in the area of care work, are not mentioned. It is possible that women migrants from poor countries work as care providers for families in rich countries precisely because women in rich countries pursue gender equality in the labour market. Not unexpectedly, then, housework and care work are considered in the 2012 report, but global power relations are, as always, silenced. Global *differences* exist in the World Bank universe (according to national income: low, middle, high), but global power relations do not. The bank partially acknowledges that economic growth and gender equality are not always mutually supportive, and that things may sometimes be more complex. However, the basic belief is that that gender disparities belong to a more or less remote past, persisting only in some particularly 'sticky domains' because of special constraints and/or 'deeply entrenched gender roles and social norms' (2012a: 13). The implicit timeline, from a dark past replete with gender inequalities to a bright future of equality, has not been abandoned, even if it is less explicitly stated than before.

Southern feminist critiques of universalizing Western/Northern conceptualizations of feminism and development

The relevance of the tensions between Northern and Southern/post-colonial conceptions of gender issues has not diminished in the post-Beijing years. Increasingly, feminist scholars of the global South are calling attention to ways in which dominant notions of gender are rooted in Western/Northern epistemologies. For example, the writings of Oyèrónké Oyewùmí point to limitations of second-wave feminist ways of conceptualizing gender. In this way, the post-colonial critique of the 'fixed global language on gender' becomes a critique not only of the limited and limiting economy-focused approach of the World Bank, but also of the often universalizing, ethnocentric views within feminist thinking from the global North.

Chandra Mohanty's critique of the concept of 'universal sisterhood', as applied by Robin Morgan in her much-read anthology published in 1984, reads as a critique of the Beijing PfA. The concept of 'woman' (as opposed to 'man') and the idea of 'sisterhood' (as uniting all women, irrespective of class, race and North/South location) have been transported directly from the second-wave feminist movement into World Bank notions of gender. 'Universal sisterhood,' Mohanty says, 'is produced ... through specific assumptions about *women as a cross-culturally singular, homogeneous group* with the same interests, perspectives and goals, and similar experiences' (1984: 110, emphasis added). Mohanty goes on to say that the homogeneity of women as a group is 'predicated on a definition of the experience of oppression where difference can only be understood as male/female' (1984: 112). In this setup, differences among women, due to different positions in relation to (global) power, become invisible. Traces of difference due to inequality and dependence are erased, as are 'the history and effects of contemporary imperialism' (1984: 111).

Since the start of the second wave, universalizing tendencies in Western feminist thinking, taking the white, western, middle class, heterosexual woman as its point of departure, have not really changed, despite encountering women from elsewhere through UN conferences on women. Instead age-old imperialist relations, were repeated, with power inequalities of race and class being erased or glossed over. This does not mean that global/transnational feminisms or shared struggles are impossible. It does mean, however, that unity of women cannot be taken for granted; it must be constructed through a process of mutual learning. Northern women must listen to, and learn from, dissent and alternative knowledge, rather than push it aside as ignorance.

Conclusion

Post-colonial African feminists have criticized the notion, shared by Western feminists and developmentalists, of an implicit timeline leading out of a gender-oppressive 'traditional' past to a bright 'modern' future of gender equality. Researchers generally agree that colonialism and development in Africa have brought new opportunities for women, but post-colonial feminists question the implicit assumption of a move from gender oppression to women's liberation. The gains for women brought about by modernity may be ambiguous; after all, the past – often dubbed 'tradition'/'traditional culture' – can be interpreted in different ways. Oyèrónké Oyewùmí argues that 'gender' was not, in itself, a dimension of hierarchy in pre-colonial Nigeria, where hierarchies of age and lineage were vastly more important. Given that the bulk of knowledge about African culture and tradition was recorded by European anthropologists, missionaries and colonial civil servants, all of them Christians – mainly British and mostly male – African feminists have found it worthwhile to make their own investigations, from different vantage points. These endeavours are resulting in an emerging body of knowledge, of importance for future feminist politics.[6]

Thus, different visions for feminist futures might be rooted in different interpretations of feminist pasts. Feminist engagements on the battlefields of knowledge are an ongoing enterprise.

[6]   Sylvia Tamale's seminal volume, *African Sexualities: A Reader*, is an important outcome of this endeavour.

References

Adomako Ampofo, Akosua and Signe Arnfred, eds. (2010) *African Feminist Politics of Knowledge: Tensions, Challenges, Possibilities*, Uppsala: Nordic Africa Institute.

Amadiume, Ifi (2000) *Daughters of the Goddess, Daughters of Imperialism*, London: Zed Books.

Arnfred, Signe (2011) 'Women, men and gender equality in development aid: Trajectories, contestations' *Kvinder, Køn og Forskning*, 20 (1): 46-56.

Arnfred, Signe (2012) 'Gender equality has become a central part of World Bank politics' *NAI Forum* (23 March), http://www.naiforum.org/2012/03. accessed 30 November 2012.

Cornwall, Andrea and Karen Brock (2006) 'The new buzzwords' in Peter Utting ed., *Reclaiming Development Agendas*, Hampshire and New York/Geneva: Palgrave/UNRISD.

Ilumoka, Adetoun (2010) 'Advocacy for women's reproductive health and rights in Africa: Between the devil and the deep blue sea' in Akosua Adomako Ampofo and Signe Arnfred. eds, *African Feminist Politics of Knowledge*, Uppsala: Nordic Africa Institute.

Mama, Amina (1997) 'Postscript: Moving from analysis to practice?' in Ayesha Imam, Amina Mama, Fatou Sow, eds, *Engendering African Social Sciences*, Dakar: CODESRIA.

Mohanty, Chandra Talpade (2003) 'Sisterhood, coalition and the politics of experience' in Chandra Mohanty, *Feminism Without Borders*, Durham and London: Duke University Press.

Morgan, Robin (1984) *Sisterhood is Global: The International Women's Movement Anthology*, New York: Feminist Press.

Oyewùmí, Oyèrónké (1997) *The Invention of Women. Making an African Sense of Western Gender Discourses*, Minneapolis and London: University of Minnesota Press.

Oyewùmí, Oyèrónké (2000) 'Family bonds/conceptual binds: African notes on feminist epistemologies', *Signs: Journal of Women in Culture and Society*, 25 (4): 1093-1098.

Oyewùmí, Oyèrónké (2002) 'Conceptualizing gender: The Eurocentric foundations of feminist concepts and the challenge of African epistemologies', *JENdA: A Journal of Culture and African Women's Studies*, 2 (1): 1-6.

Pereira, Charmaine (2010) 'Reflections of a feminist scholar-activist in Nigeria', in Akosua Adomako Ampofo and Signe Arnfred, eds, *African Feminist Politics of Knowledge*, Uppsala: Nordic Africa Institute.

Riles, Annelise (2000) *The Network Inside Out*, Ann Arbor MI: University of Michigan Press.

Roy, Ananya (2010) 'Millenial woman: The gender order of development', in Sylvia Chant, ed., *The International Handbook on Gender and Poverty*, Northampton, MA: Edward Elgar.

Sen, Gita (2006) 'The quest for gender equality' in Peter Utting, ed., *Reclaiming Development Agendas*, Hampshire and New York/Geneva: Palgrave/UNRISD.

Spivak, Gayatri (1988) 'Can the subaltern speak?' in C. Nelson and L. Grossberg, eds, *Marxism and the Interpretation of Culture*, Basingstoke: Macmillan.

Tamale, Sylvia ed. (2011) *African Sexualities: A Reader*, Nairobi: Pambazuka Press.

UN (United Nations) (1995) *Report of the Fourth World Conference on Women* (Beijing 4-15 Sept 1995). New York.

World Bank (2000) Engendering Development, A World Bank Policy Research Report, (Consultation Draft), www.worldbank.org/gender/prr, accessed November 2000.

World Bank (2001) *Engendering Development Through Gender Equality in Rights, Resources, and Voice* (January). Washington.

World Bank (2012a) *World Development Report 2012: Gender Equality and Development*, Washington.

World Bank (2012b) 'Main messages' in *World Development Report 2012: Gender Equality and Development*, Washington.

4 Knowing Time
Temporal Epistemology
& the African Novel
Bill Ashcroft

History, time and Afromodernity

We cannot approach the question of an Africa-centred epistemology without addressing the trauma of colonialism. Whether this period caused irreparable damage to African societies, or whether African subjects successfully appropriated and transformed the technologies and discourses of imperial powers (including the colonizing language), or both, frames a continuing argument in postcolonial studies. The example of literature is instructive, because the adaptation of a global language allowed writers to represent their own reality to a world audience. In turn, literary appropriations are a model for the transformed and transformative modernity created by Africans. Afromodernity is one model in which the past is folded into the present in much the same way that contemporary writers transform literary discourse. Traditional knowledges either inform or exist alongside the modern, in ways that demonstrate the irrepressible adaptability and transformative agency of cultures. Far from a sense of fracture or brokenness, which we might assume to be the effect of colonialism (Eze 2008: 25), the key to an Afro-modernity is a multiple or layered sense of time. Furthermore, the African novel has been critical in producing 'knowledge' of such layered time, and in the process disrupting our sense of what constitutes 'knowing' and what constitutes 'time'.

The issue of knowing time is obviously tied up with the production of history. 'What does the thought of history in fiction tell us about suspended histories of peoples, traditions, societies and cultures in modern Africa, including Africa's experiences of its own pasts?' (Eze 2008: 28). The novel provides a path to an answer by distinguishing between history as a source of facts, and history as a source of wisdom about the meaning of time. The question of 'knowing time', therefore, lies at the centre of a far more familiar question: 'How can the novel provide a different way of knowing tradition, a broken time, to appear at another level of consciousness as intense, if suspended history?' (Eze 2008: 34).

We might add: how can the novel provide a transformed knowledge of historical time without objectifying the past as the past? The problem with history-making is not merely its unavoidable objectification of the past, but the unavoidability of History – the master discourse of European imperialism. As Dipesh Chakrabarty famously put it: 'There is a peculiar way in which all these other histories tend to become variations on a master narrative that could be called 'the history of Europe' (1992: 1). Representations of human time and human space have been the most powerful and hegemonic purveyors of Eurocentrism in modern times. History and its associated teleology has been the means by which European concepts of time have been naturalized for postcolonial societies.

Colonial reality is excluded from History in the same way that colonial literary production was excluded from English Literature. Hegel's infamous declaration that Africa was 'no part of History' (trs. 1956: 99) was simply the statement of a European reality. The response of post-colonial writers' to their exclusion from Literature was to launch a stunning array of transformations of language and form, unimpeded by any filiative connection to the discipline. The consequence of their exclusion from History – and this applied to postcolonial experience of all kinds – was to tell the story of history through literature. This was never the 'true' history, given in response to the imperial discourse, but a different history, the very difference of which announced its radical departure from historiography. Its most widespread mode in postcolonial societies was that of allegory, which enabled the scientific discourse of history to be opened up to radical imaginative revision, and to a different kind of truth.

To examine the knowledge of time in the African novel, we start with an observation: epistemology is fundamentally determined by method: *how* we know determines *what* we know. This 'how we know' covers a great deal more than method, for it encompasses history, culture and, for most of us, modernity itself. We 'know' the earth travels around the sun, we know it abstractly, and we know it because we have learned it. But who does not 'know' also that the sun travels from horizon to horizon, frames our day from dawn to twilight, gives shape to our lives, as well as heat and life, travels, also, around the earth? The knowledge that we may have outside 'epistemology' – a knowledge gained in our bodies, our senses, our moods, our unconscious – never finds its way into epistemology because, according to science, the idea that the sun travels around the earth, an idea that has generated centuries of myth, worship and cultural identity, and a 'knowledge' that may even frame our daily life, is *wrong*. It may be knowledge nonetheless, something we 'know', and perhaps something we know outside 'meaning'. For this very reason it is an orphan, doomed to wander outside the city walls of modernity, rejected by the guardians of knowledge. But such 'knowledge' may be rescued by literature and, for our purposes, a different experience of time, an alternative modernity perhaps, may be offered by the narrativity of the novel.

The beauty of a literature that opens up the threshold between languages is that it immediately puts 'knowing' under scrutiny. The 'threshold' of the African novel, with its appropriated and transformed language, puts into question the supremacy of 'epistemology' in contemporary Western thinking. Given that language articulates an understanding that may be quite distinct from our inner experience, can we 'know' what we do not fully understand? Extending this question further: is there a form of knowledge that is accessible beyond meaning? Can literary form frame knowledge beyond hermeneutics? On the face of it, this question seems absurd: how can we know without interpreting? What kind of knowledge might exist beyond meaning? The reason this seems absurd is that not only literary studies but also the humanities themselves have revolved around interpretation. So deeply embedded in humanistic discourse is the idea of the prominence of meaning and its discovery that it has become completely invisible. But what if there is a form of understanding, a level of engagement that lies beyond our usual conception of interpretation; what if there is a meaning beyond meaning?

This possibility is suggested by Hans Ulrich Gumbrecht's *Production of Presence: What Meaning Cannot Convey*, in which he challenges 'a broadly institutionalised tradition according to which interpretation, that is, the identification and/or attribution of meaning, is the core practice, the exclusive core practice indeed, of the humanities' (2004: 3). Gumbrecht's dissatisfaction arose from a sense that 'materialities of communication' were completely ignored in the humanities. Different media affect the meaning they carry, he argues. When we engage the work of art as a 'thing', we discover that the tangible effects of the particular communication media (sound, print and computer screen, for instance) affect the meaning. This production of presence occurs in any form of communication in which its material elements 'touch' the bodies of the persons communicating (2004: 17).

Poetry and drama produce 'presence' much more readily than prose, but we can also see this production of presence within the novel genre adopted by many African writers, in which the materiality of the communication conforms to the temporal narrativity of the genre, but often employs language in which the link between word and referent is so disrupted that it pushes us past the traditional process of interpretation. In this respect, the language, structure or narrative process of the novel may be so *materially* different from any accepted form of the genre that it tempts us to 'bracket' it out as indeterminate, or simply alien. However, the production of presence in these texts may produce a knowledge that lies beyond the accepted principles of interpretation and meaning. One of the ways in which novelistic narrative may achieve this is by intimating a particular experience of time without referring to time itself.

Another way to conceive of an epistemology beyond hermeneutics is to consider the 'thingness' of the literary text, for it is precisely this materiality that enables us to encounter presence. As Steven Connor explains, some things are reflexive. Things can give a thought:

> Thought and writing constitutively call for and call on things, precisely because they are themselves always something more or less than a thing. Writing and thought are bound together, not just for the powerful though ultimately banal reason that words are the medium of thought, but because writing is the same kind of substantial no-thing as a thinking thing. (2010: 3)

The 'thinghood', the materiality of the text, may be more important than we think in its negotiation with language, because it always offers something beyond representation. But what about time? More precisely, how does the materiality of the African novel offer a way of knowing non-linear time? Is not time, like thinking, 'simultaneously short of and in excess of thinghood?' (Connor 2010: 3) Time, which was abstracted, universalized and 'disembedded' by modernity (Giddens 1990: 17-26), is never, as we well know, *experienced* as the relentless mathematical march of the clock or the calendar, together providing the modern organization of world time. It operates in cycles, slows or speeds up, sometimes even seems to stand still. Our experience of time differs from our knowledge, just as our experience of the sun's progress round the earth differs from our knowledge of the solar system.

The perception of form as materiality leads us towards a link between knowledge and form, and, in particular, a knowledge that might 'present' itself to us in a way that eludes tried-and-tested hermeneutic processes. One such form of 'knowledge', offered by the novel, beyond the strictures of interpretation, is what may be called a knowledge of time – particularly of the 'fractured,' 'multiple' or 'layered' time of the colonized society. The narrativity of the novel has a particular function in the construction of a different knowledge of time. This may not be as remarkable as many other forms of knowledge that the novel may offer 'beyond meaning'. But for several reasons – not the least of which is its disruption of the power of History– it may be one of the most strategic.

In a very obvious sense we cannot know time apart from the way in which we live within it. Technically, the 'present moment' does not exist but is always a process of the future becoming the past. What we can 'know' is a flow of 'prospections' becoming retrospections. And yet, the relationship between the future and the past is extremely important to the African novel because the experience of time is a constant projection of a future based on an inherited past. This is very different from nostalgia, very different from the yearning for a paradisal pre-colonial culture. It is a projection of the cultural past onto the future, beyond the traumatic fracture represented by colonialism; a projection designed to transform the future on the basis of inherited cultural realities; a strategy Edouard Glissant calls 'a prophetic vision of the past' (1989: 64).

The crucial characteristic of the genre of the novel is its engagement with time. Stories are the way in which we have a world, and the telling of stories appeals to us because they recount the progress of a world in time and thus can become narratives of temporal order. But magically, by unfolding in time they take us out of time. It may be that narrative, whose materiality is isomorphic with temporality, provides a way (although not the only way) of communicating different experiences of time. How then can the novel convey a different knowledge of time, specifically knowledge of what has been called the 'broken' time of the traumatized colonized subject? One way of communicating a different knowledge of time is through 'circular time', developed from forms of oral storytelling. This is not limited, of course, to the African novel. Salman Rushdie explains that the techniques of *Midnight's Children* reproduces the techniques of the Indian oral narrative tradition, going 'in great swoops, it goes in spirals or loops' rather than beginning, middle and end (Rushdie 1985: 7-8).

This technique of circling back from the present to the past, its structure of building tale within tale, and its persistence in delaying climaxes, are all features of traditional narration and orature. While this technique offers a way of articulating circular time, there is a further dimension in the post-colonial novel: the circularity of the narrative is overlaid on an ontological circularity that revolves around the cultural disruption of colonialism.

This disruption leads the African philosopher Emmanuel Eze to suggest that a prominent feature of the African novel is the presentation of 'broken' time. The African writer not only writes about African cultures as 'broken' by the experiences of colonialism but also appears to experience language itself – in this case, the language of writing – as a re-enactment of otherwise de-centred traditions ... It is as if in the writing, the writer historically inaugurates a different order of language and time, *a different sense of place* (2008: 25, 35, original emphasis).

On first consideration, the idea of a broken time that reflects the broken cultures of post-colonial African societies is persuasive. The colonial experience represents a moment of fracture between the traditional and the modern that is constantly negotiated in the language of the text. But it implies a culture that is a static object, suddenly fractured and 'denatured' by colonialism – a fracturing that, just possibly, may be mended by a return to an essential cultural reality. This myth of return is common in postcolonial writing, but cultures are never static. They are always in process, in response to various historical influences. Without diminishing the traumatic historical event of colonialism, and recognizing the immense upheavals caused in African societies, the assumption of 'brokenness' underestimates the adaptability, the transformative power and *coeval* nature of African modernities.

Although Eze uses the term 'broken', he has an astute sense of the way in which African writing captures the fluidity of culture:

> ... on one level, post-colonial African writing is a language in movement: it is a language *in* time. On another level, however, just like the best of the modern African compositions in music, such a language, literally and figuratively, composes itself and its what [sic] in hiddenness: it is a language *of* the movement of time. (2008: 34, emphasis in original)

It is a language in time because it is a transformed and appropriated English, but at the same time it is a language of time because African culture is deeply affected by the movement of time. This is not to say, however, that African time is 'broken' or that brokenness is the only way in which post-colonial time is known. Eze's main interest is in language but also in the way that fiction operates in communicating the experience of time. The novel, in particular, is a form that hinges on temporal movement and is adept at communicating a different experience of time. This may occur most often through the materiality of the form rather than through the narrated subject matter, although when the novel talks about language, the two may coincide.

To refute Eze's claim that African time is broken, I want to look at three African novelists who employ very different forms of the genre, all of whom invoke a 'knowledge' of time beyond interpretation. Chinua Achebe, the father of the realist tradition of the African novel, established the form through which African novels have been engaging with colonial domination and post-independence corruption ever since. The realist form, on the one hand, shows us that a condition of creative ethnography can give a 'layered' perception of time by offering an unmediated representation of traditional experience. Dambudzo Marechera, on the other hand, produced a fantastic, hallucinatory prose that, according to many commentators, completely revolutionized the realist tradition of the African novel. Specifically, Marechera offers an ideal sounding board for the idea that time is broken. Ben Okri, whose writing has often been termed 'magical realist', has produced an engagement with time through a transformation of African history.

Chinua Achebe: tradition and circular time

The realist form employed by Achebe was a specific strategy to contest the longstanding stereotype of unfathomable darkness, in which Africa had existed in the European imagination. Achebe's primary achievement in *Things Fall Apart* was his success in presenting the African village of Umuofia as a real place, and his protagonist Okonkwo as a real human being. In this well-documented writing back to Conrad's *Heart of Darkness* (1901), a task for which the realist mode of expression is ideally suited, the temptation for Achebe to simply reverse Conrad's view of the incomprehensible frenzy of prehistoric man – 'a whirl of black limbs, a mass of hands clapping, of feet stamping, of bodies swaying, of eyes rolling, under the droop of heavy and motionless foliage' (Conrad 1968: 68) – must have been almost overwhelming. But it is the very subtlety of Achebe's description, his presentation of Okonkwo as a deeply flawed and complex man, and his exposure of Umuofian society as one that had its own share of ethical dilemmas, that underlies the transformative power of *Things Fall Apart*. Achebe rejects Marlow's stereotyping in *Heart of Darkness* by confirming the complexity and even ambivalence of African culture.

   Achebe also initiated a deeply influential mode in the African novel by producing a form of cultural ethnography, involving a considerable amount of phenomenological bracketing, to present as fact, usually without comment, a totally different world. When he describes the celebration of the ritual of the *egwugwu* in Umuofia village, we witness a powerful demonstration of the slippage between performance and being that is also a slippage in time. The *egwugwu* are the ancestral spirits of the clan. It is clear to all that they are humans dressed up for the ritual, but in the act, the boundary between human actor and spirit disappears:

Okonkwo's wives, and perhaps other women as well, might have noticed that the second *egwugwu* had the springly walk of Okonkwo. And they might also have noticed that Okonkwo was not among the titled men and elders who sat behind the row of *egwugwu*. But if they thought these things they kept them within themselves. The *egwugwu* with the springly walk was one of the dead fathers of the clan. He looked terrible with the smoked raffia body, a huge wooden face painted white except for round hollow eyes and the charred teeth that were as big as a man's fingers. On his head were two powerful horns. (1958: 63-4)

The knowledge of the performance does not lessen the terror of being in the presence of the spirits. The critical feature of this occasion is the description of an experience in which the ontological distinction between acting and reality, the human world and the spirit world, has dissolved. 'The land of the living was not far removed from the domain of the ancestors' (1958: 85). Achebe's account reinstalls a boundary in the guise of an ethnographic irony, when he considers the recognition of Okonkwo by his wives. But clearly, in the performance of the *egwugwu*, this boundary does not exist, because it does not exist in the language. The experience of the *egwugwu* is contingent upon an experience of language in which signifier and signified dissolve into one another, or more specifically, in which the subject and object have not yet been separated by representation. The performance becomes an enactment of circular time, a historical performance of the past circling in the present. It is not magical realism, but *realism*. Nevertheless, it predicts the magical real in African fiction by disrupting the realist mode with a very African moment in which the entire *egwugwu* scene becomes a *folding* of time. The author's commentary, made in the interests of the realist novel, narrates what might seem to be the fracture of time characterizing the post-colonial experience of modernity in African society.

Yet we might equally see this as *coalesced* or *layered* time, in the same way that the participants in the *egwugwu* ritual can simultaneously accommodate two orders of reality. Such a bipartite experience could be called 'ambi-valent' in the sense of being 'two-powered', a facility that has become almost a defining characteristic of post-colonial cultural production. The remarkable strength of the African novel, then, is not to present an experience of fractured time so much as a powerfully transformed sense of circular time. This is not circular narrative of the kind discussed by Rushdie above, but it is a 'circular' experience of time in which past and present are folded into each other. Such folding elides historical 'brokenness' with an experience of tradition in modern form. The African novelist is, in a very direct way, creating an African modernity.

Dambudzo Marechera: brokenness and layered time

We might assume there is no better description of the brokenness and disruption caused by colonialism than the fragmentation we find in Dambudzo Marechera's novels. Marechera is a unique, and uniquely difficult, figure in African literature. Despite his short life, chaotic career and his wildly non-linear, non-narrative prose, he paved the way for a different kind of African writing that flourished towards the end of the twentieth century. In his essay 'The African writer's experience of European literature', he says of his time as a student: 'I would, with Jorge Louis Borges, have written a dissertation on the refutation of Time itself' (Marechera 1987: 99). In keeping with this, his work is beset by a constant disruption and dislocation of narrative convention. Brokenness and dislocation are particularly evident in his description of bilingualism:

> I was being severed from my own voice. I would listen to it as a still, small voice coming from the huge distances of the mind. It was like this: English is my second language, Shona my first. When I talked it was in the form of an interminable argument, one side of which was always expressed in English and the other side always in Shona. At the same time I would be aware of myself as something indistinct but separate from both cultures. (1978: 30)

It is arguable that this brokenness lies at the source of Marechera's choice to exile himself from both cultures, and in turn, to play out, both in his novels and in the performance of his own life, the pathology of colonialism, brokenness and 'deconstructedness' (Buuck 1997: 119), appearing to operate at the level of subjectivity. But although the effect of his form and content is fragmenting, the subject of the novel can still be regarded in terms of variable subject positions, of 'layering' rather than disjunction. While Marechera's novels might narrate both the pathological psychic and social consequences of colonialism, their mode of *performance* is not necessarily deconstructive but radically hybrid. In short, while brokenness might seem to be the implication of Marechera's writing, in regard to time and cultural hybridity, his strategy is to layer past, present and future, as well as different cultural traditions.

The appropriation of English in the post-colonial text often leads to a transformation of the received language by the mother tongue. But it also becomes the meeting point of different traditions. In the passage quoted above, the resonant Biblical phrase 'still small voice' (1 Kings 19:12 KJV), one of the many Biblical allusions in the novel, enters the text seamlessly, indicating a very different form of interaction between language realities, a layering of different cultural realities that might open the way for an understanding of the layering of time. The apparent performance of broken subjectivity in Marechera's work is the consequence of a very intricately woven (though often confusing) Menippean satiric structure, as adapted from Bakhtin by Marechera.

In other words, Marechera's complex representation of layered time is supported by his adoption of Bakhtin's concept of 'Menippean satire' to describe his own writing (Marechera 1987: 101). Bakhtin has an importance in Marechera's work because conversation, as in dialogism and the heteroglossia of multiple kinds of speech and language, illuminates both Marechera's own use of language and, correspondingly, his representation of time. For Bakhtin, the novel form provides a particularly rich medium for the many-voiced appearance of different languages. 'For the novelist working in prose, the object is always entangled in someone else's discourse about it' (Bakhtin 1981: 330). Here, Bakhtin is talking about a putatively monoglossic text, unhampered by the issues of cultural communication and cultural tension that we find in the post-colonial novel. For him, such a text is already heteroglossic, already engaged in dialogue *within* the text – a dialogue, which to all intents and purposes, is a *cross-cultural* dialogue between 'belief systems'. This heteroglossia is resoundingly evident in Marechera's work, even in his objection that the English in which he writes fractures his 'authentic' world.

Marechera's writing suggests that in the very performance of 'brokenness', which his own commentary described as a separation from his voice, he is utilizing a heteroglossic facility for ontological and temporal multiplicity. Indeed, we can refute the idea of a broken tradition and broken time by examining the extent to which many African novels contest history, providing a radically and assertively different sense of time from the modern linear time with which we are familiar (but which, as I have said, is already contested by our own experience). The 'brokenness', to which Eze refers, comes from a sense of the engulfment of African society by modernity as a consequence of colonialism. However, it may be more useful to think of the exuberant linguistic intertextuality of Marechera's prose as a layering of the temporal realities of colonial and postcolonial experience. The African novel's representation of ambivalent or layered time can then be seen as a potent example of an alternative post-colonial modernity.

Ben Okri: the transformation of historical time

Ben Okri demonstrates brilliantly the layering of time, reproducing in his narrative the kind of layering that Achebe *describes* in his account of the *egwugwu*. Okri provides a particularly interesting portrayal of non-linear time because his work is so readily appropriated by appellations such as post-modernism. But if post-modernism applies to his disruption of realism and modernism, it is a 'pre-modern' post-modernism of a kind developed by the alternative discourse of Afro-modernity. The oxymoron 'pre-modern post-modernism' conveys very well the layering that occurs in his work, both in imagery, style and the temporality they adumbrate.

Okri's style is characteristically obtained by a layering of details and images, producing a sense of excess and superabundance. Exuberant description extends almost seamlessly from apparently innocuous situations to more complex ones. Lyrical excess is a critical feature of his perception and description of the world, because it is in the energy of this excess that the spiritual enters the material. In a description of a storm, the interpenetration of spirit and material world is almost imperceptible:

> The world was still, as if it had momentarily become a picture, as if God were The Great Photographer. The clearing turned into a new world. Out of the flash came the sharp outlines of spirits rising into the air with weary heads. And then they fell down and bounced and floated over the stillness of the world. The spirits passed me, passed through me, their eyes like diamonds. And when the next explosion came, followed by another blinding flash, the spirits were obliterated. The heaviness of the air settled, the clouds opened, and the first torrential drenching of the land began. (1991: 285)

Most commentators refer to this as 'magic realism'. Yet the harnessing of two orders of reality, the layering, in effect, of two modes of time – one which the spirit world automatically inhabits, and one representing a demotic present – is not substantially different from Achebe's description of the *egwugwu* in *Things Fall Apart*, a layering of traditional time upon modernity to produce an alternative modernity. The knowledge of Africa that this produces is one from which neither order of reality can be bracketed out.

Although Okri's imagining of a different history occurs very often in his imagining of a different, multi-layered, phenomenal world, the most direct narrative about the writing of African history is in the chapter entitled 'The battle of rewritten histories', in *Infinite Riches*. This provides one of the most imaginative depictions of the struggle involved in the writing of African history, when the Governor General, clearly a symbol of the entire institution of imperial knowledge-making, puts pen to paper:

> He rewrote the space in which I slept. He rewrote the long silences of the country which were really passionate dreams. He rewrote the seas and wind, the atmospheric

conditions and the humidity. He rewrote the seasons and made them limited and unlyrical. He reinvented the geography of the nation and the whole continent. He redrew the continent's size on the world map, made it smaller, made it odder. (1998: 110-11)

This is not only a summary of the effects of historiography but a powerful condemnation of the function of *naming* in imperial geographies and historical accounts.

> He changed the names of places which were older than the places themselves. He redesigned the phonality of African names, softened the consonants, flattened the vowels. In altering the sound of the names he altered their meaning and affected the destiny of the named... The renamed things lost their ancient weight in our memory. The renamed things lost their old reality. They became lighter, and stranger. They became divorced from their old selves. (1998: 111)

In this enterprise of 'knowing' the other, the embodiment of the empire is shown to rob the colonized place of its reality. Although the principle is the very recognizable link between knowledge and power that we find in Saïd's *Orientalism* (1978), colonial history offers a particular rewriting of history because it reinvents beginnings.

> The Governor General made our history begin with the arrival of his people on our shores ... in his rewriting of our history [he] deprived us of language, of poetry, of stories, of architecture, of civic laws, of social organization, of art, science, mathematics, sculpture, abstract conception, and philosophy. (1978: 111)

This is an astute and comprehensive perception of the function of imperial control, the actual effects of the 'civilizing mission'. The country had to be erased, wiped clean so that it could be invested with life and history at the moment of colonial contact – 'with a stroke of his splendid calligraphic style, he invested us with life ... and we awoke into history, stunned and ungrateful, as he renamed our meadows and valleys, and forgot the slave trade' (1978: 111). In his rewriting, the Governor General wiped out Africa's ancient civilizations, its religions, spiritual dimensions, its art and music, and in so changing the past 'he altered our present'.

But in this novel, a different history, a layering of different orders of time that now projects into the future, occurs when the old woman of the forest weaves the secret history of the continent. As the narrative unfolds, the immense energy of her 'retelling', and thus re-historicizing a different kind of Africa, produces a (pan-)Africa that is not only vast but powerful in its potential effect on the entire world, for the history she weaves is 'Frightening and wondrous, bloody and comic, labyrinthine, circular, always turning, always surprising, with events becoming signs and signs becoming reality' (1978: 112).

This is more than a history, it is a laminating of different orders of time. The old woman codes the secrets of plants, the interpenetrations of human and spirit world, the delicate balance of forces:

> She even coded fragments of the great jigsaw that the creator spread all over the diverse peoples of the earth, hinting that no one race or people can have the complete picture or monopoly of the ultimate possibilities of the human genius alone. With her magic she suggested that it's only when all peoples meet and know and love one another that we begin to get an inkling of this awesome picture, or jigsaw, or majestic power. The fragments of the grand picture of humanity were the most haunting and beautiful part of her weaving that day. (1978: 112-13)

This is a richly utopian view of the capacity of the African imaginary to re-enter and reshape the modern world. It is not merely a hope for African resurgence, but a vision of Africa's transformative potential, a potential that will be realized, as the teleological, expansionist and hegemonic tendencies of the West are gradually subverted. In one sense, *Infinite Riches* is an attempt to show the scope of that cultural possibility by infusing the language of excess with the enormously expanded vision of the horizons of African cultural experience.

Conclusion

From the observations of these three novelists, we can see much more in their writing than the mere communication of narrative meaning. Through the resonance of their materiality, literary texts, even prose texts, may produce a different form of knowing – of 'knowing beyond meaning', as the 'thingness' of the text unlocks a vast hermeneutic surplus. While unfolding in time, the African novel may also produce a 'knowing' of a different form of time, a circular, folded or layered time in which a past is apprehended within the present. This folding of time is a model for Afro-modernity itself, a significant model, because Africa has commonly been held to be the antithesis or the other of modernity. By offering a 'knowledge' of circular time, of a past folded into the present, African novels reveal that an alternative modernity may proceed in a very different way from the linear progression that has defined the modern. 'Circular' time, 'layered' or 'folded' time are all ways of describing the complex imbrication of past and present in the African novel, an imbrication that introduces the reader to a form of knowing that exists beyond referentiality. Where Achebe transformed the perception of the traditional African village, and Marechera revolutionized the tradition of African realism, Ben Okri demonstrates the ways in which an African knowledge of layered time might suggest the utopian possibility of a transformation of global modernity itself.

References

Achebe, Chinua (1958). *Things Fall Apart*, London: Heinemann.
Bakhtin, Mikhail M. (1981). *The Dialogic Imagination: Four Essays* (ed. Michael Holquist, trans. Caryl Emerson and Michael Holquist). Austin, TX: University of Texas Press.
Buuck, David (1997). 'African doppelgänger: Hybridity and identity in the work of Dambudzo Marechera', *Research in African Literatures*, 28 (2): 118-31.
Chakrabarty, Dipesh (1992). 'Postcoloniality and the artifice of history: Who speaks for 'Indian' pasts?' *Representations* 32 (Winter): 1-26.
Connor, Steven (2010). 'Thinking things' *Textual Practice*, 24 (1): 1-20.
Conrad, Joseph (1901/1986). *Heart of Darkness*, Harmondsworth: Penguin.
Eze, Emmanuel Chukwudi (2008). 'Language and time in post-colonial experience', *Research in African Literatures*, 39 (1): 24-47.
Giddens, Anthony (1990). *The Consequences of Modernity*, Cambridge: Polity Press.
Glissant, Edouard (1989). *Caribbean Discourse: Selected Essays*, trans. J. Michael Dash, Charlottesville VA: University Press of Virginia.
Gumbrecht, Hans Ulrich (2004). *The Production of Presence: What Meaning Cannot Convey*, Stanford CA: Stanford University Press.
Hegel, George Wilhelm Friedrich (1956). *The Philosophy of History*, New York: Dover.
Marechera, Dambudzo (1978). *House of Hunger*, London: Heinemann.
Marechera, Dambudzo (1987). 'The African writer's experience of European literature' ,*Zambesia*, 14 (2): 99-111.
Marechera, Dambudzo (1992). *The Black Insider*, (comp. and ed. Flora Veit-Wild), Trenton NJ: Africa World Press.
Okri, Ben (1991). *The Famished Road*, London: Jonathan Cape.
Okri, Ben (1998). *Infinite Riches*, London: Phoenix House.
Rushdie, Salman (1985). 'Interview with Rushdie', *Kunapipi*, 7 (1): 1-10.

5 Black Boxes & Glass Jars
Classification in the Hunt for Africa-centred Knowledge
Brenda Cooper

Classification: 'less of a pigeonhole, than a pigeon'[1]

In this chapter, I explore the ways in which systems of classification contribute to producing the knowledges that they are supposedly designed simply to store. I ask how classification contributes to producing Africa-centred knowledge or to inhibiting its production. Specifically, I explore some of the consequences of placing *Africa* (as traditional and archaic) in one pigeonhole and *modernity* (meaning Europe) in another, which presents the challenge of how to confront and dismantle this binary in the service of creating Africa-centred knowledges. There are many different ways of rising to this challenge. As we shall see, some projects retain the binary of modernity versus the pre-modern, but shuffle the content of which falls under what heading. Other projects work towards obliterating the binary and contesting its existence as a tool for understanding history. In describing some of the latter, I particularly emphasize the manipulation of the English language and its capacity for facilitating the invention of new sub-languages. I do this in terms of the fiction of Helen Oyeyemi, whose diasporic language gymnastics are exemplary of some of the dismantling endeavours in the field of African literature.

Finally, I suggest that these different ways of challenging the determining power of entrenched classification codes do not deal with the conundrum presented by the following two statements: i) classification is a necessary tool for meaning making; and ii) classification inhibits meaning making. Classification creates codes for meaning making that are as necessary as they are potentially toxic. However, I conclude with the proposal that *articulation* might present a malleable and more dynamic form of classification. This surfacing of the design plan, which propels classification, is difficult because organizing principles are as invisible as they are powerful.

[1] Fowler 1982: 37.

Bowker and Star define a classification system as 'a set of boxes (metaphorical or literal) into which things can be put to then do some kind of work' (1999: 10). The crux is that the design of the boxes – their size, shape, quantity, site and substance – mediates what can be put into them. This design is what is so hard to see. This invisibility of the design is what Lakoff is getting at when he rejects the folk theory of classification, which is based on the belief that 'things come in well-defined kinds, that the kinds are characterized by shared properties, and that there is one right taxonomy of the kinds' (quoted in Bowker and Star 1999: 33).

What this folk theory conceals is that the shared properties that appear so natural and intrinsic are, in fact, ways of seeing and acting in the world that are constructed. The formula on which their construction is based, is sealed up in what Bruno Latour has called the 'black box'. The black box holds all the 'common sense' that a culture shares that turns questions, priorities and interests into facts. As Latour puts it, the box is 'well sealed' and people generally do not 'live in a world of fiction, representation, symbol, approximation and convention: they are simply *right*' (1987: 206, emphasis in original). According to Latour, in a later work, what this concealment enables is a focus on 'inputs and outputs' and not on the complex processes that produce these effects (1999: 304).

I am not suggesting that the design of the classification constructs reality. Those complex processes to which Latour refers, are the interests and material realities of power and privilege. These are what dictate the design and limit the options. Their political rationale is buried in the sealed black box. And lest this sounds too conspiratorial, we have to understand that this process is normalized and archived in such a way as to be inherited and accepted as common-sense reality. This includes common knowledge about the nature of Africa. What is buried is the analysis that leads from colonial interests to metaphors such as the dark heart of a savage and homogenous continent.

The reality is, of course, not so clean as to present us with either totally and unambiguously good or bad classification systems. Globalization, collusion, opportunistic alliances and unexpected deals cut across continents. This ensures that a tangle of mixed designs and codes have to be unravelled in order to detect what can end up being complex crosscurrents of interests and consequences. As Bowker and Star discovered regarding the classification of illnesses, there is 'a panoply of tangled and crisscrossing classification schemes held together by an increasingly harassed and sprawling international public health bureaucracy' (1999: 21). This tanglement, tenuously held together by invisible ties, is vulnerable and unstable, which is why this project of delving into the nature of our accepted codes and columns is so challenging and potentially transformative.

The black box is, therefore, a somewhat blunt analytical instrument as seepage occurs both into and out of the box and, given that black and white are notorious in their own concealment of grey, partial visibility is a more likely condition (1999: 161). The core argument holds, however – black boxes seal up the arbitrariness and constructedness of coded classifications, as well as their social and political consequences. Building portholes into these black boxes, hammering hinges and handles onto them, so as to prise them open and make visible these hidden tentacles of meaning, becomes a form of epistemological politics.

This struggle for transparency is the entry point into Helen Oyeyemi's novel, *White is for Witching*, and illuminates the intriguing epigraph from Gwendolyn Brooks with which it opens:

> I hold my honey and I store my bread
> In little jars and cabinets of my will.
> I label clearly, and each latch and lid
> I bid, Be firm till I return from Hell. (Oyeyemi 2009)

Oyeyemi was born in Nigeria and her parents migrated to London when she was only four years old. What might be Gwendolyn Brooks' meaning and why does this African American poet speak to Oyeyemi as she begins her third novel, and to us, as we ponder the knowledge produced by the sorting pattern into jars and cabinets?

The difference between black boxes and glass jars is between that which allows access and that which is cemented up. Brooks' cabinets are clearly labelled. The jars are see-through glass, and have lids that lift up; her boxes have hinges, which make themselves accessible to the hungry travelling artist on her return. Brooks' poem may be lit by only a puny light, but there is enough visibility to enable it to be itself a receptacle both for Brooks' protagonist, and, through her for Oyeyemi, to raid on her return from her descent into gloom and disarray. There is 'a differential pattern of activities that occurs within spaces that are well lit and spaces that are shadowy and dark' (Lee and Stenner 1999: 96). Latour's black boxes are hermetically sealed, this being a condition of their effectiveness. In the rest of the chapter, I struggle to prise open the black box, and to hold the classification binary of modernity versus the pre-modern, and its consequences, up to the light.

Modernity versus the pre-modern: retaining the binary, contesting the contents

Probably one of the most powerful and stubborn binaries buried in the black box is the polarization between modernity and the indigenous, or between pre-scientific/pre-industrial societies and their post-opposites. This categorization gives rise to a proliferation of assumptions about African culture, politics and social life against a backdrop of a supposedly more advanced Europe. One way of contesting these assumptions is to retain the binary – to see modernity as desirable, and as an inevitable progression into the global, technological world – but to insist that there are multiple routes and pathways to achieving this. In other words, the content of the particular route to modernity that Europe happened to follow should be interrogated, and not confused with the form or mechanism of transformation from older to newer ways of operating in the complex world of the twenty-first century.

Manthia Diawara's project is to show how Africans might 'find their own way in the modern world' (1998: 107). This he does by taking us into West African markets – supposedly domains of 'tradition' that operate outside of global capitalism. He suggests that if you can read the code of 'the seeming disorder', of 'curvilinear paths', in the cacophony of goods ranging from tomatoes to Dutch fabrics, you could discover an effective challenge to the modernity of nation states and World Bank hegemony (1998: 116). Diawara demonstrates that West African merchants were familiar with places such as 'Paris, New York, Hong Kong, Tokyo, and Johannesburg before African students set foot in those places' (1998: 118). He suggests that the African nation 'believed too much in the new man' and 'confused him with the European man and his culture' (1998: 118-19). This confusion sums it all up. The new man [*sic*] is desirable within this paradigm, but this need not mean that he looks, talks and dresses like a European. And so:

> the merchants are the first to introduce radios, sunglasses, watches, televisions, and Mercedes cars to the remote places of West Africa. They revitalize traditional cultures through the introduction of these new elements in the market, resist the takeover of businesses by multinational corporations, and compete with the agents of the state for the role of modernizing the masses. (1998: 119)

The accoutrements of material life – sunglasses and radios – are grounded in the African market at its hub, and become the launching pad for an exploration of changing social and cultural forms from within an African perspective. Diawara does not bypass the magnetic field of Western goods and chattels, but he examines their integration and transformation into African cultural life, starting from the local market, and thereby taking a different path from the more commonly accepted routes. What he is contesting is that the African market is archaic.

In a similar vein, Brian Larkin explores what he terms 'parallel modernities' in his paper on 'Indian Films and Nigerian Lovers'. The Northern Nigerian Hausa population of his study, do not necessarily invest all of their imaginaries in Western cultural forms but, in avidly partaking of Hindi film, find other models as catalysts for their emerging identities (2002: 18). What Larkin is calling for is 'a revision of conceptions of global cultural flows that privilege the centrality of the West' (2002: 19). He is emphatic that he is not minimizing 'the hegemony of Western culture', but he is stressing that it is 'only part' of the range of choices, which include 'Hausa or Yoruba videos, Indian, Hong Kong or American films or videos of Qur'anic *tafsir* (exegesis) by local preachers' (2002: 20).

Interestingly, Larkin does not reify these Hindi movies as somehow providing better models than Western films. The point is that the conundrums, consequences and solutions posed by Indian movies are sufficiently similar and simultaneously also different from African issues to provide the roughage enabling African modernity to find local expression. This line of argument retains the binary of modernity in opposition to the archaic or pre-industrial, but refuses to place Africa in one column and Europe in another. It makes the content of both columns more muddied and complicated. This shuffling of what goes into the modernity column is what Dipesh Chakrabarty is driving at with regard to India in his book, *Provincializing Europe*. He does not necessarily reject modernity itself (2000: 42), but rather 'the narratives of "modernity" that ... point to a certain "Europe" as the primary habitus of the modern' (2000: 43).

Detonating the binary and hunting the factish

A more radical position dismantles the opposition between modernity and its opposite entirely. It contests the existence of modernity itself as a goal and a benchmark. It argues that the binary inevitably sets up a uni-directional flow of knowledge from North to South, and suggests that a different model be built on journeys taking place back and forth in multiple directions. This changes the way one classifies cultural geneses, influences, and possible futures.

For example, Eileen Julien explores the genealogy of African fiction and its assumed origins in the genre of the European novel in her paper, 'The Extroverted African Novel'. Her goal is no less than to 'rewrite the history of the novel' in all of its manifestations, popular and bourgeois, local and migrant, and thereby to 'rethink inherited wisdom on modernity' (2006: 669). The inherited wisdom that she singles out for disruption is the assumption that the form of the novel is European, a form which is dressed up in some exotic African content, like oral tales, resulting in 'alien, imported modernity, touched up with local African color' (2006: 673). For this syndrome, she coins the term 'ornamentalism', with its apt, though not alluded to, overtones of Edward Saïd's Orientalism. Her critique goes way beyond the question of novels. This 'ornamentalism' is part of the discourse that suggests that 'modernity and the democratic nation state are fundamentally Western and must be imported into Africa, Asia, and Latin America, where they can, at best, be "ornamented" by indigenous culture' (2006: 679). In other words, at the heart of 'ornamentalism' is a presumed tension between 'whatever it means to be modern and whatever it means to be African' (2006: 673). Instead of this superficial window-dressing of the European novel form, Julien suggests that Europe and Africa mutually influenced each other in the construction of a new paradigm, a refiguring of subjectivity and language and in the invention of new knowledges. And these new knowledges are always constituent of the old in complex combination with multiple pasts, forms and imaginaries – 'the modern novel is *creole*, ... born from the contact of peoples and cultures' (2006: 675, emphasis in original).

In the same vein, Bruno Latour asserts that 'modernization has never occurred' in his book *We Have Never Been Modern* (1991: 76). Only by means of 'harsh disciplining' (1991: 72) are some entities compelled to become contemporary, and others designated as 'archaic' or 'irrational'. This brutal cleavage of the modern from the indigenous corrals time into 'a fine laminary flow' instead of the 'great hotchpotch' that it is (1991: 76). Latour suggests that any adjudication of the constituents of modernity involves a suspect 'classification principle' (1991: 75). The question remains as to how, precisely, to demolish this suspect classification? In his 2010 book, *On the Modern Cult of the Factish Gods*, Latour suggests that this can be achieved by inventing new words in order to wrest language from its so-called common-sense assumptions.

The new word that Latour invents is 'factish'. This word cuts right through the binary by combining the notion of so-called scientific facts with so-called traditional African fetishes. This is necessitated because 'moderns' are convinced of the 'essential difference between facts and fetishes' (2010: 11), and, furthermore, they understand modernity as Western, and as based on facts, science and rationality, while places like

Africa are assumed to be backward, and filled with inhabitants who believe in magic and supernatural tokens like the fetish (2010: 60).

The factish obliterates the binary between fact and fetish and, more importantly, between Africa and Europe in that, while the cultural and political substance of our factishes may differ, all human beings, without exception, require that mix of belief and verifiable evidence in order to make meaning, and to pass through our rites of passage as we become adults in a social world. In defining a factish, Latour emphasizes what it does. It is a tool of practice, whose theory remains invisible to actors. The factish enables us, personhood as a whole, to '*pass*' (2010: 23, emphasis in original), 'to live' (2010: 28). It is '*the wisdom of the passage*' (2010: 35, emphasis in original). What Latour also seems to imply is that to take an alternative path from the designated route of power and domination, we need to be armed with a different language. With made-up words, like 'factish', the binary between modernity and Africa can be dismantled. And so, 'lights cross paths' and African divinities are welcomed into the science laboratory (2010: 66). Lights that flit and shine freely across paths, create new routes and portals across them. It creates the possibility that religious rituals and brews bubbling in laboratory test tubes may share as much as they dispute with each other. Moreover, Latour's invention of *a new word* compels us to think outside of pigeonholes, and takes us to the fundamental question of *language*, as well as its relationship to classification, and to knowledge-making more broadly.

In using European languages to express their creativity, African writers, from the very beginning, recognized the imperative to bend language to their own wills, to make it work as their slave and not their master. This was a gargantuan task; it is not merely a case of using a few proverbs and words from indigenous languages, nor is it about depicting African rituals in the mode of anthropological interpreters. Far more deeply concealed in the very intestines of the black box of the English language are its stories of conquest, its tropes of light and darkness, its multiple codes and maps and keys, which reinforce the necessity of a civilizing mission to enable savages from the dark continent to be liberated into the modernity of church and crown.

Many writers have argued that Africa-centred knowledges can emerge only through a transformation of the languages in which they are expressed. Most famously, Ngũgĩ wa Thiong'o (1986) called for writers to use indigenous African languages for their thoughts and desires, and thereafter have them translated into English if they so wished. I cannot go into this debate here, but I focus instead on the mechanisms whereby diasporic writers, such as Helen Oyeyemi, who has no African language, bends and wreaks havoc on English and its genre classifications, in expressing her Africanness as it entwines with her Englishness.

For example, in *White is for Witching* (2009), Oyeyemi spins words around so that they perform double functions, in order to link different dimensions and to open up the simultaneous existence of history, reality, and the intervention of gods. Look at her use of the word, 'that' in the following quotation. The first context refers to Oyeyemi's fictional character, Miranda, knocking on the door of the room of two girls, Deme and Soryaz, who are living in her house. The second seemingly unrelated context is the breakup of the relationship between Miranda's brother and his girlfriend, Emma:

> Miranda went to see if Deme and Soryaz were all right.
> 'Who is it?' The girls said together
> 'It's me,' she said.
> They wouldn't answer after
> 　　　　　　　　　that
> evening, Emma and I broke up. (2009: 41)

The word 'that' enables the narration to change from the omniscient third person, describing Miranda's actions, to the first person of her brother. What were separate categories of narration and action become strangely linked. This happens repeatedly in the novel and is a stylistic and political device of interrogating categories. Look at the use of the weighty word 'white', especially significant as it echoes the title. We see it act as a portal between the harsh, contemporary political realities of race where illegal immigrants are housed in detention centres, and the terrifying psychological realities of Miranda's haunting by her weird, gothic, and ghostly ancestors, such as Anna Good, who also live in her house:

> Miranda had known the address of the detention centre before she had come, she knew that the place was called the Citadel, but she had forgotten that it actually looked like a citadel. She had re-imagined the building as white and similar to a hospital. But now she understood that that would have been silly. A building of this size would not blend on the Western Heights if it was
> white
> was a colour that Anna Good was afraid to wear. Her fear reflected her feeling that she was not clean. (2009: 115)

White, then, is for witching, being the race of the witches in the novel; it is for the white lack of knowledge of the oppression of black people, who are hounded and deported, and who are not from nice, clean hospital-type buildings; it is the colour that the grandmother, Anna Good, shuns, both because she is a enveloped in the tradition of fear and internalized inferiority that women inherit from their forebears, and also because she is indeed unsavoury in the blood-sucking witchy qualities she passes on to generations of sad women. The singsong of nonsense connects two dimensions metonymically by the chance alphabetical resonance of the letter 'w'. This results in the scrambling of common-sense systems of classification.

Such words, as I have described elsewhere with regard to Biyi Bandele's, *The Street* (Cooper 2008: Chapter 2), enable different, usually incompatible dimensions to engage each other. The enabling capacity of made-up words, like Lewis Carroll's 'snark', was highlighted by Gilles Deleuze in his detailed analysis of Carroll's deceptively simple poem. The word snark provides a segue between the literal and the figurative, thereby becoming an organizing principle in an otherwise chaotic world of obliterated categories (Deleuze 1990: 26). The entire logic of Carroll's 'The Hunting of the Snark', in fact, rests on the co-existence of different kinds of dimensions, such as:

> They sought it with thimbles, they sought it with care;
>   They pursued it with forks and hope;
> They threatened its life with a railway-share;
>   They charmed it with smiles and soap. (1990: 250)

The snark will only be found if forks and hope, the material and the spiritual, are united in the hunt. In this way, a snark word acts as a kind of hinge that opens new knowledge by enabling seemingly incompatible connections in old systems of classification. A snark is a factish.

The suggestion that Oyeyemi is hunting her own snarks is less fanciful than may at first appear, given that Oyeyemi has acknowledged Lewis Carroll's influence. In an interview, she is asked about how she devised the technique of poetically shaping words on the page in *White is for Witching*, as illustrated above. Oyeyemi's intriguing response is that this style emerged 'like falling down a dark rabbit hole' (Armitstead 2009:). In other words, the language itself provides a tunnel, a sighting of a snark, into a different Wonderland world. Oyeyemi entitles the parts of *White is for Witching* after Carroll, the first being 'Curiouser' and later 'And curiouser'. So, the rabbit hole becomes a portal across columns, and refuses the teleology always waiting in the wings to shuffle all that appears new into old hierarchies, evolutions and powerful interests.

Then again, it is difficult to take language by the jugular and open up gates to other knowledges in it, without the possibility of tearing it apart and making no sense at all. Communal codes of understanding and labelling enable social interaction. An excess of words in mad spin and play could detoxify old categories or degenerate into gibberish. Indeed, Oyeyemi's novels are extremely difficult to understand, and only the most intrepid readers get through their lack of narrative, their dizzying play, their verbal gymnastics and their refusal of narrative tradition.

It is possible, in other words, that Oyeyemi goes too far in her pulverizing of dominant codes and accepted meanings. The process of exposing the politics of classification is a dangerous endeavour, given that classification is such an important and unavoidable part of our ability to navigate and decode the challenges of our daily lives. This takes us back to the hell into which both Brookes and Oyeyemi descend as they confront the dominant power concealed in the black boxes – a hell from which they might only return with the aid of their own, alternative system of labelled and see-though jars. It is a painful process to prize open a black box, and to move from box to glass, from concealment to visibility, from colonial archive to Africa-centredness. This is why Oyeyemi calls on the African-American tradition of Gwendolyn Brookes and her little, labelled 'jars and cabinets', which are of their own construction; their system, expresses their 'will'. What this means is that classification is also an enabling tool when designed to enable the interests of less-dominant groups to prevail. What this also means is that we have to 'design classification systems that do not foreclose on rearrangements suggested by new forms of social and natural knowledge' (Haraway 1992: 321).

The question then becomes, how might we classify without re-inventing forms of power, where glass jars inexorably become the black boxes? Are there more fluid and provisional forms of coding? All these questions might be summed up by the concluding one of this chapter: What would it mean *to articulate* instead of to classify?

Articulation instead of classification?

> to articulate ... is to put things together, scary things, risky things, contingent things (Haraway 1992: 324).

To articulate is to put hope and soap together, not out of semantic logic, but because they contest this logic for a moment. And their rhyme is their reason. To articulate is to make alliances that are contextual and mobile, rather than fixed and separated by silos of established interests. With her concept of articulation, Haraway enters, Latour's 'amodern' world, which insists on the absence of beginnings, enlightenments, and endings: the world has always been in the middle of things, in unruly and practical conversations, full of action and structured by a startling array of actants and of networking and unequal collectives. (Haraway 1992: 304)

Elements align and link, not permanently within groupings – the logic of which has long disappeared from conscious knowledge – but within the contextual urgencies and political necessities of the historical moment. In this lego-wonderland of shape-shifting potential, new creatures may emerge out of an alternative system of procreation than from the heterosexuality of the nuclear benchmarks. These could be called cyborgs, as imagined in Donna Haraway's handbook of articulation, her 'Cyborg Manifesto'. The cyborg is not a hybrid, but its body is historically contingent, flexible and changing as in articulation, rather than syncretism (Haraway 1991: 324). These multiple, risky things, thrown metonymically into contiguity, are arrangements that fly in the face of any ordered evolution of progress journeying inexorably from North to South. An articulated world

has an undecidable number of modes and sites where connections can be made. The surfaces of this kind of world are not frictionless curved planes. Unlike things can be joined – and like things can be broken apart – and vice versa. Full of sensory hairs, evaginations, invaginations, and indentations, the surfaces which interest me are dissected by joints. (Haraway 1992: 324)

The cyborg appeals to diasporic writers, whose allegiances are multiple. She is Octavia Butler's Shori, the black, genetically modified vampire, who lives in a symbiotic and benevolent state with humans; she is Okorafor-Mbachu's Zahrah, the windseeker, in her novel of that title; or Okorafor's meta-humans in *Who Fears Death*, one of whom carries with her a favourite book entitled *My Cyborg Manifesto*. Okorafor's parents are Nigerian, and she grew up in the United States. And so, 'the cyborg's transracial, transnational body conjures forth an identity no longer split between First and Third World, between metropole and native home, but rather, *a body so fragmented that its morphology is a diaspora*' (Apter 1999: 217, emphasis added). Apter's description of the cyborg as having a 'morphology' that is diaspora is highly suggestive. Morphology most commonly refers to the shape and structure of words, or of biological beings. Thus it is a word that sums up the cyborg's capacity for being modular, for embodying multiplicity, for being writers who are verbal magicians, wordsmiths, heir to continents, and to the world. 'Evaginations, invaginations, and indentations' is the visceral language of poetry, of metonymic connections.

Perhaps Mami Wata, the African water spirit, who occupies a suggestive crossroads between rewritten African myth, the material and mutation, is a form of cyborg. She is exemplary of Warner's (2009) definition of the fantastic literature of metamorphosis, tales of which 'often arose in spaces (temporal, geographical, and mental) that were crossroads, cross-cultural zones, points of interchange on the intricate connective tissue of communications between cultures' (2009: 17). She is the past and the present of Africa, and it is likely that 'she emerged from the head of a slave ship', at the very moment, in other words, of the emergence of diaspora (Davies 1998: 138). She embodies crossover diasporic writers, who are playing with language, stories and alternatives. She is everywhere and nowhere:

> Because she has no feet, she cannot walk. Because she has no wings, she cannot fly. She is the person who has to be made over constantly to discover who she is. She is *the floating signifier*. (Davies 1998: 138, emphasis added)

As floating signifier, she is a snark, an anchor, an enabler, connecting normally disparate zones. Mami Wata is a shape-shifter incarnate, unsettled and mobile. It is no surprise, then, that Helen Oyeyemi depicts multiple incarnations of Mami Wata in her novel, *The Opposite House*, where she is known as Yemaya, or Aya for short. Yemaya had been a Yoruba water spirit, and became a goddess of the ocean when she travelled across the waters with the slaves, becoming Mami Wata: 'Aya's family is large. Each member of Aya's family has aspects, and those aspects have aspects' (2007: 111). And so, 'Yemaya Ataramagwa was never still for a minute; light jumped in her hair' with overtones of its mermaid blondness (2007: 111). By contrast, the fishiness of the mermaid Yemaya Achabba, 'was as cold and limp and quiet as a fish-scale coat' (2007: 111). Then again, 'Yemaya Oqqutte made eyes at men and swung her hips lazily' (2007: 111).

The articulated cyborg Mama is not only diasporic. She is also to be found in Diawara's market, where the assumptions of the traditional versus the global world were confounded, and where the World Bank is not the only option:

> Articulation may better explain the ways in which those Lagos market women navigate the contingencies of identity by *articulating* different subject positions strategically, not as cosmopolitans, but as navigators. (Ashcroft 2010: 79, emphasis in original)

Conclusion

It is important to conclude on a cautionary note. The navigation that
articulation entails takes place in dangerous waters, even when a
provisional way of articulating the world, rather than a rigid system
of classification, is deployed. The compass guiding this voyage is the
existence of realities of social, political and global life. In other words,
in order to catch sight of the magical snark, or to travel armed with the
password factish, we need to understand that the principles driving our
systems of articulation are historical and material contexts, which do
not themselves float and fluctuate. These are the still points where tricky
currents are negotiated. Or not. When the hunt for the snark backfires,
instead of the enabling word, annihilation can take place. Instead of a
snark, a dreaded boojum may be sighted:

> For, although common Snarks do no manner of harm,
>   Yet, I feel it my duty to say,
> Some are Boojums – (Carroll 2011: 239)

If a boojum surfaces from the deep, then you will 'softly and suddenly
vanish away'(Carroll (2011: 241). A boojum: a mix of boogey-
man and jumble? Whatever it is, it is bad. Articulation carries its
own perils. Drawing on new allies, some of which are unstable and
possibly untrustworthy, involves entering the belly of the whale. The
threat is of disintegration, the kind of meltdown that, I suspect, may
have contributed to Helen Oyeyemi's suicide attempt while she was
still at school. Her protagonist engages in a fearful dance of fictional,
wild poetry, echoing with syncopated sound, and challenging settled,
figurative language and finite codes of fiction's conventions.

> she saw the moon turn away
> and the trees thrashing to save their roots
> dogs in every house around that still stood, *their barking distant as if from inside a
> single locked safe, the metal syncopating the sound of fear,* saying dance, dance, don't
> look around, dance
> which she did, kicking and yelling ... (2009: 79, emphasis added)

In *White is for Witching* (2009), the black box, from whose sacred,
secret knowledge she is excluded, drives Oyeyemi's Miranda mad.
Miranda is the embodiment of the impossibility of easy systems of
binary classification. She is white and she is also black; she is diasporic
like her creator, whose origins are Nigerian and upbringing is English.
Her manic, mad dance is enacted in poetic, rhythmic, non-sequitorial

metonymy. Metonymy's site of happenstance, rather than quests and holy grails, enables it to contest the hidden foundations of modernity's tropes and metaphors. But Miranda is a mad woman, a white vampire witch, a Caribbean hag, a *soucouyant*, who eats chalk and sucks blood.

Nevertheless, as she transforms herself into the Mami Wata cyborgs of her imaginary, Helen Oyeyemi challenges us, the readers, to make sense of her Africa, which is as much about the white, English male, Lewis Carroll, as it is about a Yoruba water spirit, who journeys across the perilous Atlantic. Finally, it is worth emphasizing that, while this Yoruba spirit-cum-European mermaid is a floating signifier, the slavery that sent her on her journey is an historical truth. The hunt is on for changing, articulating realities to become transparent organizing principles of how we see the world. In the process, we may construct new, Africa-centred knowledges.

References

Apter, Emily (1999) *Continental Drift*, Chicago and London: University of Chicago Press.

Armitstead, Claire (2009) 'Book of the Week: *White is for Witching* by Helen Oyeyemi', *The Guardian*, 19 June. http://www.guardian.co.uk/books/audio/2009/jun/18/helen-oyeyemi-white-is-for-witching. Accessed online April, 2011.

Ashcroft, Bill (2010) 'Transnation' in Janet Wilson, Cristina Sandru and Sarah Lawson Welsh, eds, *Rerouting the Postcolonial: New Directions for the New Millennium*, London: Routledge.

Bowker, Geoffrey C. and Star, Susan Leigh (1999) *Sorting Things Out: Classification and its Consequences*, Cambridge, MA: MIT Press.

Butler, Octavia E. (2005) *Fledgling*, New York: Grand Central Publishing.

Carroll, Lewis (2011 [1876]) *The Hunting of the Snark*, London: The British Library.

Chakrabarty, Dipesh (2000) *Provincializing Europe: Postcolonial Thought and Historical Difference*, Princeton NJ: Princeton University Press.

Cooper, Brenda (2008) *A New Generation of African Writers*, Melton: James Currey.

Davies, Ioan (1998) 'Negotiating African dulture: Toward a decolonization of the fetish' in Fredric Jameson and Masao Miyoshi, eds, *The Cultures of Globalization*, Durham NC and London: Duke University Press.

Deleuze, Gilles (1969/1990) *The Logic of Sense*, New York: Columbia University Press.

Diawara, Manthia (1998) 'Toward a regional imaginary in Africa' in Fredric Jameson and Masao Miyoshi, eds, *The Cultures of Globalization*, Durham NC and London: Duke University Press.

Fowler, Alastair (1982) *Kinds of Literature: An Introduction to the Theory of Genres and Modes*, Oxford: Clarendon Press.

Haraway, Donna (1991) *Simians, Cyborgs, and Women. The Reinvention of Nature*, London: Free Association Books.

Haraway, Donna J. (1992) 'The promise of monsters: A regenerative politics for inappropriate/d others' in Lawrence Grossberg, Cary Nelson and Paula Treichler, eds. *Cultural Studies*, London: Routledge.

Julien, Eileen (2006) 'The extroverted African novel' in F Moretti, ed., *The Novel, Volume 1: History, Geography and Culture*, Princeton NJ and Oxford: Princeton University Press.

Larkin, Brian (2002) 'Indian films and Nigerian lovers: Media and the creation of parallel modernities' in Stephanie Newell, ed., *Readings in African Popular Fiction*, Bloomington IN and Oxford: Indiana University Press and James Currey.

Latour, Bruno (1987) *Science in Action: How to Follow Scientists and Engineers Through Society*, Cambridge MA: Harvard University Press.

Latour, Bruno (1991) *We Have Never Been Modern*, New York: Harvester Wheatsheaf.

Latour, Bruno (1999) *Pandora's Hope: Essays on the Reality of Science Studies*, Cambridge MA: Harvard University Press.

Latour, Bruno (2010) *On The Modern Cult of the Factish Gods*. Durham NC: Duke University Press.

Lee, Nick and Paul Stenner (1999) 'Who pays? Can we pay them back?' in John H Law, ed., *Actor Network Theory*, Oxford: Blackwell.

Ngũgĩ wa Thiong'o (1986) *Decolonising the Mind: The Politics of Language in African Literature*, London, Nairobi, Portsmouth NH: James Currey, Heinemann Kenya, Heinemann Inc.

Okorafor, Nnedi (2010) *Who Fears Death*, New York: Daw.

Okorafor-Mbachu, Nnedi (2005) *Zahrah the Windseeker*, Boston MA: Houghton Mifflin.

Oyeyemi, Helen (2007) *The Opposite House*, London: Bloomsbury.

Oyeyemi, Helen (2009) *White is for Witching*, London: Picador.

Warner, Marina (2004) *Fantastic Metamorphoses, Other Worlds*, Oxford: Oxford University Press.

6

'This is a Robbers' System'
Popular Musicians' Readings
of the Kenyan State

Mbugua wa Mungai

Globalization has tended to give force to particular knowledges, privileging them while at the same time marginalizing and subverting other, often local, knowledges. An entirely understandable response from below has been to assert the primacy of local knowledge. It is often asserted that local knowledge has greater explanatory power, is more sensitive to context, and has local resonance. Following from this, it can be argued that local knowledge can constitute a form of resistance and empowerment. Within nation states there is a contestation over knowledge that pits states against citizens. States are themselves invested in creating knowledge as a way of legitimizing themselves. As such, nation states are also enemies of local knowledge that expresses dissonance and opposition to the inequalities over which they preside.

In this chapter, I examine the local knowledge produced by popular musicians in Kenya, as well as how they address local issues and express local concerns.[1] What emerges is that this local knowledge is politically unstable, simultaneously mirroring and critiquing the excesses of greed and violence within the nation state. This it does by way of its own particular style, both musically and rhetorically. Intriguingly, its greatest oppositional power may be embodied in the music itself in ways that are quite difficult to pinpoint. In other words, even as this music-based knowledge acts as a catharsis, it also reminds its audiences of their global peripheralization, and reflects their collusion with that system. It is a local knowledge that speaks in many tongues and does not necessarily set the musicians or their audiences free.

---

[1]   The lyric quoted in the title of this chapter is a translation of the line, '*hii ni system ya majambazi*', which features in a song called 'Majambazi' by Kenyan rappers, Mashifta. The rap first became popular in 2000, and represents Kenyan society as a robbers' system.

93

Music and knowledge

One of the most visible spaces for the public production and expression of local knowledge in Kenya is popular music. Partly due to this, the music industry has also tended to be a perilous and intensely contested space. Dominant political culture, influenced by its relationship to private capital, has sought to determine and regulate the content of popular music, sometimes even violently.

The state has also intervened in the popular music industry's processes of production, and sought to influence public 'consumption' of the 'knowledge' that emanates from its collective practices. Seen as simultaneously 'critical', 'subversive', 'prophetic', 'explanatory', 'analytical' and 'entertaining', popular musicians in Kenya are crucial shapers of their communities' knowledge of themselves, and their relation to other sites of knowledge. Indeed, Kenyan musicians have created a kind of folk knowledge through a tradition of critique, the roots of which can be located in subversive, anti-colonial music. Successive generations of post-colonial performers have adapted this model to specific political situations and contests. While I acknowledge the historical role played by popular musicians in Kenya's anti-colonial movement, in this chapter I have chosen to focus more on urban life after 1980, to demonstrate how musicians construct knowledge about poor urban communities and their possible futures.[2] I draw on Baba Otonglo's 1984 song, 'Budget Iko High',[3] which I consider to be seminal in instantiating the sorts of creative subterfuge I have alluded to, and I argue that its modality of social critique has aided the concretizing of urban space as a platform through which Kenyans formulate creative forms of vernacular knowledge. I also acknowledge that this critique simultaneously colludes with state power.

'Budget Iko High' forms the backdrop against which I develop the argument that although, through their lyrics, Kenya's popular musicians contribute to the construction of knowledge about their communities, ironically the 'truth' that is thus generated does not enable true liberation for their audiences because the music is circumscribed by the political and economic context in which the musicians operate. The force of this context is manifested in how it

[2]   The early 1980s saw the beginning of severe repression by the regime of former president, Daniel Arap Moi. These were also the years in which the World Bank and IMF-supported structural-adjustment programme began to bite, with disastrous consequences for the urban poor; social protest was, therefore, a function of both state repression and economic bondage.

[3]   Baba Otonglo is a stage name sometimes used by Osumba Rateng, a Luo musician. The title of the track, which was released on an album with the same name, translates from Kiswahili as 'expensive budget'.

co-opts the musicians, even as they create a form of alternative and oppositional local knowledge.

A thread that runs through this chapter relates to the ambivalence and perils of (local) knowing. Knowledge comes with physical, emotional and psychological risks, and an assessment of this risk can prompt a healthy scepticism about calls for the localization of knowledge. While not wishing to minimize the validity of the social critique that can be achieved through music, I argue that in this case the musicians' knowledge offers but a symbolic critique of material realities of Kenyan life. Musicians, as creative practitioners, loop audiences into an 'imagined community' (*pace* Anderson)[4], which is ultimately forced to cede ground to ideas and practices determined by larger processes, such as those of nation-formation.

Urban Kenya – of which Nairobi is the epitome – was deliberately chosen as the site of this study. The city is a space of vibrant cultural production and experimentation yet, at the same time, it is fraught with often risky and intense capitalistic ventures, especially in the symbiosis between private capital and state corruption. The cohabitation of government and capital conspires against indigenous capital, and ignites conflict between, for example, Nairobi's hawkers and the city council,[5] or *matatu*[6] (taxi) drivers and the Kenya Bus Company. The intensity of this conflict illuminates a clash of knowledges while, at the same time illustrating how interdependent these knowledges are.

Baba Otonglo's 'Budget Iko High': popular music in a time of structural adjustment

'Budget Iko High' was a highly popular song in Kenya in 1984, a year that saw one of Kenya's severest droughts. The track was briefly played on national radio, then known as the Voice of Kenya, before it was banned by the government. In the song's introduction, the speaker, Baba Otonglo – which literally translated means 'Father of Coins' – is the finance minister of an unnamed country, the identity of which is not difficult to fathom as Kenya, given the obvious pointers in the song. The song is set in parliament as the finance minister makes his budget speech. Recognizing that the country is facing steep inflation, the minister presents a set of expenditure rules, the implementation of

---

[4]   Anderson, Benedict (1983). *Imagined Communities*, London: Verso.
[5]   For a detailed exploration of the nature and politics of conflicts between informal-sector workers and urban authorities in Nairobi, see Macharia (1992).
[6]   *Matatu* are privately owned passenger vans and minibuses.

which will hopefully see the country through the troubled financial times ahead. After the official presentation, and in what is clearly a parody of the usual, erudite post-budget analysis, the voice of a dejected speaker in the role of the 'common man', *mwananchi*, is heard. He laments the fact that prices of basic commodities – maize flour, sugar, milk and tea – have increased. Once-affordable and popular consumer commodities such as meat and chapatti will henceforth be exclusively found on the menus of the rich; the poor can, at best, hope to savour such delicacies once a year, during Christmas celebrations. The gist of the song is that life has become unbearable for the common folk. Aware that he cannot directly blame the government for the precarious financial situation that his family finds themselves in, the speaker blames his misfortunes on price deregulation – the policy by which the government, conceding to the IMF's blueprint for market liberalization, removed price controls on basic consumer goods in the 1980s. The song's audiences easily identified the connection between (poor) government policy and citizens' suffering, mapped in the personal humiliations experienced in the speaker's private/domestic life: he no longer feels man enough as he cannot adequately provide for his family.

There was another aspect of the work that was seldom remarked upon: by adopting a stage name with the Kiswahili appellation *baba* (father), the artist playfully contested and consequently subversively arrogated to himself the title 'Father of the Nation', which was then reserved for President Moi. In political panegyrics, the president was called 'Baba Moi', while his ruling party, the Kenya African National Union, was known in Kiswahili as *'chama cha baba na mama'* (the father/ mother party). Operating formally as a multi-party democracy but *de facto* as a single party state, Moi's government sought to convert Kenyans into unquestioning, state-supporting citizens. The image of the paterfamilias symbolically presented the state as benign, but the strategy failed. The image found little resonance among Kenyans, and state repression further undermined the government's credibility. In practice, Kenya's president appeared to be a dictator, a cannibal who devoured members of his own family, and who allowed mismanagement and corruption to run rife. After 1982, the one-party state under Moi systematically cracked down on political dissent. Academics were detained or forced into exile, and anti-establishment politicians were sent to jail for long periods. In the face of this, the role of speaking to power fell to popular musicians and theatre practitioners.[7] At the time, the state hardly imagined that the spaces in which these artists

---

[7]   For a detailed analysis of theatre and popular music performances as platforms of anti-government critique during the late 1980s, see Haugerud (1997: 28-32).

practised, let alone the content of their creative work, could be deployed for serious anti-government critique.

This was the context in which Baba Otonglo's 'Budget' emerged and gained wide popularity. The song presciently alluded to the idea of 'belt-tightening' under the highly controversial and unpopular structural adjustment programmes that the IMF and World Bank demanded that Kenya institute from the mid-1980s as a way of reducing government investment in public projects. These included cutbacks in the education sector, a field in which the educated classes, often the beneficiaries of state largesse, were invested. Not surprisingly, within a short time of its release, 'Budget' had become a rallying point around which citizens' critiques of the government coalesced. The song was swiftly banned. 'Budget' disappeared from the airwaves, but the foundations of knowledge formulation by popular musicians had already been built.

Urban 'youth nation': the case of Nairobi rappers

Kenya's urban youth have not succumbed to the blandishments of the state, nor have they readily accepted state definitions of citizenship. For a state to rule successfully it needs, among other things, inhabitants to accept the idea that they are all united as residents of a country. Far from accepting this definition, or its corollary that the state fairly represents all citizens, Kenya's young urban musicians deconstruct state values. In what follows, I examine the worldview of these young people, and explore the agendas they have for their 'youth nation' (*pace* Samper 2002). Self-knowledge, as we shall see, leads these musicians and their audiences into deep dilemmas precisely because they neither have the material resources nor the organizational capacity to confront the problems their music identifies. Simultaneously, and somewhat contradictorily, therefore, they sometimes adhere to the materialist values of the capitalist state.

One of the most remarkable things about Nairobi's rappers is their successful appropriation of American rap models to speak to local audiences. Obviously the genre's outer trappings are 'American' – the dress, the 'bling' and the generally spectacularized body, of which CMB Prezzo[8] is arguably the ultimate exemplar. However, the content of such music remains localized, at least in the case of Kenya, following the tradition set by Hardstone, one of Kenya's pioneer rappers. In his track, 'Uhiki' (1999), Hardstone successfully wove Marvin Gaye's 'Sexual

---

[8] Prezzo is a young male rapper known for his penchant for flashy jewellery, glitzy cars and wanton spending.

Healing' into traditional Gikuyu wedding songs, to critique some of Gikuyu society's forms of engagement with modernity, such as the reformulation of traditional wedding ceremonies to address matters of economics and sexuality (Nyairo 2007: 128-132). Further localization is evident in the fact that much of the music is created using Sheng,[9] Kiswahili, and, in some instances, other local languages such as Dholuo and Kikuyu. This dynamic ensures that the musicians reach even rural audiences. It is instructive that a musician such as Redsan, who also raps in English, seemed to attract less attention from the youth than when he sang in Sheng, as demonstrated by the popularity of his track, 'Apakatwe' (2002). At another level, it is worth noting that while it is true that artists from different East African countries usually anchor their music in specific geographical landscapes, the content of their work appeals to audiences across the region because of shared historical experiences: colonialism, rapid social change and various other crises of modernity. In line with this, it seems natural that youth identity is one of the most widely rapped-about themes.

The identity that Nairobi rappers express, is a complex one, shaped as it is by elements that the mainstream society often frowns upon. This might explain the older generation's antagonistic view of contemporary urban music. However, given the realization by the youth that Kenyan society is no guardian of youth interests, and that following its dictates inevitably means that young people will make little headway in their lives, rappers are increasingly focusing on the need to put their own individual interests first, before those of anyone else. Here lies the fault line between the rappers forming part of an alternative, subversive community, and their inability to free themselves from the values of a corrupt society. Narcissism is what modernity has taught them: to succeed in life, at least in Kenya, one must deliberately look out for oneself, but also, and here is where we see the tension, one must eschew following the herd. For instance, in rapper DNG's Sheng rap, 'Iyoo', the musician addresses a conflict between himself and society's authorities, here pointedly represented by the church: *Maisha pia ni yangu ... Nakula hepi kivyangu ... Jumapili nasali tena nauliza maswali,/Mbona siwezi fanya hivi na hivi?/Ati kwa sababu haikubaliki* (My life is mine ... I choose my own way of having fun ...On Sundays I go to church, and I ask questions./ Why can't I do this or that?/I am told these things are forbidden).

---

[9]   Sheng is a sociolect that works mainly by hybridization; words from various languages are added on to Kiswahili stems. Word meanings are also reversed and the syntax is often marked by playful metathesis. For a full discussion of Sheng, see, for example, Githinji (2006, 2007, 2008), Githiora (2002), Nzunga (2002), Ogechi (2007) and Samper (2002). In this section, the following legend is used for non-English words: G=Gikuyu, K=Kiswahili and S=Sheng.

The song then goes on to depict what these forbidden things are: sex, beer and generally having fun. The (decadence of the) city is celebrated, not because the speaker is unaware of the possibilities of being 'corrupted' by it, but rather because its ways can be fulfilling and liberating for the individual. If, for mainstream culture, community is the point of focus, for the speaker in 'Iyoo', the individual is the *centre* of social experience. In this work, the idea of space and authority are predominant to the extent that the *persona* can appropriate them for his own purposes; he seizes the authority to talk about his life, constantly invoking *his experience* as a legitimate basis for self-representation. The speaker's incredulity about the explanations given in church as to why he cannot do certain things is his way of calling into question, and rejecting, mainstream institutions as well as their forms of knowledge. The authority of such institutions is repudiated because the answers they provide to questions posed by the youth make no sense to them. It is little wonder, then, that few youth in Nairobi affirm finding any relief in spirituality.

Aware of the unsuitability of mainstream values as a charter for city living, some rappers opt to develop what they call 'philosophy *sedi*' (seditious philosophy) – an explanation of life that is firmly drawn around the vagaries and risks of urban living. This is the central theme of the rap group Ukoo Flani's 'Dandora L.O.V.E', which laments society's view of rappers as mad people who should be locked away in psychiatric institutions. Again, what comes through in the song is the clash of world views between these self-declared 'street philosophers' and a mainstream society that does not comprehend the sordid realities of young people's life in Nairobi, and particularly in the area of the city known as Eastlands – where arbitrary police arrests, crime, drugs, joblessness, poverty and violence are daily realities. Thus, the rappers recognize Nairobi's urban slums as spaces of possible regeneration, acknowledging that the youth can use their creative talents to transform their lives through music. Again, there is something of a tension here, as this transformation would, to some extent, set them free. Thus, these rappers are not motivated simply by selfishness; they are also creatively contributing to an alternative youth culture.

Dandora, a seedy neighbourhood in the Eastlands area where life is generally grim, is imagined as 'hip hop city' and Githurai, another run-down slum to the north of Nairobi, is seen as the home of 'tough rappers' in Mr Googz and Vinnie Banton's 'Githurai'. Generally, rappers map the stories of their lives in relation to the sordid narratives of the city's wastelands. In these circumstances it seems inevitable that youth experiment with ways of making the '3K' – *kuhanya, kuheng* and *kuwaka*

(S: sex, partying and drinking) – their mantra. It is relevant to mention here that Kenyans are perceived as being increasingly addicted to alcohol, and given the proliferation of cheap brews packed in sachets for quick consumption (see Willis 1996), rappers have naturally spoken to this phenomenon, which afflicts many youth in both urban and rural areas.

This perception of Kenyans is evident in rapper Nonini's immensely popular 'Keroro' (G: beer). The rap is a critique of the perceived national culture of drug addiction (see Nyassy and Kihara 2008; Orengo 2009). The same theme is also clear in Risasi's 'Watu Wote' (K: everyone), as well as in Nonini and Nameless's collaboration 'Furahiday', a pun on the words Friday and *furahi* (K: be happy), which is depicted as a weekly fun day, ruled by a clubbing ethic and filled with barbecues, beers and women. In Nonini's 'Keroro', the speaker describes the inverted world of bar-room culture – where womanizing, drug abuse and a general lack of decorum are expected – and decries the tendency for city residents to drink at the expense of their families' welfare. Ironically, where the men are depicted eagerly pursuing illicit sex in these bars, they are simultaneously ridiculed for their inability to meet their conjugal obligations when they get home because they are usually too drunk: '*ndio unaona mabibi zetu siku hizi wanazusha juu ya kuwaka daily tunashindwa na kuchangamsha*' (S: our wives are always complaining these days because we drink daily, and we are unable to fulfil their needs). Esther Wahome's 'Kuna Dawa' (K: there is a cure), a gospel track, has been appropriated by youth culture and *matatu* drivers to speak to their own more secular realities; they have seized upon the song, and use it to name alcohol, which is also known as *dawa* (medicine) in street culture, as the cure for their problems.

In addition, and this is again indicative of the tension between their subversiveness and their co-option into the mainstream, it is notable that for local rappers, sexism is a major source of the metaphors through which they present the theme of sexuality in their music. In their texts, women are explicitly framed as *makabati* (S: literally translated, this word means cupboards, but in this context it refers to buttocks). Women therefore figure primarily as objects of the male gaze and sexual consumption. This thread runs through Kleptomaniax's 'Swing Swing', Q Chillah's 'Cheza' (K: Play), Longombas' 'Vuta Pumz' (S: Hold your breath) and 'Shika More' (S: Feel up),[10] The Bugz's 'Kamoja Tu' (S: Just once), Nonini's 'We Kamu' (S: You come') and 'Manzi wa Nairobi' (S: Nairobi girls), Ken Razy's 'Ti Chi' (S: Teach), Jua Kali and Pilipili's 'Kamata Dame' (S: Grab a girl'), Deux Vultures' 'Mona

---

[10]   The title of this song plays on the word '*shikamoo*', a respectful form of greeting in Kiswahili.

Lisa', Jimw@t's 'Under 18', Risasi na Suzuki's 'Miss Digida' and Jose Chameleon's Tingisha (S: Shake your booty) among others.

Beyond this, the women that young men meet in clubs are depicted as two-timing gold-diggers, who lose their morality as soon they come into contact with rich men, as in Professor Jay's Kiswahili 'Nikusaidiaje?' (K: How can I help you?).[11] It is no coincidence that nearly all of Nairobi's male rap groups have female dancers, whose purpose in music videos seems to be merely to gyrate their bodies – usually with excessive focus on their breasts and derrières – as the male rappers make suggestive comments about them, and about women in general. These female dancers are never named, a phenomenon which, like in *matatu* subculture, ascribes to them purely supporting roles in the performance of youth masculinity.

In contrast, Tanzania's Bongo Flava has female rappers who take centre-stage in the group's video productions, appearing either as main performers or collaborators. At any rate, their names appear in the production credits, suggesting the existence of a significant difference between Kenyan and Tanzanian rappers' views on gender.

However, despite the apparent glorification of the 3Ks in youth culture, Kenyan rappers do sometimes point out the dangers inherent in pursuing hedonistic lifestyles. In this regard, they encode the HIV/ AIDS narrative in their work, but they tend to represent HIV as a female disease. This too relates to the *matatu* subculture, where the idea of the female body as contaminating to the social body is rife. Young, beautiful women are presented as the purveyors of the social death that HIV represents, while men self-servingly figure as innocent victims.

This theme comes through in Circute and Joel's 'Juala', (S: Condom), in which the female body is referred to in a derogatory way as *manyake* (S: hanging meat), the Sheng word for the female body. The same theme is evident in Jimmy Gait's gospel track 'Muhadhara' (S: HIV / great trouble), which *matatu* drivers have appropriated and turned into a secular commentary about the dangers posed to young men by rich older women looking for 'toy-boys'. In the song, a 'sugar mummy' plots to ensnare the speaker, a young born-again Christian singer, who is down on his luck, by promising him instant wealth and all of modernity's fancy goods, so long as he agrees to have a sexual relationship with her. This reversal of roles is a significant indicator of the kinds of social changes that have taken place in Nairobi, where women who would traditionally wait for men to pursue them, have turned the tables, leaving males in utter confusion in the wake of such relationships.

---

[11]   Professor Jay is Tanzanian but his music is popular amongst Nairobi youth.

Such relationships can also portend pleasant surprises for men, however, especially in situations when the female is a younger woman who, unlike a sugar mummy, has more marriage potential. For example, in Softonia's 'Chocolate', a Gikuyu rap set to a Bhangra beat, a beautiful rich man's daughter rams into the speaker's car, occasioning a heavy traffic jam. However, instead of this resulting in an altercation as might be expected, the ensuing negotiations end up with the young man going back to the woman's fabulous house and jumping into bed with her, crooning about the delights of 'devouring' his newly-acquired chocolate. What is remarkable about the idea of identity suggested through the appropriation of Bhangra rhythms (originally from the state of Punjab in India) is that young people in the city are looking not only to America for ideas of cosmopolitanism, but are also willing to incorporate eastern culture(s) into their experiments with identity. The United Kingdom is always deliberately bypassed, however, which is, in itself, a contradictory gesture that merely replaces one form of cultural domination with another.

The idea of young urban women turning the tables on men is also evident in Professor Jay's 'Zali Za Mentali'. In this rap, the speaker is a cart-pusher whose first attempt at chatting up a woman ends up in a stinging rebuke from the woman: '*Wee vipi? Hebu nipishe! Wee kinyago, hebu yaishe!*' (K: What is it with you? Let me pass. You cartoon, stop it right there.) However, the man is soon relieved of his agony when a younger and more beautiful girl drives up, strikes up a conversation with him, and expresses her sympathy and 'love' for him. After a second meeting, the young woman, who reveals herself to be 'Vicky, an only child from a rich family', begs the cart-pusher to come and live with her. This soon leads to marriage, financial bliss, and a happy-ever-after ending. Very matter-of-factly, the cart-pusher does not in any way allow his manly pride to come in the way of his fortune, and effectively ends up as a 'kept man'. This is not to say that young people in the cities never pursue relationships according to the normative romantic template. Serenades are a universal phenomenon in this music, and indeed they constitute the predominant theme in the work of female rappers. However, the depiction of non-normative relationships enables us to make deductions about the nature of social change, since they can be taken as indications of the kinds of gender makeovers that are becoming possible in Nairobi.

Another pet topic among urban rappers is disappointment with the current social order. Such disillusionment arises out of rampant joblessness, the perceived corruption of the political elite and the lack of space for youth to participate in governance processes. This theme features more prominently in the politically-conscious music produced by Eastlands-based rappers, particularly those who work under the Ukoo Flani-Mau Mau grouping, which includes actors, acrobats, fine artists, poets and rappers (see wa Mungai 2008). That the work of these rappers evinces a higher political consciousness than that of their counterparts from more affluent parts of Nairobi should not surprise. The area known as Dandora, which is also home to Nairobi's main rubbish dump, is the epitome of marginality – whatever the city feels the need to eject, whether physical waste or human beings who are unwelcome in the central business district, gets discarded there. The rest of the city regards Dandora residents as criminals of an assorted nature and their material despair as the index of a depraved moral condition. Life in Dandora is thus a castaway existence, but one which rappers hope to overcome by singing about the desperate circumstances of their slum kinsfolk. It is little wonder then that the language of uprising and rebellion against *gava* (S: government), and society in general, is pre-eminent in raps that are forged literally at the very edges of life.

A call to arms is seen clearly in Mashifta's 'Majambazi' (K: Robbers), and it is illustrative that the group's name means 'bandit', the term given to Somali bandits in Kenya's often violent North Eastern Province. These bandits began as a secessionist movement in the 1970s which was swiftly crushed by Jomo Kenyatta's government. In the track, which opens to the sound of background gunshots, the speaker narrates the woes that bedevil those living on the margins of the city. They die of AIDS and poverty, and find no sense in the government's call for them to practise family planning. Young people in these slums are forced to make difficult choices, and often make wrong ones. They get involved in crime; young women become prostitutes, some abandon their new-born babies in the hope that someone will adopt them and give them better life opportunities. However, while acknowledging these genuine problems, the speaker sees them as part of a deeper social malaise. He notes that Kenya has a national culture of robbery where everyone is full of *tamaa*, (K: greed), for quick money and success. Businessmen, government ministers, lawyers, and the police, are accused of using their respective institutions to make money crookedly, and live in the fear of being found out. Even religious leaders – and religion is taken fairly seriously in a mainstream culture that prides itself on the claim that 'Kenya is a God-fearing country' – are regularly censured for hypocrisy. The choral chant 'hii system ni ya majambazi' (S: this is a robbers' system) makes it clear that slum youth also take part in this ethos of stealing. Equally telling, however, is the song's metaphor which portrays youth as 'a stillborn generation', conceived as a result of faulty condoms. The youth are seen not only as a malformed category, but the possibility of their living healthy lives within a generally diseased social body is thrown into serious doubt. 'Nairobi is populated by thieves and prostitutes shedding diamond tears in guesthouses', the speaker concludes.

If the topic of sex is preponderant in Nairobi youth music, the reason is that musicians perceive it as part of a critical currency with which the business of Kenya's politics is transacted. This idea is presented in another of Mashifta's raps, 'Pesa pombe' (K: Money and booze), in which the speaker points out that alongside these two commodities, sex complicates the nature of Kenya's governance; the elite are always immaturely chasing (and quarrelling over) money, beer and women, and this, in turn, leads to a generally corrupt political culture.

In these circumstances, some rappers see the need for a violent revolution if the social-political order is to be reformed. This is the sense that comes across in Kalamashaka's 'Fanya Mambo' (K: Do something), in which the speaker says that he is ready to commit violence using spears, guns and machetes in order to effect social change. This theme is reinforced by Girongi's 'Fear Tour', which puns on the Kiswahili word *fyatua* (fire the gun). Quite subversively, the rap is dedicated to 'everyone who knows how to use a gun but doesn't work for the government', thereby playing to the outlaw image that is popular in youth culture. The name Girongi is derived from the Gikuyu word, *njirungi* (bullets), a term used by the self-proclaimed descendants of the Mau Mau, in the phrase *matigari ma njirungi* (lit. those who survived the bullets). It seems that this phrase was fashioned after the title of Ngũgĩ wa Thiong'o's 1989 novel, *Matigari*, the central theme of which is an elusive quest for social justice and truth by the hero, Matigari. While it might very well be that the track 'Fear Tour' offers a critique of gun-related violence, Girongi's work also seems to refer to the ongoing class struggle, and the unfulfilled nationalist dream of land (resources) and freedom for which the Mau Mau waged war against British colonialism. For these youth to achieve their place in society, it seems necessary to rise violently against those in Kenyan mainstream society who stand in the path of such achievement. Similarly, the *'risasi'* (K: bullet) in the name of rap duo, Risasi na Suzuki, seems to speak to the idea of violence as a regular phenomenon, a fact of city life, as common as the Japanese cars found on Kenyan roads.

If followed to their logical conclusion, the threads of popular youth music lead to other connecting points in Nairobi's larger cultural web. Through their work, rap musicians continuously contest the dominant narratives of Kenyan identity and aspirations, not in order to delegitimize them but, more significantly, as a way of showing that variant identities can and do co-exist within the Kenyan nation.

This youth culture has become a way of claiming space within the interstices between narcissism and political engagement, between self and community, between corruption and integrity. In the end, in fact, one might argue that even though these urban youth have genuine grievances about their social marginalization, their aspirations are not radically different from those expressed by other citizens in mainstream Kenya culture. Hence the dilemma: what to do with the passions of rebellion that they arouse in their audiences? Once the truth has been uncovered, it seems to bind these individuals to a sense of self-doubt, inadequacy and despair.

Conclusion: the (im)practicability of local knowledge

The scenarios outlined in this chapter challenge one to contemplate whether it is better 'to know or not to know'. In Kenya, both positions have merits, but for the country's popular musicians, this dilemma not only haunts them daily but, paradoxically, almost always leads them implicitly to concede that other forms of knowledge (the practices of the mainstream) will always define them, their art, and the processes of its production.

There is also a degree of danger in knowing too much; hence the often-heard claim, '*Sitaki kujua. Mambo mengine Kenya ukiyajua unajiletea shida tu*' (K: I don't want to know because in Kenya knowing certain things guarantees you deep trouble). 'Trouble', which might take the form of social exclusion, arrest or even death, is the consequence of breaching borders in order to catch on to certain forbidden, exclusivist knowledge. Passing on such knowledge is a risky enterprise, as popular musicians in Kenya have come to realize. This is so for more than one reason. It can lead to police harassment, or to an awareness that, as musicians, they cannot direct their knowledge into channels that will lead to the achievement of a greater social good.

This can engender an attitude of calculated resistance to knowing, especially if the consequences of possessing and purveying such knowledge are self-deleterious. Thus the Kiswahili phrase '*sitaki kujua*' (I don't want to know), while apparently disavowing desire for knowledge, at the same time hints at the dilemma that those who hold certain kinds of knowledge find themselves in: what does one ultimately do with such knowledge?

A key argument in this chapter has been that, through their own identities and sense of nationhood, Nairobi's popular musicians have brought to the fore 'new' ways of thinking; these ways are new to the extent that they are not part of the canonical state ideology of identity, which hinges on the axis of formal education and career development. In fact, the musicians critique the canonical views, derived from foundational institutions such as churches and schools – the critical socialization platforms of the state (see Prazak 1999; Silberschmidt 2001). At another level, knowledge constructed and expressed in these spaces is new because it is local; it is produced by 'boys and girls of the hood'. In other words, these knowledge producers bring up 'facts' of their life from an emic perspective, demonstrating how the vagaries of life in the marginal spaces of the urban quagmire necessarily lead individuals to question the dominant narrative of nationhood and identity that has been propounded by the state since Kenya's independence.

Yet if Kenyan society is understood to be generally fixated upon ideas of social advancement that are exploitive, gendered and violent, then the world of Nairobi's popular urban musicians at times tends to be more so. What this means is that, embedded in this rap culture, is a knowledge which is simultaneously contradictory and multiple, a knowledge in which class, gender, and greedy, narcissistic and materialist ethics constitute the critical fault lines of Kenyan society.

What may, in fact, be the case is that the musicians' knowledge of themselves and their communities only differs from other mainstream narratives of identity, place and value in terms of generational articulation. It is the rhetorical flavour, rather than the ideological content, that delineates the knowledge purveyed in the work of these musicians. It is also apparent that the musicians themselves do not always fully understand the limitations and contradictions of their own knowledge.

References

Anderson, Benedict (1991). *Imagined Communities: Reflections on the Origin and Spread of Nationalism*, London and New York: Verso.

Githinji, Peter (2006). 'Bazes and their shibboleths: Lexical variation and Sheng speakers' identity in Nairobi', *Nordic Journal of African Studies*, 15 (4):. 443-76.

Githinji, Peter (2007). '*Mchongoano* verbal duels: Risky discourse and sociocultural commentary', in Kimani Njogu and G Oluoch-Olunya, eds, *Cultural Production and Social Change in Kenya: Building Bridges*, Nairobi: Twaweza Communications.

Githinji, Peter (2008). 'Sexism and (mis)representation of women in Sheng', *Journal of African Cultural Studies*, 20 (1): 15-32.

Githiora, Chege (2002). 'Sheng: Peer language, Swahili dialect or emerging creole?' *Journal of African Cultural Studies*, 15 (3): 159-81.

Haugerud, Angelique (1997). *The Culture of Politics in Modern Kenya*, New York: Cambridge University Press.

Macharia, Kinuthia (1992). 'Slum clearance and the informal economy in Nairobi', *Journal of Modern African Studies*, 30 (2): 221-36

Nyairo, Joyce (2007). '"Modify": Jua Kali as metaphor for Africa's Urban Ethnicities and Cultures', in James Ogude and Joyce Nyairo, eds, *Urban Legends, Popular Culture and Popular Literature in Kenya*, Trenton NJ and Asmara: Africa World Press.

Nyassy, Daniel and Githua Kihara (2008). 'Kenya risks losing an entire youth generation to drugs' *Saturday Nation*, 27 December. http://www.nation.co.ke/News/-/1056/507536/-/u0p955/-/index.html. Accessed online 29 December 2008.

Nzunga, Michael P. K. (2002). 'Sheng and Engsh: The booming offspring of linguistic intermarriage' in Ingrid Rissom, ed., *Languages and Communication in East Africa*, Bayreuth African Studies 51, Bayreuth: Bayreuth University.

Ogechi, Nathan Oyori (2007). 'Building bridges through trichotomous youth identities in Kenya: Evidence from code-choice', in Kimani Njogu, ed., *Cultural Production and Social Change in Kenya: Building Bridges*, Nairobi: Twaweza Communications

Orengo, Peter (2009). 'Our steady decline into substance abuse', *Standard Digital*, 15 January. http://www.standardmedia.co.ke/?articleID=1144004099&story_title=Our-steady-decline-into-substance-abuse Accessed online 15 January 2009.

Prazak, Miroslava (1999). '"We're on the run": Ideas of progress among adolescents in rural Kenya', *Journal of African Cultural Studies*, 12 (1):. 93-110.

Samper, David Arthur (2002). Talking Sheng: The Role of a Hybrid Language in the Construction of Identity and Youth Culture in Nairobi, Kenya. PhD thesis, University of Pennsylvania.

Silberschmidt, Margrethe (2001). 'Disempowerment of men in rural and urban East Africa: Implications for male identity and sexual behavior', *World Development*, 29 (4): 657-71.

wa Mungai, Mbugua (2008). 'Made in Riverwood: (Dis)locating identities and power through Kenyan pop music' *Journal of African Cultural Studies*, 20 (1):. 57-70.

Willis, Justin (1996). *Potent Brews: A Social History of Alcohol in East Africa, 1850–1999*, Athens,OH and Oxford: Ohio University Press and James Currey Publishers.

Discography[12]

Baba Ontonglo [Osumba Raten'g] (1984) 'Budget iko High' *Budget Iko High*. Nairobi: Music Copyright Society of Kenya/The Orchard.

Circute and Joel (uploaded May 2007) 'Juala', http://www.youtube.com/watch?v=ziF-HAATRGU. Accessed online 27 April 2013.

Deux Vultures (uploaded August 2012) 'Mona Lisa', http://www.youtube.com/watch?v=NKf2dEQLyHs. Accessed online 27 April 2013.

DNG (n.d.). 'Iyoo', http://www.myspace.com/kenyadng. Accessed online 27 April 2013

Gait, Jimmy (uploaded Feb 2009) 'Muhadhara', http://www.youtube.com/watch?v=1lDXRDxL5-g. Accessed online 27 April 2013.

Girongi (uploaded Feb 2007) 'Fear Tour', http://www.youtube.com/watch?v=L27j1jlPxrg. Accessed online 27 April 2013.

Hardstone (1999). 'Uhiki' (Pinye's remix), *Nuting but de Stone*. Nairobi: Sync Sound Studios and Kelele Records.

Jimw@t (uploaded April 2012) 'Under 18', *http://www.youtube.com/watch?v=emMYCDIKNrE*. Accessed online 27 April 2013.

Jose Chameleon (uploaded December 2007). 'Tingisha', http://www.youtube.com/watch?v=iHHw7MnhA6E. Accessed online 27 April 2013.

Jua Kali and Pilipili (uploaded August 2011). 'Kamata Dame', http://www.youtube.com/watch?v=NZTvCV1tUxk. Accessed online 27 April 2013.

Ken Razy (uploaded Feb 2008). 'Ti Chi', http://www.youtube.com/watch?v=NFi--HWNUks. Accessed online 27 April 2013.

Kleptomaniax (uploaded September 2006). 'Swing Swing',http://www.youtube.com/watch?v=1TqQM4BD4ww. Accessed online 27 April 2013.

Kalamashaka (2001). 'Fanya Mambo' *Ni Wakati*. Nairobi: Own release.

Longombas (2006). 'Vuta Pumz', http://www.youtube.com/watch?v=U5TPhlwujE4. Accessed online 27 April 2013.

Longombas (2006). 'Shika More', http://www.youtube.com/watch?v=vQJBGlr3hy0. Accessed online 27 April 2013.

---

[12]   Much of the music discussed in this chapter is informally distributed, and in some instances full publication details have been difficult to trace. If copyright holders come forward, appropriate arrangements will be made.

Mashifta (uploaded Jan 2009). 'Majambazi', http://www.youtube.com/watch?v=kHcVgdC0irA. Accessed online 27 April 2013.

Mashifta (uploaded April 2011). 'Pesa Pombe', http://www.youtube.com/watch?v=j7DjNpSyOLk. Accessed online 27 April 2013.

Mr Googz and Vinnie Banton (2002). 'Githurai'. Nairobi: Ogopa Deejays.

Nonini (uploaded March 2007). 'We Kamu', https://www.youtube.com/watch?v=Ne2DXjIzOxk. Accessed online 27 April 2013.

Nonini (2004). 'Keroro' *Hanyaring Game.* Nairobi: Homeboyz.

Nonini and Nameless (2008). 'Furahiday' *Mwisho Ya Mawazo.* Nairobi: Pro Habo.

Professor Jay (2001). 'Nikusaidiaje?' *Machozi Jasho na Damu.* Dar es Salaam: Own release.

Professor Jay (n.d.). 'Zali Za Mentali' Dar es Salaam: Own release.

Q Chillah (uploaded Aug 2008). 'Cheza', www.youtube.com/watch?v=mLf-sxlvz5k. Accessed online 27 April 2013.

Redsan (2002). 'Apakatwe' on *Seasons of the San.* Nairobi: Ogopa Deejays.

Risasi (2006). 'Watu Wote', *Mummy.* Nairobi: Sasita Entertainment.

Risasi na Suzuki (n.d.). 'Miss Digida' *Mziki Yangu.* Mombasa: Tabasam records.

Softonia (n.d.). 'Chocolate'. Own release (copy in possession of the author).

The Bugz (uploaded Feb 2008). 'Kamoja Tu', http://www.youtube.com/watch?v=fviro9-RDko. Accessed online 27 April 2013.

Ukoo Flani (2007). 'Dandora L.O.V.E', *Subira.* Nairobi: Ukoo Flani-Mau Mau.

Wahome, Esther (2009). 'Kuna Dawa' *Yahweh.* Nairobi: MMC Productions.

Part II

POLICY & PRACTICE
– APPLYING THE KNOWLEDGE

7 Science, Fishers' Knowledge & Namibia's Fishing Industry

Barbara Paterson, Marieke Norton
Astrid Jarre & Lesley Green

In the [first] decade, management of the hake resource has been confounded by uncertainties surrounding the size of the resource. There were two conflicting estimates of abundance, depending on whether the survey or the commercial [data] was used, complicating the recommendation of a [total allowable catch]. The survey index indicates ... that the population is currently overexploited. In contrast, the estimate obtained from a surplus-production model, based on commercial catch and effort data, indicates that abundance is currently close to pristine levels. (Van der Westhuizen: 313)

And now I feel the fish have really now evolved into these learned [creatures]. They got doctorates. They're really clever now. Now you gotta wake up. And the fish that pops it's head up ... you must jump on it and take your cut ... Either [the fish] has gone, or it got clever. (Bob, Namibian hake longline skipper (3 July 2009))[1]

The world's oceans are overfished (Pauly et al. 2007). One of the responses to this from the fishing industry has been to try to fish more 'scientifically'. However, as indicated in the first of the above quotes, the science of fisheries management is not without uncertainties, conflicts and contestations. The failure of conventional science to provide the basis for managing the world's fisheries in a sustainable manner has sparked a countermovement towards an ecosystem approach to fisheries management (FAO). This approach aims at holistic management; it considers fisheries as components of complex social and ecological systems requiring a balancing of diverse and often conflicting goals (Paterson et al. 2007).

In this chapter we explore the meanings that scientists and fishermen share with regard to fish stocks. We show that while there are differences in approach, both groups share the same concerns, and ultimately their perspectives may well be complementary and contribute to preserving the threatened fisheries.

This chapter has been written by an interdisciplinary team of researchers based in South Africa and Namibia. All share an interest

---

[1] Interviews with Namibian longline and trawl fishers took place in Walvis Bay Namibia in 2009 and 2010. Names were changed to maintain their anonymity.

in fishing and fish stocks. Paterson is a German-trained modeller of knowledge-based systems who lives in Namibia and who conducted all the interviews. Jarre is a marine-systems ecologist who worked in Denmark before moving to Cape Town. Green and Norton are both anthropologists and are based in Cape Town.

The trawler and longline hake fishers in the northern Benguela have a perspective on sustainable fishing that is often ignored or neglected. Their knowledge is often treated either as anecdotal or as simply filling a gap that more 'scientific' measures or approaches offer. Within the science community, however, there is increasing sensitivity towards alternative ways of knowing about fish (Ommer et al. 2011), such that it is not always easy to distinguish between 'a scientist' and other kinds of fish researchers.

In this chapter we provide narratives of Namibian trawlers and long-line captains, which illustrate how they make sense of catching hake. The narratives were collected via interviews conducted between 2009 and 2010 following the methodology for local-knowledge interviews described by Neis, Schneider et al. (1999). Namibia's hake longline and trawl fleet is comprised of corporately owned vessels. When the interviews were conducted, 63 demersal trawl vessels and 13 longline vessels were licensed to operate in Namibian waters, but it is not known how many were active. Following the recommendations of Davis and Wagner, snowball sampling was used to identify eight trawler and six longline captains who were reputed to be highly experienced. To honor our obligation to consider the risks and benefits that may derive from participation in research (Carruthers and Neis 2011) we provided sufficient information to allow participants to give free and informed consent.

We show how the captains determine where the fish are, how many and which species to catch, as well as how best to do so in a context where: i) the resource is threatened; ii) quotas are set by the government for their highly capitalized employers; iii) they have to ensure their own livelihoods, and those of their families.

Scientists who provide advice for managing fishing, and the fishers who actually catch the fish, have shared interests but their respective understandings of fisheries provide insights at different temporal and spatial scales, and at different levels of detail. On the one hand, fisheries management has traditionally focused on determining the maximum amount of fish that may be harvested. This calculation is invariably based on a set of assumptions that are often inexplicit, and generally ignore the possibility of different modes of calculation, as well as different understandings of the nature of the resource. Moreover its very rationale is to catch as many fish as possible within what the resource will allow. Fishers, on the other hand, aim to create value from fishing, which involves deriving economic benefits from their catches, as well as maintaining their particular way of life at sea. Although profits from high catch rates are not unimportant to fishers, the daily processes of fishing and being at sea involve complex interactions between fishers and the marine environment, and give rise to more complicated considerations than simply aiming to catch as many fish as possible on any given day.

Neither governments nor the fishing industry can guarantee the recovery and future sustainability of depleted fish stocks by relying simply on contemporary scientific understandings of fish and fishing, as if these are somehow value-free. Any decisions made about fishing in Namibia would benefit from including fishers' knowledge, and from a conversation between scientists and fishers that develops a holistic and shared eco-knowledge.

Counting fish: catch targets and bio-economic models

The focus on profit making with little regard for the preservation of fish stocks emerged in Europe in the late nineteenth century, with the development of industrialized trawling. At the time, eminent biologists such as Thomas Henry Huxley believed that the natural abundance of fish populations could never be overfished. Nevertheless, concern was soon expressed about the decline of cod catches. As early as 1902, this concern led to the establishment of the International Council for the Exploration of the Seas – an intergovernmental European body tasked with co-ordinating research, and later with providing management advice.

Fluctuations and failures in the fishing industry spurred the desire to control the variability of catches, whether these were considered natural or induced by the impact of fishing (Smith 1994; Bavington 2009). This wish to understand and minimize fluctuations in catch rates in order better to guide capital investment and trade, led to the widespread acceptance of mathematical modelling to predict the reproductive behaviour of fish populations. This early and close link between classical fisheries science and economics is reflected in the terminology of the field, which reflects the seamless transition through which biological organisms become objects of accountancy, and were then seen as 'stocks', 'assets' and 'resources'. In their paper titled 'The Actor Enacted: The Cumbrian Sheep in 2001', John Law and Annemarie

Mol present an argument that led them to consider Cumbrian sheep as 'a sheep multiple' (2008: 65). They emphasize, however, that this multiplicity is not a plurality, but rather a convergence of complex and intricate relations between the variant versions thereof. Similarly, it can be argued that reducing fish to value-bearing economic units reduces the 'fish multiple' by emphasizing certain relations and ignoring others.

For nearly a century, fisheries science regarded fish as discrete, unrelated populations, and assumed that the productivity of such fish populations was largely independent of their physical and chemical environment as well as of the social-ecological changes in the fishery. In this paradigm, mainstream fisheries science assumed that the recruitment of young fish into the fishable population could be predicted based on the size of the adult population. It also assumed that the size of the adult fish population could be manipulated by fishing pressure (see, for example, Finlayson 1994). Consequently, fisheries management, guided by scientific advice, has focused on regulating fishing pressure by controlling the number of boats, the sizes of fishing nets and the total amount of fish that may be caught annually (Lalli and Parsons 1993).

In the case of Namibian hake, for instance, the total allowable catch is determined by means of a population model that includes data related to 'catch per unit effort' (that is, the amount of fish caught as a function of hours fished or days spent at sea), as well as abundance indices derived from research surveys. Although information extracted by scientists from fishers' logbooks and catch-data offers a potentially rich source of information, fisheries management tend to be reactive rather than pro-active. That is, as Neis and Kean (2003) have shown, scientists and managers tend to assume that fishing practices remain constant and thus formulate their ideas and policies using outdated information.

The collapse of many of the world's most important fish populations such as Atlantic cod, Californian sardines and Peruvian anchovies indicates that the scientific approach has not been successful (Daw and Gray 2005; Degnbol 2003; Finlayson 1994). Consequently fisheries science is divided on questions regarding forms of modelling and the effectiveness of management interventions (Bavington 2009). In Namibia, quantitative stock assessment, and associated concepts and processes, are increasingly contested as it becomes clear that the notion of discrete fish populations as a unit of management has limitations (Roux and Shannon 2004).

The use of catch per unit effort as an index of abundance is also considered problematic by many scientists (see, for example, Maunder et al. 2006) because it assumes that effort is constant. In fact, effort is influenced by gear changes and corresponding changes in fishing efficiency. Data obtained from research surveys can also be problematic because such surveys tend to be conducted with specific equipment, and confined to certain times and areas. Furthermore, fish mortality is difficult to quantify accurately because landings and catches are not the same: harvesters discard fish at sea, both intentionally (if a catch is unwanted) and unintentionally (when fishing nets tear, for example). In addition, the two species of hake that live in Namibian waters – the shallow-water hake and the deep-water hake, with their specific life-history strategies and population dynamics, are currently assessed together because industry catches allegedly cannot be separated into species. Yet, as Roux and Shannon demonstrate, research findings using the concept of single stocks in the Namibian context cannot adequately account for the environmental effects on the two fish populations, the variability of natural mortality, the many interactions of organisms in the ocean, or the effects of fishing on the food web.

The consideration of wider ecosystem structures and functions is a major challenge for fisheries research and management in the Benguela in the 21st century (Degnbol and Jarre 2004; Roux and Shannon 2004). Calls for more integrated management in accordance with the ecosystem approach to fisheries have generally gained ascendancy over the last two decades. Many scientists are now emphasizing the need for better knowledge about the structures and functioning of marine social-ecological systems under variability and change, and aiming to integrate both qualitative and quantitative information into management advice (see, for example, Ommer et al. 2011).

Scientific knowledge is the product of social as well as ecological factors (Finlayson 1994; Latour 1999; Neis, Felt et al. 1999). Fisheries science seems to be shifting away from an accountancy approach and towards a more qualitative ecosystem approach in acknowledgment of the complex social-ecological interactions that shape fisheries systems. One important aspect of this shift is the recognition that closer attention to, and increased understanding of, the ways in which fishers make sense of fishing, as well as of their experience and knowledge, may contribute to improving the status and quality of fisheries.

Navigating social-ecological seascapes

Hake-trawler and longline skippers in Namibia are usually employed by fishing companies who own the boats and fishing gear (Draper 2001; Paterson 2010). Hake trawlers in Namibia use sophisticated fishing gear and navigation equipment, and can carry up to a hundred metric tons of fish. As noted earlier, skippers have three primary considerations – the fish, their employers' interests, and their own livelihoods, including those of their crew. These considerations create a context of often-competing goals.

In 1990, newly independent Namibia inherited over-exploited fish populations, including various kinds of hake. Subsequent management of the fishing industry was geared towards rebuilding its capacities along more inclusive lines, and ensuring that fish populations were large enough to ensure the industry's longevity. The need to rebuild fish stocks is a tricky target, as the interests of capital require generous total allowable catch quotas in order to grow and maintain company income from year to year. The Namibian government faces a dual and contradictory imperative. On the one hand, the state has to ensure the longevity of the industry through healthy fish stocks. On the other hand, it has to protect the interests of capital because it is both a gainful employer of their citizens and a source of tax revenue.

The skippers earn a substantial income from fishing, and obviously want to maintain the lifestyles to which they have become accustomed. While their basic salaries are fixed, they earn 'fish money' based on landings, as well as on the seasonal and market-based calculations of their employers. Depending on the nature of the target market at any given time, companies will ask for either quantity or quality – that is, many small fish to sell to a depressed market, or larger, better-looking fish to sell to markets where consumers are spending more. Fishers change their practices according to what their companies demand, the fish they are able to find (often not the same thing), and what they think the fish populations can sustain in order to make sure that they can fish again the next day. In other words, skippers hardly ever have one simple overriding interest when deciding when, where or what to fish. By the time they are on their boats, their context has already shaped the range of possibilities open to them.

The status of the resource, the economic interests of the government and the fishing companies, as well as the living standards of the skippers and their crews, all come together in the notion of 'the quota'. Fishing permits or 'rights' are held not by the skippers but by fishing companies, and the permits are linked to quotas allocated by the government. Each quota represents a share of the total allowable catch. Quotas are set at the end of April each year, when the fishing companies are informed of their allocated quota. Prior to this, the fishing companies do not know if they will receive a quota, what size it will be, or on what grounds it will be calculated. The size of the quota allocated to each company determines the pace and intensity of subsequent fishing activities. Some companies aim to catch as much fish as possible in the hope of securing an additional quota either from the government or from other companies; others spread their quotas out to ensure that they have at least some work throughout the season. If there is no quota, vessels will not be sent to sea, and the skippers and their crews will earn no commission. Thus the quota frames the politics of fishing.

Narratives from fishing captains

The skippers whose views are presented here have between 12 and 40 years of fishing experience. The trawlers catch fish by dragging a net over the seabed behind their vessels, whereas longliners use a 20-mile-long fishing line from which they suspend hooks. The line is set close to the ground and held in position by anchors, weights and floats. In both cases, fishing trips take about a week depending on the catch. The need to maintain the quality of a catch, as well as the quantity of fuel and provisions they can carry, limits the length of the trips to a maximum of ten days.

The notion of a quality catch is important in determining how the fishers proceed, and this notion of quality is itself contingent on market conditions and how the company has strategized to meet market demands. A prime-quality longline hake is put on ice, and then flown to Spain to be sold whole and, importantly, looking as if it has just been pulled from the water. Trawled fish is headed and gutted on board, and then processed on shore into frozen fillets, loins and other portions that are sold in supermarkets in Europe, USA and South Africa. A company's strategy is usually a negotiation of market conditions and their fleet's cost effectiveness. The fishers' strategy, in turn, is a negotiation of the company's demands and conditions at sea. As Allan, captain of a longline vessel, explains (9 July 2009):

> You'll end up with say 35 tons of fish for a very good trip. And you can do that in three days if it is possible, but you work your people to death ... If you catch fish in a five-day period, your quality is excellent, very good, because you can space it out nicely. If you catch like eight tons every day, then your people get tired and you start to lose quality, because the guys work too fast. They leave the fish too long in the bin, and then they handle it too roughly, and scales come off and your fish doesn't look too good.

To maintain catch rates the skippers need to ensure that their boats follow the fish. As a trawler moves away from a shoal there will be fewer live fish in the net, so the skippers turn around to get back to the fish. Once a longline has been set, however, the skipper is committed to remaining in place for a 24-hour period. So, before resetting the line, the skipper tries to make sure that the fish are still in the area (Paterson 2010). Indications from the current catch are examined. If the fish are already dead when hauled in, it is likely that the shoal passed by much earlier, and the chances of catching more fish in the same spot are small. If the fish are still alive, there is a good chance that they might still be active in the same area, and might bite again if the line is reset. In addition, if the hooks are deep in the throats of the fish, it means the fish were hungry, and keen to bite.

The fishers' movements at sea are thus informed by the state of the fish, and their interpretation of the catch. Fish and fishers are intertwined through their mutual interaction with the equipment, and the production of fishing knowledge is an ongoing process that relies on the technology of fishing and fish behaviour, as much as it does on the experience of the fisher. Following Law and Mol's line of thought, and looking at the fish as actors, the perspective of the fisher illuminates other aspects of the 'fish multiple'.

A successful fishing trip is one where the catch is good and the costs are low. A skipper wants to spend as little time as possible searching for fish. Although Namibian hake longline and trawler fishers have sophisticated fish-finding equipment available, this technology allows them to 'see' only the fish that are below the vessel or going into the net. Thus, knowing *where* to fish is not only a question of technology, but also about personal experience and an ability to network with other fishers. Some fishers discuss which areas are yielding good catches, and many will choose fishing areas based on the catch rates and the quality of the fish being caught in that area by other fishers. Not all skippers follow what others are doing, however. Some have strong personal preferences for particular areas, as longliner Bob explains (3 July 2009):

> Every skipper's got his 'farm'. People say that area belongs to me, to Bob, that's Bob's grounds, leave him alone. If trawlers're here and I'm here, they say, 'Ok sorry, we give you way.' Because they know I go there. That's my place, ja, that's my area. That's where I like [to work]. Coz the fish is nice, generally the fish is nice.

Similarly, Michael skippers a 55-metre trawler, and mostly fishes in the waters off Walvis Bay, at a depth of around 800 metres. He notes:

> You can go check on the records of our vessel, we only stay in the deep water there ... and there is not a lot of vessels. Maybe one or two you get, but not every trip also ... all my trips is in the deep. I think I am now the only one here at the company that's [fishing in the deep]. (23 July 2009)

Their preferences for particular areas reflect these skippers' attitudes to the sea. Both know where to find the fish that they are looking for. But, besides these target-oriented considerations, their preferences are infused with a sense of proprietorship. Bob calls his fishing area 'his farm'; Michael talks about exploring areas where nobody has trawled. Although he is aware of the risks he takes by fishing in uncharted waters, he is reluctant to give away his hard-earned tracks to another fisherman. He prefers to do his own thing rather than fish in the company of other trawlers. Fishing in 'the deep' is infused with a sense of adventure and the added danger of strong swells.

Finding 'a piece of fish' in the vastness of the seascape is a challenge that requires an understanding of what the fish are likely to do, and this is informed by the long-term relationship that fishers have with the sea. Knowledge of the impact of the weather, the seasons, and the phases of the moon on fish is important. Catches are usually smaller during strong winds and high swells. At full moon, fishers expect to find shallow-water hake in shallower water, and at new moon they head for deeper waters. Bob notes that he expects the fish to move to deeper water during strong winds, while longline skipper Allan says: 'Fish tend to always go into the wind. I don't know why 'coz they're on the bottom but they know when the wind starts to blow. Especially two days before the wind, then the fish normally bite, and then they normally move up against the wind' (9 July 2009).

This tacit knowledge of the marine environment, as well as the interactions that guide the fishers' movements and actions at sea, is augmented by explicit documentation. In their logbooks, fishers record the time, date, and position, as well as information such as the weather conditions, the swell, water temperature, etc. The quality of the catch is also noted, including the species, the quantity, and the size of the fish caught. When other sources of information fail, skippers consult their own logbooks to see where they have found fish under similar conditions in the past. The information in these logbooks is the only form of fishers' knowledge that is currently shared with the Ministry of Fisheries, and used for fisheries management.

Greater than the sum of its parts: an ecosystem approach

Fishing is not simply about catching as much fish as possible. As has been shown, fishers navigate a highly complex, politicized context in order to balance different interests and objectives. The future of fisheries management depends on a greater degree of collaboration between scientists and fishers than currently practised. Focusing on the differences helps to reveal important issues that require resolution, but it can also deflect attention from what these two groups have in common. A focus on the ways in which scientists and fishers can complement one another reveals the potential for new forms of knowledge creation within fisheries management.

Traditional stock assessment science related to the productivity of fish tends to be removed from the larger marine environment, and remains isolated from the socio-political and economic context of fishing. A reductionist focus on the mathematics and statistics of stock assessment distances classical fisheries science from the phenomenological and experiential relationship that fishers have with the ocean. Fishers' knowledge tends to be regarded as unimportant in this knowledge economy as they are perceived to be closer to labour than to capital. Managers in the fishing industry, on the other hand, see themselves as subject to shareholders and profit making, and, as noted, earning short-term profit can be in tension with the sustainability of the industry because decisions are based on bio-economical, statistical ways of estimating fish population sizes, and these have been proven to be unreliable. The focus on mathematical modelling ignores questions of ontology, as well as how the various parties or actors relate to fishing resources on a personal and professional level. This means that the intentions behind research and policy decisions tend to be taken for granted, and while this approach remains unexamined, it can be considered a 'natural' way to proceed.

This reliance on quantitative information and statistical testing of hypotheses is data-intensive and requires costly and extensive at-sea surveys. Research costs, however, speak to a fundamental commonality between stock assessment science and the economics of fishing, namely the central importance of the commodity value of the resource. After all, only economically valuable fisheries can afford to be subjected to sophisticated stock assessment. The aim of the state to maximize the long-term profitability and sustainability of the high value natural resource through sophisticated assessment is mirrored in the economic strategies of individual companies, which also want to ensure long-term profitability. So called 'quota management' is a concept that some Namibian trawling companies apply to ensure that their quota will last throughout the year. Instead of catching as much as they can, they lower the frequency of fishing trips and try to keep the factory supplied with fish, and their employees with work, throughout the year. A company's lack of quota has implications for the fishers, who also prefer long-term maintenance of livelihoods and living standards above short-term financial gain. Bob explains:

> 'I saw [a guy] yesterday on the beach, and he said to me – 'What's going on, are you working again.' And I said, 'No, I'm waiting for quota'; and I thought the last time I saw you I was waiting for quota – this is my flipping life – this is no good, this is no flipping good. And it's making me sick. You see, I'm a person that before it's happened I start to worry. Before I come to my lowest financial situation possible I already start making myself sick. I know, I'm good for two months still, but I'm already sick because I'm already thinking about the end of two months' time and I'm already sick. [...] I'm very, very unsure – and also, I'm proud – I won't be able to go to the bank and say to the bank: 'listen, you know, this month [I am earning less].' No ways.' (23 June 2006)

Thus it can be argued that both fisheries science and fishers have a vested interest in the sustainability of the industry and in the continued health of the fish population that will ensure ongoing work. A more inclusive attitude, such as that reflected in the ecosystem approach to fisheries management mentioned earlier, goes beyond the central focus on the instrumental value of the commodity, emphasizing instead the intrinsic value of the species within the wider ecosystem, and the social processes that both rely on and affect it.

The extensive at-sea surveys required for stock assessment can only be carried out a few times per year. This contrasts starkly with the day-to-day engagements of the fishers, many of whom spend more time at sea than on land, and who experience an interconnected, interactive relationship between themselves and the fish, mediated through their fishing vessel and fishing equipment (Draper 2001; Paterson 2010). The GPS and sonar technologies used by scientists are not dramatically different from the technologies that fishers use. The technologies that are used for fish-finding and navigation by fishers and scientists at sea were originally developed for military purposes. In scientific surveys these technologies are combined with sampling techniques that aim to provide a comprehensive picture of a fishing area, including the distribution of fish. Scientific surveys offer an 'external' view that claims to measure resources objectively. The fishers, through their daily engagement, have a perspective of the sea space that is at the same time more localized and more detailed. This does not imply that the knowledge that fishers gain through their work is categorically different from scientific knowledge. Fishers and scientists both employ cartographic techniques, and use the same three-dimensional model of sea space determined by longitude, latitude and water depth. The use of this spatial grid and GPS technology reinforces the re-creation of space as an exploitable resource which plays a part in the functioning of capitalist economies (McHaffie 1995; Paterson 2007). Whereas the bio-economic or scientific approach claims to be objective, the fishers' insights are context specific and rich in detail. As Michael put it: 'Unless you have trawled there you don't know that area' (23 February 2009).

It can be argued that this difference in scale, while seeming to reflect a mismatch between the two forms of knowledge, offers an important opportunity for integration. Combining a large-scale overview with detailed local knowledge has the potential to provide a more complete understanding of the ecology of fishing (Neis et al. 1999). Finlayson's analysis of the collapse of Canadian cod shows how social and cultural factors influenced the production and interpretation of scientific knowledge and its application for fisheries management. On this basis, it can be argued that there are no grounds for positioning fishers with their lived experience and scientists with their statistics of stock assessment on opposite sides of the table. Both forms of knowledge are necessary, and are produced in response to social and ecological contexts.

The shift to the ecosystem approach to fisheries management demands a fisheries science that is both holistic and contextual, and the central tenet of this is a consideration of fish and fishers as part of an interconnected social-ecological system. This approach has the potential to provide a qualitative understanding of ecosystem roles and functions, as it looks at fish and fishers within the complexity of an ecosystem that includes the entire food web, as well as various energy flows and exchanges. Although, in its ideal formulation, the ecosystem approach to fisheries management seems to have more in common with fishers' daily experience at sea than the purely statistical focus of traditional fisheries science, it would be counter-productive to view either quantitative fisheries science or fishers' knowledge as coherent or 'monolithic'. This would ignore the inherent complexity of both perspectives, and prevent discussion based on common ground and partial connections, where potentially interesting new collaborations could be generated (Duggan et al. forthcoming).

Many of those involved in catching and researching fish acknowledge the value of expertise held by others. Scientists collect data from fishers (usually from their logbooks), and Namibian hake skippers acknowledge the expertise of the scientists. Examples of successful collaborations include identification of local sub-populations (Wroblewski 2000) and research around catch rates in joint demersal-fish surveys (Wieland et al. 2009; 2011).

Conclusion

Namibia's hake-trawler and longline fishing captains have a deep knowledge of the fish they hunt. They develop this knowledge amid a cluster of economic, ecological and social interests that include their own personal needs, as well as those of the companies they work for. The knowledge that fishers produce in the course of their work at sea, and how they apply it, is not categorically different from the knowledge that scientists produce and apply in fisheries management. That is, the processes by which fishers and scientists gather data are mediated by the same kinds of technologies, and both fishers and scientists create meaning from this data from the perspectives current within their own cultural, political and economic contexts. Uncertainties in cultural and political contexts can influence scientists to interpret the same set of data differently at different times (see Finlayson 1994, for example). In the case of industrial fisheries, such as Namibia's hake fisheries, both fishers and scientists are entangled in industry networks. Fishers operate multi-million dollar fishing vessels on behalf of large companies, which, in turn, generate a large proportion of the country's GDP and employ thousands of people. These factors are pertinent to the interests of the Namibian government, whose mandate it is to manage the country's resources to the benefit of the Namibian public. Fishers, fishing companies and government scientists have vested interests in maintaining fish stocks so that they yield maximum, yet sustainable, catches. However, neither fishers nor the scientists, on their own, have the means to accurately assess the status of fish stocks. As is the case with information and communication technologies (see Rivett et al. in this volume), contemporary technologies are often unable to answer certain questions or provide solutions to specific problems. Users of the technology have other critical insights, and are potentially able to contribute to making useful, context-specific knowledge. For fishers, knowledge of the fish as actors is crucial for fishing success. This knowledge reflects an important part of the fish 'multiple', and should be considered as important to fisheries management as the numerical data that informs the assessments of fish stocks.

Considering the uncertainties around stock assessment, as well as the documented need for more holistic fisheries management approaches and broader knowledge bases, it seems clear that fisheries management in Namibia, as elsewhere, would benefit significantly from creating platforms for dialogue between fishers and scientists.

References

Bavington, D. L. Y. (2009). 'Managing to endanger: Creating manageable cod fisheries in Newfoundland & Labrador, Canada', *Maritime Studies*, 7 (2): 99-121.

Carruthers, E. H. and B. Neis (2011). 'Bycatch mitigation in context: Using qualitative interview data to improve assessment and mitigation in a data-rich fishery', *Biological Conservation*, 144: 2289-2299.

Davis, A. and J. R. Wagner (2003). 'Who knows? On the importance of identifying "experts" when researching local ecological knowledge', *Human Ecology*, 31 (3): 463-489.

Daw, T. and T. Gray (2005). 'Fisheries science and sustainability in international policy: A study of failure in the European Union's Common Fisheries Policy', *Marine Policy*, 29: 189-197.

Degnbol, P. (2003). 'Science and the user perspective: The gap co-management must address', in D. C. Wilson, J. R. Nielsen and P. Degnbol, eds, *The Fisheries Co-management Experience: Accomplishments, Challenges and Prospects*. Dordrecht: Kluwer.

Degnbol, P. and A. Jarre (2004). 'Review of indicators in fisheries management: A development perspective', *African Journal of Marine Science*, 26 (1): 303-326.

Draper, K. (2011). Technologies, Knowledges, and Capital: Towards a Political Ecology of the Hake Trawl Fishery Walvis Bay, Namibia. Master's dissertation, University of Cape Town, South Africa.

Duggan, G. L., Rogerson, J. J. M., Green, L. J. F., and Jarre, A. (forthcoming). 'Opening dialogue and fostering collaboration: Thinking through different ways of knowing for fisheries research and management', *South African Journal of Science*, Vol and pp nos to come.

FAO (Food and Agriculture Organization) (2003). *Technical Guidelines for Responsible Fisheries 4: Fisheries Management 2, The Ecosystem Approach to Fisheries*. Rome.

Finlayson, A. C. (1994). *Fishing for Truth: A Sociological Analysis of Northern Cod Stock Assessments from 1977-1990*. St. Johns NL: ISER Books.

Huxley, T. H. (1883). Inaugural Address to the Fisheries Exhibition. London, UK. http://aleph0.clarku.edu/huxley/SM5/fish.html. Accessed online 3 August 2008.

Lalli C. and T. Parsons (1993). *Biological Oceanography: An Introduction*. Oxford: Pergamon Press.

Latour, B. (1999). 'Circulating Reference' in *Pandora's Hope: Essays on the Reality of Science Studies*. Cambridge MA: Harvard University Press.

Law, J. and A. Mol (2008). 'The actor enacted: The Cumbrian sheep in 2001' in Carl Knappett and Lambros Malafouris, eds, *Material Agency*, New York: Springer.

Maunder, M. N., J. R. Sibert, A. Fonteneau, J. Hampton, P. Kleiber, and S. J. Harley (2006). 'Interpreting catch per-unit-effort data to assess the status of individual stocks and communities', *ICES Journal of Marine Science*, 63:. 1373-1385.

McHaffie, P. H. (1995). 'Manufacturing metaphors. Public cartography, the market, and democracy' in J. Pickles, ed., *Ground Truth: The Social Implications of Geographic Information Systems*. New York: Guilford Press.

Neis, B. and R. Kean (2003). 'Why fish stocks collapse: An interdisciplinary approach to understanding the dynamics of "fishing up"', in R. Byron, ed., *Retrenchment and Regeneration in Rural Newfoundland*. Toronto: University of Toronto Press.

Neis, B., L. Felt, R. L. Haedrich, and D. C. Schneider (1999). 'An interdisciplinary methodology for collecting and integrating fishers' ecological knowledge into resource management', in D. Newell and R. E. Ommer, eds, *Fishing Places, Fishing People: Issues and Traditions in Canadian Small-Scale Fisheries*. Toronto: University of Toronto Press.

Neis, B., D. C. Schneider, L. Felt, R. L. Haedrich, J. Fischer and J. A. Hutchings (1999). 'Fisheries assessment: What can be learned from interviewing resource users?' *Canadian Journal of Fisheries and Aquatic Sciences*, 56 (10): 1949-1963.

Ommer, R. E, R. I. Perry, K. Cochrane and P. Cury, eds. (2011). *World Fisheries: A Social-Ecological Analysis*, Oxford: Wiley-Blackwell.

Paterson, B. (2007). 'We cannot eat data: The need for computer ethics to address the cultural and ecological impacts of computing', in S. Hongladarom and C. Ess, eds, *Information Technology Ethics: Cultural Perspectives*, Hershey PA: Idea Group Reference.

Paterson, B. (2010). Fishermen's experience and knowledge in the Namibian Hake Fishery. Unpublished Research Report. Marine Research Institute, University of Cape Town.

Paterson, B., A. Jarre, C. L. Moloney, T. P. Fairweather, C. D. van der Lingen, L. J. Shannon, and F. G. Field (2007). 'A fuzzy-logic tool for multi-criteria decision making in fisheries: The case of the South African pelagic fishery', *Marine and Freshwater Research*, 58 (11): 1056-1068.

Pauly, D., V. Christensen, S. Guénette, T. J. Pitcher, U. R. Sumaila, C. J. Walters, R. Watson, and D. Zeller (2002). 'Towards sustainability in world fisheries', *Nature*, 418:. 689-695.

Roux, J-P., and L. J. Shannon (2004). 'Ecosystem approach to fisheries management in the northern Benguela: the Namibian Experience', *African Journal of Marine Science*, 26 (1): 79-93.

Smith, T. D. (1994). *Scaling Fisheries: The Science of Measuring the Effects of Fishing, 1855–1955*, Cambridge: Cambridge University Press.

Van der Westhuizen, A. (2001) 'A decade of exploitation and management of the Namibian hake stocks', *South African Journal of Marine Science*, 23 (1): 337-346.

Wieland, K., E. M. Fenger Pedersen, H. J. Olesen, and J. E. Beyer (2009). 'Effect of bottom type on catch rates of North Sea cod (*Gadus morhua*) in surveys with commercial fishing vessels', *Fisheries Research*, 96 (2-3): 244-251.

Wieland, K., H. J. Olesen, E. M. Fenger Pedersen, and J. E. Beyer (2011). 'Potential bias in estimates of abundance and distribution of North Sea cod (*Gadus morhua*) due to strong winds prevailing prior or during a survey', *Fisheries Research*, 110 (2): 325- 330.

Wroblewski, J. (2000) 'The colour of cod: Fishers and scientists identify a local cod stock in Gilbert Bay, southern Labrador', in B. Neis and L. Felt, eds, *Finding Our Sea Legs: Linking Fishery People and Their Knowledge with Science and Management*, St. Johns NL: ISER Books.

8 ICT for Development
Extending Computing Design Concepts

Ulrike Rivett, Gary Marsden*
& Edwin Blake

Information Communication Technologies (ICTs) such as cellphones have become a part of our daily lives. The technology has rapidly been adopted throughout the world, and this is particularly true in Africa. ICTs provide opportunities for development but the expectations they tend to raise, of improved services and a general modernization, are often not realized.

The failure rate of ICT systems in the developing world is astonishingly high (Heeks 2002). Initiatives such as telecentres (centres in rural villages with computers and internet access) have been shown to fail both in the software engineering sense (they are unsustainable and need repair), and in terms of human-computer interaction (no one uses the computers as they are seen as unnecessary) (Benjamin 2001). Disciplines such as Software Engineering and Human-Computer Interaction have been successful in creating ICT systems for the developed world. In Africa, however, the picture is very different.

Together with colleagues we have developed ICTs for under-resourced and rural communities in South Africa and other developing countries; a field that has become known as Information and Communications Technology for Development (ICT4D). Our focus has been on using devices such as cellphones to develop context-appropriate and easily accessible tools that can support communities and governments in advancing their developmental goals.

In this chapter we provide some examples of our successes and failures in designing ICT4D systems. In assessing these examples, we question basic concepts used in computing such as efficiency and effectiveness, as well as scalability and efficacy. In addition, we explain why we seek to include the voices of actors other than engineers in our design processes. Echoing the findings of Thesen and Cooper in this

---

* We would like to dedicate this chapter to our friend and colleague, Gary Marsden, who died suddenly on 27 December 2013. He was instrumental in establishing the Centre of ICT4D at the University of Cape Town and championed the integration of African Knowledge in Design and Human-Computer Interaction (HCI).

volume, we show that questions of assessment invariably involve issues of power and location, and that some voices, generally of the most marginal actors in a process, can easily be overlooked.

Some systems are reported as successful when they work in a single location, even if their deployment does not move beyond a single community (Sørenson et al. 2008). However, many existing system design methodologies do not respond satisfactorily when applied to specific development contexts. A major reason for this is that the assumptions on which such systems are based do not fit all contexts, and the outcomes they generate end up being unsustainable or inappropriate. South African society, for example, is characterized by the diversity of its population groups, languages, cultures and religions. Yet, most system methodologies assume that societies are homogenous, and adopt a one-size-fits-all approach that is designed to be scaled throughout a society. In a heterogeneous context, such as South Africa, system methodologies have to respond to the diversity that exists rather than expecting society to adapt to the system by becoming more homogenous.

Our quest in this chapter is to explore what happens when we build a system, by first identifying a need, and then ensuring that the system addresses the need appropriately through a blend of methods from many disciplines. The end point (and goal) we aim to achieve is feasibility and sustainability. We probe current methods of identifying starting points that can lead to our goals of feasibility and sustainability within a local context. We then explore end points, critiquing existing measures of achievement, and suggesting new ways of understanding success in ICT projects in a social-development context. Our approach involves exploring the contexts in which ICT systems are envisaged as solutions, and how the disciplines of human-computer interaction and software engineering respond to this approach to system development. We also explore how the existing methods can be improved and made more effective through the use of methodologies such as action research. We conclude that contemporary understandings of success need to be challenged and changed, and engineers and software designers in developing contexts need to recruit users as co-designers, and work with them to agree on the problem to be solved, the means of solving it, and contribute to determining measures of success.

In a water quality project in Cambodia, Mozambique, South Africa and Vietnam, discussed in further detail below, the goal was to ensure delivery of safe drinking water to rural communities. Approximately 1.8 million people die annually from water-borne diseases, with the developing countries of Asia and southern Africa having the highest mortality rates. Ensuring the provision of safe drinking water at a national level requires not only an understanding of the chemistry and microbiology of water, but also of the workings of institutionalized water systems.

An assumption was made that drinking water quality and its testing are well understood globally, given the influence of the Millennium Development Goals and the efforts of the World Health Organization. However, we identified a gap between the real and perceived needs for water-quality monitoring, as well as the effectiveness of water testing across the different countries. While ICT engineers identified what they considered to be an essential tool in improving the water-quality testing process, this did not necessarily accord with the organizational structures in each of the countries that managed drinking water delivery. While the quality of drinking water might be globally defined, social, political and institutional relationships define how a tool is used, even in contexts in which international standards seem to be accepted and well understood.

What should be built? Modernization as a desired path?

When analysing existing ICT systems, much of the discussion is positioned within the discourse of development-as-modernization (Gurumurthy and Singh 2009; Moodley 2009). This discourse assumes that modernization is a universally desired path for economic and technological growth, and that such growth will maximize the achievements of advanced capitalism (located primarily in the industrial North) by transferring these to the periphery. While such discourse is highly contested within the terrain of development studies, it is virtually taken for granted in the ICT field. Most projects follow a top-down, 'functionalist' model (Hirschheim and Klein 1989), seeing ICTs as instrumental and essentially value-free. The ultimate goal of systems development is seen as creating efficient and effective technical systems, exemplifying what Avgerou (2002) calls the 'techno-economic rationality of western modernity'. Wilson (1997), drawing on the work of Habermas sees positivist ICT research as adding a scientific gloss to the implementation of technical systems that are presented as being politically neutral.

When investigating ICT systems that have failed, it is apparent that the initial suggestion to develop and implement a system often comes from a technocratic source, such as a research institution, a donor agency or a government department. The failure of such ICT systems is often attributed to background of the user community, and the question of the appropriateness of the ICT system as a solution is rarely tackled. Failure is analysed by assessing aspects such as staffing skills, infrastructure limitations and financial constraints, which speak to the shortcomings of the user community rather than of the system itself (Heeks 2002). An analysis of the relative power and intentions of the stakeholders suggesting a system, versus the stakeholders who are expected to use the system, rarely forms part of analysing design, development, success or failure.

The case study that follows provides an example of an ICT solution that considered the influence of various stakeholders as part of the system design. This enabled the design team to evaluate the likely relevance of the tool in relation to the various stakeholders.

The Water Quality Reporter: who are the stakeholders?

The iCOMMS (Information for Community Oriented Municipal Services) team, which forms part of the Department of Civil Engineering at the University of Cape Town, developed a cellphone application called the Water Quality Reporter between 2008 and 2011. The development of the application formed part of the Aquatest project, which was funded by the Bill and Melinda Gates Foundation. The purpose of the application was to allow water-supply managers in remote rural villages to provide information on the water quality to government officials. The cellphone application was implemented and tested in the rural areas of South Africa, Cambodia, Vietnam and Mozambique.

As part of the design process, we analysed stakeholders by developing an importance/influence matrix. The first matrix as shown in Figure 8.1 (p. 130 overleaf) focused on those stakeholders that are routinely considered when investigating the challenge of water quality monitoring in a country (Loudon and Rivett 2010). However, when reviewing the matrix, based on the engagement with the various groups, it became apparent that our own group, namely researchers, had been ignored as a high-importance, high-influence stakeholder. Equally, the funder and the overall project consortium had a high influence in the design of the system, and they too had been excluded from the matrix. A revised stakeholder matrix was then drawn up, which represented the situation in a far more appropriate way (see Figure 8.2).

The more realistic representation of the influence of the various stakeholders gave us a greater understanding of the impact of each group's power and intentions on the design of the system. The need for information flow in the water-quality sector is relatively well defined, based on the roles and responsibilities prescribed by legislation, as well as a fairly widely held understanding and

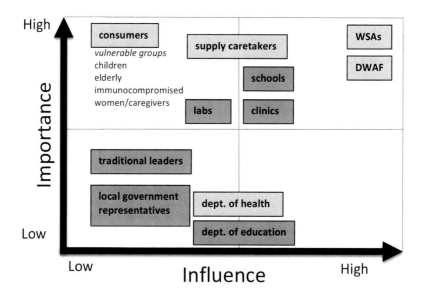

Figure 8.1 Initial assessment of stakeholders

Note: DWAF stands for the Department of Water Affairs, WSA stands for Water Service Authority

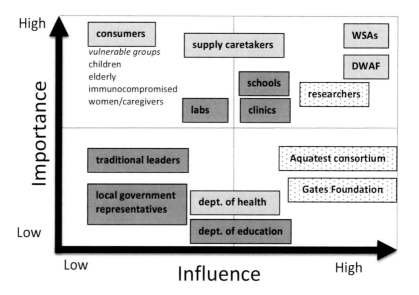

Figure 8.2 Revised assessment of stakeholders

acceptance of what constitutes best practice. Challenges may still arise in the implementation of legislation, given different local arrangements, but there is general agreement on the information flow. Among the researchers, the project consortium and the funders, roles and spheres of influences are continuously negotiated, and the ICT-systems we developed invariably reflected this. For example, we developed a technically challenging mobile-image processing system (Loudon et al. 2009) that was of great interest to the funders, the project team and ourselves, but it did not satisfy any of the particular needs expressed by other South African stakeholders such as the Water Services Authorities, the Department of Water Affairs or local communities.

Obtaining a clear analysis of stakeholders at the outset of a system design, makes it possible to understand the many influences a system has to satisfy. It also allows a more critical understanding of real and perceived needs. Whereas a system design might have to respond to certain requirements for project–political reasons, a 'Southern theory' approach (Connell 2007) allows us to assess the impact that such a design, and each of the stakeholders, has at various points in the process. At the outset, the identification of an ICT system as a solution to a particular societal need requires that we critically consider who suggested the solution, and how much influence they have on the overall design. Similarly, when a particular system has been identified as a solution, the interests of those involved in its design and development have to be investigated.

Users as co-designers

Within the disciplines of Human-Computer Interaction and Interaction Design, much has been published on how to create appropriate systems for users in the developing world. However, these approaches tend to assume that ICT users, and the tasks that ICTs are employed for, are largely universal. In terms of this model, context is seen as irrelevant. For example, the approach adopted in *International User Interfaces* (Del Gado and Nielsen 1996) took a very mechanical approach to creating systems for different cultures. Tasks were assumed to be identical, even if the language through which tasks were mediated might vary. It was thus seen as acceptable to simply translate elements of a user interface from a source language into a target language: so the 'home' key in an English interface becomes a '*maison*' key in a French interface.

The notion of interface translations have been shown to be severely lacking when applied to the diversity of needs and cultures of around 80 per cent of the planet's population that now own a cellular handset (ITU Telecom World 2011). Users often struggle to understand unfamiliar icons or the concepts they represent. For example, the work of Gitau et al. (2010) shows us that the main reason South African participants in her research could not access the internet from their cellphones was simply because the icons used were inappropriate and misleading.

In an effort to overcome the shortcomings of these superficial notions of culture, many ICT designers in the developing world started to use ethnographic design-led methods (created for well-resourced, primarily urban Northern contexts) to try to uncover the needs of ICT users in developing contexts. However, these methods have been found to be based on similarly mechanical notions of culture (Kimaro, Honest and Titlestad 2008).

It is essential, therefore, that designers develop some common ground with the end users before they engage in any design. This interaction-design approach attempts to focus broadly on: i) observing users in a naturalistic setting to ascertain their needs; and ii) designing new systems and building prototypes, preferably with input from such users.

The idea behind observing users in their own contexts is predicated on the notion that some systems are already in place in their environments. Whether or not these systems are ICT related, the assumption is that the new system is being created to improve on an existing one. In many situations in the developing world, there are few systems in place on which one can base a design: for example, the HPI Research School at the University of Cape Town in 2011 created a system allowing users to create CVs using their cellphones, and then submit the CVs to prospective employers. Prior to this system being built, users had no access to systems that would allow them to create a CV or find jobs online.[1]

In relation to designing new systems with input from end users, it is very difficult to engage users in co-design when they may have no idea of how ICTs work, or even of the basic separation between hardware and software. Co-design methods also advocate, for example, coming together to sketch ideas on paper, yet in some contexts participants refused to participate, claiming that the process was wasteful of paper (Bidwell et al. 2010). In other words, a co-design approach can also fail if the users' context is not carefully factored in. In short, existing human-computer interaction methodologies cannot show

---

[1]   See www.ummeli.com

us where to start; cultural models are too abstract and irrelevant, whilst ethnographically inspired design methods are predicated on assumptions that do not hold.

The imperative for users to be co-designers is also manifest in software engineering (that is, methods developed to produce quality computer software). What constitutes good quality changes from 'fit for purpose' to an increasing understanding in cases where clients or users find it very difficult to say exactly what the purpose of a product should be at the outset.

The first attempts at requirements analysis in the early 1980s (Liskov and Berzins 1986) attempted to elicit very detailed requirements from users by means of careful and painstaking analysis. When this proved unsatisfactory as a way of dealing with complex design problems, cyclical or iterative methodologies were adopted, whereby intermediate systems were developed and presented to users in partial fulfilment of their requirements. Based on feedback from users, systems are then refined further until the systems and the desired outcomes converge. Not only does this approach address users' inadequate understandings of how computer systems might meet their requirements, it also allows unexpected technical problems to be addressed in a flexible fashion.

These iterative methodologies are collectively known as 'agile' software engineering. Central to such methods is communication between users and engineers. For example, a method, known as 'Extreme Programming', emphasizes discovering common metaphors that allow users and engineers to understand how systems work. However, when such methods are used to build ICT4D systems, 'users' and 'developers' may not share a common basis for communication. Sometimes, the very means of communication has to be discovered by both parties. Thus the foundations for agile engineering development may not exist in developing-country contexts, where a common language and understanding still has to be created. This process is frequently assisted by an *intermediary*, a *human access point* or a *champion*, who serves as a 'translator' between users and developers. In our experience, such an agent has to be firmly based within the user community, and must be able to identify the possibilities ICTs offer without raising expectations on either side.

The case study that follows highlights the challenges that communication can pose to users and developers. The missing link of local-context information resulted in a system failing, and then being re-contextualized by the community so that the system is now useful to them, even though it does not fulfil the purposes it was designed for.

Teleconsultation in rural South Africa: who are the co-designers?

The University of Cape Town's Department of Computer Science designed a teleconsultation system (Tucker and Blake 2008) to enable nurses at a rural health clinic in South Africa's Eastern Cape province to consult doctors at the local hospital, and thus provide better health care to local people. A feature of rural areas in South Africa is that people are not concentrated in small towns or villages, but are spread out in scattered settlements throughout the countryside. Rural hospitals support satellite clinics situated in these settlements.

While designing the system, we successfully solved several technical challenges involved in building a reliable, long-range WiFi network, that allows users to make calls via the internet. We built a mixed synchronous (real-time) and asynchronous (store-and-forward) communication system. Solar-power and battery backups overcame the problem of frequent power outages. We installed relay stations in secure places (such as the headman's house in the settlement where the clinic was located). The asynchronous feature helped over-burdened doctors and nurses who could rarely talk in real-time. We iteratively improved the user interface from a basic design on a laptop to an eventual system that worked via mobile phones.

From an agile design point of view, the system was effective and reliable. The network remained live without interruption for many months at a time. The system was usable and designed to fit into the work patterns and availability of the users. Nevertheless, the system was never used on an ongoing basis. As a teleconsultation system it cannot count as a success.

It has since become clear that there were a few issues that we did not anticipate. For example, despite stating that they used the system, logs revealed that the nurses seldom did. One possible explanation for this is that, in local culture, one does not criticize, and it is seen as important to remain agreeable and connected with the researchers. Eventually, we also discovered that the nurses believed that the system allowed doctors to check on their attendance at the clinic, so they distrusted it, seeing it as a source of managerial surveillance. We had observed that the nurses were frequently absent when they should have been on duty. One reason for this is that the local health department seems to have a policy of appointing nurses to posts far away from their homes. For these nurses, getting home on weekends involved an expensive and time-consuming trip of several hours on bad roads. Thus Fridays and Mondays could be lost to travel time.

Much later, however, the system was put to use for an altogether different purpose. Since it allowed some people in the community to gain access to the internet, the doctors added a satellite connection for their own use, and our WiFi system gave internet access to other people along the network, notably the headman's son. Other nodes were subsequently added to the network to provide more coverage for communication services to other settlements and a local community-supported backpackers operation.

We suspect that had we linked the clinics to one another from the start, so that the nurses could talk to each other, the attitude to technology may have been different. However our mindset at the outset was to set up a doctor-nurse consultation system and so linking clinics for chat between nurses was not initially an apparent need. It turned out subsequently that an earlier (and abandoned because no longer supported) citizen-band radio from the previous decade had apparently enjoyed more acceptance possibly because it allowed inter-clinic discussions.

This example illustrates how technology can sometimes not fit in with local communities even if, up to a point, participative and agile approaches have been used to design the system. Rapidly changing local circumstances, combined with difficult-to-detect (and even unconscious) subterranean social circumstances, require a constant interrogation of processes, as well as a willingness to rethink both the starting point of a design and its final outcome.

Technology and 'good ideas' may not be appropriate for local communities, but this does not necessarily mean that local communities won't appropriate a 'failed' system for their own ends. Even the notion of what defines a 'failed' system has to be interrogated further.

How do we evaluate ICT4D? The limitations

One of the challenges of assessing the success or failure of ICT4D systems is the approach adopted to evaluating success. For example, users often define the success of a system by how it responds to their needs, noting simply that 'it works'. This refers mainly to a technical 'working'; that is, the system does not crash and it responds – at least for some stakeholders – to the identified need. As noted earlier, designers and funders assess and evaluate systems in terms of efficiency and effectiveness as well as efficacy and scalability. However, we would argue that these evaluation methods have limitations that can result in ICT4D design remaining stagnant.

'It works'

In engineering terms, software is considered a success when it meets performance metrics related to efficiency or robustness. So, for example, telephone switching software might be considered successful if it takes less than a second to establish a call, and drops fewer than 0.001 per cent of calls. Typically these success metrics are set at the start of a development process and software engineers consider the software complete when those metrics have been met. In the context of ICT4D, however, there are two critical problems with this approach.

The first relates to the notion that success metrics can be defined at the start of a design process. In the technology-saturated developed world it is often apparent what technology is missing, and therefore, the steps involved in resolving any deficiencies can easily be identified. In the developing world, however, the introduction of technology radically alters other structures and practices, making it impossible to foresee all that may be required of a technology before it is introduced.

The second problem relates to spurious success. Much software engineering is built on the premise that ICT problems exist outside of, and apart from, any development process. A problem is given to engineers who go off to create the best solution that they can, while assuming that 'development problems' will be solved by 'other' people (such as anthropologists, economists or sociologists). Therefore success metrics tend to be defined in terms of the technology, and success is spuriously claimed when these metrics are achieved, regardless of whether users actually benefit or not. Coming back to the example of telephone-switch software, it is possible to build a piece of software that is efficient in terms of dropped calls and connection times but does not fulfil any useful purpose such as allowing people to chat remotely.

For ICT4D to be effective, on the other hand, it must:

- be measured in terms of the impact it makes on users (not just in terms of the performance of the technology);
- acknowledge that problems change over time and that a 'working' solution may only be one step towards a better understanding of the real problem.

Efficiency and effectiveness

The discipline of Human-Computer Interaction overcomes some of the limitations found in other software-engineering approaches, as it centres success criteria on the end user of a system. The internationally agreed standard for usability requires designers to create systems that are 'effective, efficient and satisfactory' for a user. While this definition has the user at its core, it does not require that any steps be taken to ensure that the correct problem is being solved.

This can be illustrated with reference to the teleconsultation case study described earlier. Our initial prototype was PC based, requiring nurses to undergo six months training to become comfortable with an unfamiliar device (the PC), the operating system (Windows), and our software. Seeking to improve efficiency, effectiveness and satisfaction, we worked with the nurses to develop a mobile phone application with the same functionality as the desktop system. This required only two weeks of training, and met all the usability criteria. However, even this efficient, effective and satisfying system was never used by the nurses, as we simply did not understand well enough their perceptions of their power in relation to the doctors at the hospital. Essentially, no system built along similar lines would have succeeded.

The failure of usability and much human-computer interaction comes from the focus on the individual, with the intention of optimizing the individual's performance. If ICTs are to be developed to serve communities, then success criteria need to be determined by, and for, the community as a whole, and not just by and for individuals from within that community.

Scalability and efficacy

In the context of system design, scalability refers to the notion of being able to use the same system multiple times, either in different settings or for a variety of users. A good example of scalability is Microsoft Office, which is used globally and can be described as a highly scalable product.

Scalability is possible when a system is developed against a highly homogenous background, or when users are able to change their workflow to match that of the developed system. If a system provides enough incentive (for example, when word processors allow us all to write neater and faster), the system is more likely to be easily scalable than when the incentive is less clear. Scalability requires the user to be able to respond to various system requirements, including being able to afford the necessary hardware or software.

Notions of homogeneity and users adapting to system requirements are profoundly in conflict with the needs of communities in under-resourced settings. South Africa has a highly heterogeneous population, to which our eleven official languages bear testimony. In addition, rural communities respond differently to daily challenges based on the resources available to them. A system that responds to the needs of one community may not respond to the needs of another. The notion of creating a single system that can be used by many is not wrong when one can expect the users to adapt. For example, a finance software package that is used throughout the world may require organizations to change their workflows, and result in the software creating a level of homogeneity across communities of users. Yet, in a developing-world context, the notion of 'one system for all', tends to arrogantly assume that the solutions for seemingly similar challenges in different contexts are the same.

Efficacy is another challenging notion when considering system success in the context of ICT4D. Efficacy refers to the notion of how many people 'like' a system, and the degree to which it fulfils the intended outcome. In the context of the Water Quality Report described above, it was possible to assess how much information was flowing between water-supply caretakers and municipalities. However, it was not possible to assess whether the information had an impact on improving attitudes towards water quality within the community, or even whether community health improved as more information was collected. This has been a key problem in a number of system developments. The tracking of the Millennium Development Goals is a good example. The success of Millennium Goal 7C – to ensure environmental sustainability by halving the proportion of the population without sustainable access to safe drinking water and basic sanitation by 2015 – is assessed by tracking how many people have been given access to safe water. However, we do not know if these people still have access to safe water: all we know is that, at one point in time, they had access, but the pump may have since broken. Existing methods of determining efficacy are, to a great extent, self-referential, and the degree to which they assist in developing systems that truly improve design is doubtful.

The beginning of the end and the end of the beginning: methodologies for building ICT4D systems

As we have shown in this chapter, from the starting point of identifying a need for a system to the end point of feasibility and sustainability, ICT4D systems are defined and constrained by software engineering and design. The purpose of design and engineering is to modify reality in ways that suit users and transform their lives for the better in some way. This is what we mean by our extended understanding of 'fit for purpose'. The engineering endeavour then focuses on uncovering a basic common understanding between all participants and the design methodology used is intended to facilitate this. While consciously aiming at transformation via our engineered interventions we critically question which purposes at the beginning and end of the process are best suited as goals for designs.

From an engineering or design perspective, we believe that far more emphasis has to be put on mutual learning and knowledge discovery. We never lose sight of the primary aim of design, which is to facilitate improvement of some aspect of the lives of users. From a research perspective, on the other hand, we are intent on intervening in the lives of users while continually increasing our understanding of the situation, our discipline and ourselves.

Our solution to the issue of goal setting lies in involving the community where our intervention is to become active. We regard the community as partners in design, and we call this aspect of the method 'community-based co-design'. By having the community as co-designers, we start to address the issues identified above, namely:

- Understanding the community's needs: having community members as active partners in the design process means that we stand a greater chance of understanding and responding to their needs;
- Avoiding paternalistic notions of development: by engaging the community directly, we do not need to rely on external, top-down, notions of development.

The question, of course, is how best to identify and engage potential users in this new methodology. Several options are possible. We make use of three, depending on the nature of the various situations we work in.

The first is to communicate with communities via an intermediary; that is, a person or a group (such as an NGO) who have the trust and respect of a community. In this situation, communication shifts from being a dyadic exchange between co-designers towards a triadic inter-preted design of a system artefact. This has important consequences, and leads to a mediated design process.

The second is to build partnerships with community members (with or without the help of intermediaries) that result in deep mutual understanding. In such situations, the co-design conversation is easier because concepts and values are shared. This is a very long-term process, and can require decades rather than years. This approach raises important ethical issues of reciprocity between engineers and community members.

The third involves splitting the design process between building tools to support artefact production, and the production of the system artefacts themselves. This means that, rather than always creating a finished solution, we may create tools that enable people to create their own solutions. The tools are also created with the community in a joint design process. The essential idea is that engineers limit their role to procuring tools, and training others in the use of those tools; the community then takes over the tools to produce their own systems. This co-design conversation, which mostly involves an intermediary, has the benefit of being more short term, and is aimed at discovering needs and training requirements.

The epistemology of effectiveness

Engineers understand 'fit for purpose' in terms of the extent to which a system meets the stated needs of users. Once we accept that identifying such needs is very difficult, and that once we include users as co-designers, then discovering a practical purpose for which an artefact can be designed is problematic. It is also possible that the academic needs of researchers to know and understand will conflict with the needs of the community.

Our 'solution' to this is to conflate *practice* with *knowing*. Creating knowledge is inextricably intertwined with effective action. Knowledge that does not lead to effective action is not really knowledge, and the failure to create effective systems is equivalent to a failure of understanding. This is the position of pragmatist epistemology – an epistemology that is compatible with action research (Oquist 1978).

Conclusion

We have argued that mediated design processes, or user-needs analyses that include communities as co-designers, result in a more holistic approach to software design and engineering. The shift represents a move from a closed system of expertise, with the engineer as the expert and other participants as subjects, to open collaboration and co-ownership of the design process. This challenges the traditional role of the designer profoundly. Instead of the designer setting the agenda, deciding on the methodologies and owning the outcomes, the emphasis moves to a shared learning approach. This fundamental shift results in the designer giving up control, and becoming a facilitator.

References

Avgerou, Chrisanthi (2000) 'Recognising alternative rationalities in the deployment of information systems' *Electronic Journal of Information Systems in Developing Countries*, 3 (7): 1-15.

Benjamin, Peter (2001) 'Community development and democratization through information technology: Building the new South Africa' in Richard Heeks ed., *Re-inventing Government in the Information Age*, London: Routledge.

Bidwell, Nicola J, Thomas Reitmaier, Gary Marsden and Susan Hansen (2010) 'Designing with mobile digital storytelling in rural Africa' in *Proceedings of the 28th International Conference on Human Factors in Computing Systems* (CHI '10). New York: ACM.

Connell, Raewyn (2007) *Southern Theory: The Global Dynamics of Knowledge in Social Science*, Sydney: Allen & Unwin.

Del Gado, Elisa *and* Jakob Nielsen (1996) International User Interfaces, *New York: John Wiley & Sons.*

Gurumurthy, Anita and Parminda Jeet Singh (2009) 'ICTD: Is it a new species of development?' Bangalore: IT For Change, http://www.comminit.com/ict-4-development/node/306946 Accessed online 26 November 2012.

Heeks, Richard (2002) 'Information systems and developing countries: Failure, success and local improvization' *The Information Society*, 18 (2):. 101-112.

Hirschheim, Rudy and Heinz K Klein (1989) 'Four paradigms of information systems development' *Communications of the ACM*, 32 (10): 1199-1216.

ITU Telecom World, *The World in 2011: ICT Facts and Figures*, http://www.itu.int/ITU-D/ict/facts/2011/material/ICTFactsFigures2011.pdf Accessed online 28 November 2012.

Kimaro, Honest and Titlestad, Ola (2008) 'Challenges of user participation in the design of a computer based system: the possibility of participatory customization in low income countries', *Health Informatics in Developing Countries*, 2(1): 1-9.

Liskov, Barbara Huberman and Valdis Berzins, V. (1986) 'An Appraisal of Program Specifications' in Gehani Narain and Andrew McGettrick, eds, *Software Specification Techniques*, New York: Addison Wesley.

Loudon, Melissa and Ulrike Rivett (2010) 'Methods and conceptual tools for success in local government information systems', a paper presented at the IDIA Conference, Cape Town 3–5 Nov 2010, http://www.developmentinformatics.org/conferences/2010.

Loudon, Melissa, Tahmina Ajmal, Ulrike Rivett, Dirk de Jager, Robert Bain, Robert Matthews and Stephen Gundry (2009) 'A "human-in-the-loop" mobile image recognition application for rapid scanning of water quality test results', a paper presented at the First International Workshop on Expressive Interactions for Sustainability and Empowerment (EISE 2009), 29-30 October, London. http://ewic.bcs.org/content/ConWebDoc/33637. Accessed online 6 March 2013.

Moodley, Sagren (2005) 'The promise of e-development? A critical assessment of the state of ICT-for-poverty-reduction discourse in South Africa', *Perspectives on Global Development and Technology*, 4 (1): 1-26.

Oquist, Paul (1978) 'The epistemology of action research' *Acta Sociologica*, 21 (2): 143-163.

Sørensen Tove, Ulrike Rivett and Jill Fortuin (2008) 'Review of e-health systems for HIV/AIDS and antiretroviral treatment management in South Africa', *Journal of Telemedicine and Telecare*, 14 (1): 37-41.

Gitau, Shikoh, Gary Marsden, and Jonathan Donner (2010) 'After access: Challenges facing mobile-only internet users in the developing world', *Proceedings of the 28th International Conference on Human Factors in Computing Systems (CHI 2010)*, New York: ACM.

Tucker, William and Edwin Blake (2008) 'The role of outcome mapping in developing a rural telemedicine system' in Paul Cunningham and Miriam Cunningham eds, *IST-Africa 2008: Conference Proceedings*. Windhoek: International Information Management Corporation.

Wilson, FA (1997) 'The truth is out there: The search for emancipatory principles in information systems design', *Information Technology & People*, 10 (3): 187-204.

9

'Good Houses Make Good People'
Making Knowledge about Health & Environment in Cape Town

Warren Smit, Ariane de Lannoy,
Robert VH Dover, Estelle V Lambert,
Naomi Levitt & Vanessa Watson

There is increasing recognition of the importance of the physical environment of cities for the health and wellbeing of residents. Along with the social and institutional aspects of cities, the physical urban environment can play a significant role in influencing health-related behaviours and outcomes. In some ways, it may seem easier to address the physical urban environment than the social one, but without any associated upstream or downstream support or engagement, such changes do not always have the expected outcomes.

The most commonly used concepts and tools for understanding the relationships between physical urban environments and health and wellbeing are largely based on empirical work undertaken in the global North,[1] as, indeed, are the concepts of 'health' and 'urban' that underpin this body of knowledge. On the one hand, some of the existing guidelines on how to create healthy urban environments (see, for example, Barton and Tsourou 2000) are of limited use in cities such as Cape Town, South Africa, where contextual realities are very different from those in the global North, and many of the assumptions underpinning the dominant body of knowledge do not necessarily apply. On the other hand, some guidelines cannot easily be labelled as Northern, particularly where they have been adopted to address issues of global development, such as the Millennium Development Goals. For example, urban violence is a problem in the cities of the North as well as the South.

Nonetheless, different assumptions distinguish Northern and Southern planning approaches. This is largely because modern urban planning, as a discipline and practice, originated in the global North in response to earlier waves of rapid urbanization. Thereafter, these

---

[1] Slater (2004) discusses the problem of categorization of different regions of the world, and the binaries implied in terms such as First World/Third World or West/non-West, which ignore the extent of the 'interpenetrations' that have occurred. The terms 'global South' and 'global North' used in this chapter do not overcome this problem but offer a less pejorative reference to different parts of the world.

approaches were transplanted to the global South primarily to control the development of emerging colonial towns, but were still based on assumptions that shaped their emergence in their areas of origin; namely, that planning would be implemented in contexts characterized by: strong economies and public institutions, relatively high levels of employment and income, manageable populations amenable to spatial control, as well as reasonably good levels of infrastructural development. In most of the global South few of these assumptions hold, yet Northern concepts and positions on urban planning continue to dominate. As a result, one of the problems of urban planning, in South Africa and elsewhere in the global South, is that urban planners and the residents being planned for often have very different perspectives. This can lead to urban environments that do not meet the needs of all residents (Watson 2003). In response to these disjunctures between theory and context, calls have been made for research in the global South to 'extend the geographical range of empirical resources and scholarly insight for theorizing beyond the West and western-dominated forms of globalization' (Robinson 2002: 549).

This chapter draws on the work of an interdisciplinary research programme in Cape Town that aims to better understand the relationship between human health and the physical urban environment. Ultimately, we aim to contribute towards the creation of healthier urban environments in Cape Town and elsewhere in the global South. The project seeks to go beyond existing (Northern) approaches, to develop new conceptualizations of urban health, test out new methodologies, and contribute to new (Southern) theories about the relationship between the physical urban environment and health.

Knowledge about physical urban environments and health

The physical urban environment influences health in a variety of ways, determining, to a significant extent, access to shelter and services, spaces for outdoor activity, and food (Boarnet 2006; Commission on Social Determinants of Health 2008; Diez Roux 2003; Galea and Vlahov 2005; Smit et al. 2011; Vlahov et al. 2007; Vlahov and Galea 2002). Nevertheless, much of the literature that explores the links between urban environment and health adopts largely positivist approaches, relies on standardized measuring instruments, and assumes that correlations imply causation. This approach often does little to encourage researchers to pay greater attention to the specifics of local contexts.

There are at least three key assumptions in the dominant body of knowledge about the relationship between human health and the physical urban environment which do not match the realities of the global South. These are outlined below.

Conceptions of human health and wellbeing
Although the debate about whether it is possible to have an objective definition of 'health' remains unresolved (Hamilton 2010), assumptions about the nature of 'human health and wellbeing' are implicit in much of the literature. A key milestone was reached in the 1940s when the World Health Organization adopted a definition of health as 'a state of complete physical, psychological, and social well-being and not only the absence of disease or weakness' (WHO 1948).[2] Quantitative methodologies, standardized measuring instruments, and the developers of various technologies have, nevertheless, tended to work within a relatively narrow definition of 'disease' (Hofmann 2011). Contemporary global conceptions of health also do not prioritize spirituality or relationships, and effectively marginalize many traditional perspectives. Whereas Western approaches focus on the functioning of the organs and mental faculties of the individual, some traditional African conceptions of health focus on 'mental, physical, spiritual, and emotional stability for oneself, family members, and community' (Omonzejele 2008: 120). In these traditional conceptions, health and wellbeing are often seen as closely linked to the relationship with one's ancestors, and diseases are often seen as having spiritual or mystical, as well as physical, causes (Okpako 1999; Omonzejele 2008; Sarli et al. 2012).

Conceptions of the urban environment
Most of the dominant assumptions about what constitutes a viable 'urban environment' hark back to European cities, but African forms of urbanism that have evolved more recently tend to be characterized by informality, complexity, and a lack of neat separations (Freund 2007; Myers 2011). Informal settlements, for example, have few clearly defined streets or clear separations between vehicle and pedestrian spaces, public and private spaces, or between land uses (residential dwellings are often also the site of home-based enterprises) (Simone 1999, 2000; Smit 2006). Similarly, 'plots' and dwelling units are not always clearly defined, and households, too, can be fairly fluid, with extended families spread across various urban and rural homes and frequent movement of family members between these dwellings (Spiegel et al. 1996). All of this can make the relationship between residents and

[2] This definition was subsequently revised to: 'Health is a state of complete physical, mental and social well-being and not merely the absence of disease or infirmity' (WHO 2006).

their neighbourhoods more complex than conventional conceptions of modern Western cities provide for.

Conceptions of choice
The dominant conceptions assume that individuals act rationally and voluntarily in a world of many options and clear choices. As a result, when studying health-related behaviours, adequate attention is seldom given to the social and cultural factors that limit people's choices, or to the fact that, in some contexts, decisions are made by groups rather than individuals. In contexts such as Cape Town, with its high levels of poverty and inequality, entrenched socio-spatial segregation, and distorted property markets that do not function in much of the city, assumptions about the choices people have, in terms of their lifestyles and where to live, do not necessarily hold.

The Cape Town context

Cape Town has a population of about 3.7 million people (City of Cape Town 2011). As in most other cities of the global South, wealth and poverty, formality and informality are juxtaposed. The city's levels of inequality are among the highest in the world (UN-Habitat 2010) – almost 40 per cent of households are classified as poor, with insufficient income to access basic necessities such as food and shelter (City of Cape Town 2011). Slums are the most tangible manifestation of poverty and inequality, and an estimated 280,000 households live in informal dwellings (City of Cape Town 2011). The city also has high burdens of disease and levels of health inequity. The most recent age-standardized mortality rate for Cape Town is 1,011 per 100,000 people (Groenewald et al. 2010), which is considerably higher than the rate for most cities in the global North; for example, it is 60 per cent higher than the 2010 mortality rate for New York City (New York City Department of Health and Mental Hygiene). Health indicators also vary enormously between Cape Town's health districts. For example, the mortality rate for communicable diseases is about five times higher in the poorer Khayelitsha Health District than it is in the adjacent Southern Peninsula Health District (550 versus 112 deaths per 100,000 people per year) (Groenewald et al. 2008).

The burden of disease in Cape Town (and other South African cities) is particularly complex, and includes the following key dimensions:

• HIV/AIDS is the leading cause of premature mortality.

- Other communicable diseases (such as tuberculosis and diarrhoea) are in the top ten causes of premature mortality, and continue at high levels (Groenewald et al. 2008). These diseases are closely linked to poverty, overcrowding, inadequate shelter, inadequate access to basic services, and inadequate access to affordable and healthy food (Muzigaba and Puoane 2011).
- The prevalence of non-communicable diseases, such as diabetes mellitus and ischaemic heart disease (also in the top ten causes of premature mortality), is growing rapidly (Groenewald et al. 2008, Peer et al. 2012). This is linked to changes in lifestyle associated with rural-urban migration and the transition of some households to relatively more affluent lifestyles (Bradshaw and Steyn 2001). Socio-cultural factors, such as perceptions of ideal body shape have also been shown to play an important role (Mchiza et al. 2011; Puoane et al. 2002, 2010).
- Harm from injuries related to homicide and traffic accidents, are the second and fourth most frequent causes of premature mortality in Cape Town (Groenewald et al. 2008).
- High levels of psychosocial stress and depression are also reported (Peltzer et al. 2008; Seedat et al. 2004).

Improving the health and wellbeing of residents of Cape Town is a challenge. Available health data are limited and outdated. In addition, high levels of political contestation have led city policymakers to focus on short-term, tangible forms of delivery such as housing and infrastructure (Smit 2004), without explicitly considering the long-term health and wellbeing of residents.

Case study: Khayelitsha

Khayelitsha is a residential area on the periphery of Cape Town, established by the apartheid government in the mid-1980s for black Africans (Cook 1986). The 2001 Census showed that the population of Khayelitsha was 329,000, and that this was increasing by 5.3 per cent per year (City of Cape Town 2005). The city estimated that 72 per cent of households in Khayelitsha have incomes below the household subsistence level (a commonly used measure of poverty), and 65 per cent of households live in informal dwellings (City of Cape Town 2005).

We undertook fieldwork in three areas: one of the oldest formal parts of Khayelitsha (Section A), one of the older site-and-service areas (Site

B) and an informal settlement (Taiwan).[3] A five-day workshop was held in each area, using 'body mapping' to stimulate discussion about health and wellbeing, and how these are affected by living environments. At each workshop, ten participants traced their outlines and then annotated the tracings, as a basis on which to discuss their health and wellbeing, in whatever ways they understood these concepts. Participants included representations of the environments in which they live, and indicated how this impacts on their health and wellbeing (a few examples are shown in Figures 9.1-9.4). In addition, we conducted in-depth interviews with respondents, and, after handing out disposable cameras, we asked all the participants to take photographs of the aspects of their environment that they felt influenced their health and quality of life. The preliminary results of the fieldwork are discussed below, and are structured according to perceptions of health and wellbeing and the impact of the physical urban environment on health and wellbeing as this relates to the nature of available shelter and services, physical activity and sources of food.

Perceptions of health and wellbeing
Most participants had fairly biomedical understandings of health, probably as a result of their interactions with the public-healthcare system. Some older respondents were very conscious of their health status, but had different perceptions of what they could do about this. For example, one respondent had diabetes and high blood pressure, and saw herself as having poor health over which she had little control. Another respondent had a heart problem that necessitated frequent visits to a hospital, but she made conscious efforts to lead a 'healthy' lifestyle; this included eating fresh fruit and vegetables, and walking for exercise. Most other respondents had few explicit health problems and took their good health, in a biomedical sense, for granted.

Many participants highlighted the relational dimensions of health and wellbeing, and emphasized that interaction with others, as well as the health and wellbeing of neighbourhood communities as a whole, were important for individual health and quality of life. For example, some participants from the Taiwan settlement said they had found a way to 'keep their heads up high' by contributing to a soup kitchen, and helping to take care of others. Intergenerational relations and tensions

---

[3] Site-and-service areas are where residents are provided with legal security of tenure and full services, but initially lived in shacks (in many cases residents have subsequently built formal houses). Informal settlements are where residents have no legal security of tenure, live in shacks, and have access to limited services (although temporary communal services may exist).

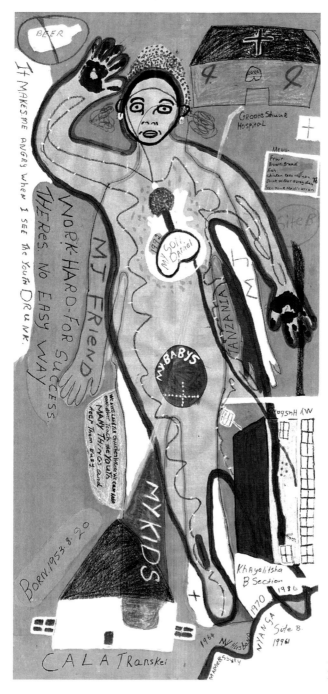

Figure 9.1
Mandisa, Section A

Figure 9.2
Sizwe, Section A

Figure 9.3
Thandi, Taiwan

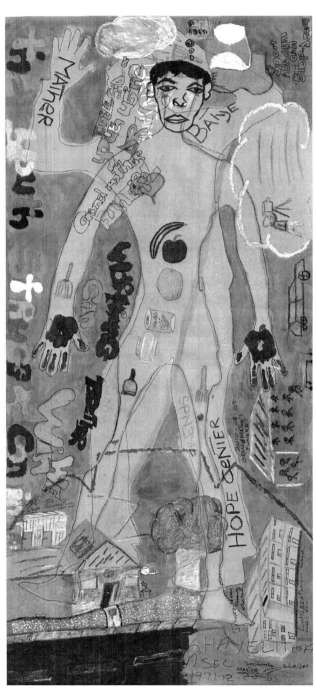

Figure 9.4
Siyabonga, Taiwan

were also highlighted by both younger and older participants. Older participants mentioned the need for spaces where they could interact with youth, to impart cultural values 'about ways of doing things in life' without resorting to crime and violence. Younger participants, in return, asked for understanding from the older generation, and admitted that they needed guidance and support.

A significant number of participants mentioned a spiritual dimension of health and wellbeing, drawing on both traditional beliefs and Christian beliefs. For example, Babalwa[4] noted that, 'Life is fine when you have faith in your God', and many participants drew bibles and crosses on their body maps, indicating these as important sources of support. While only one participant explicitly highlighted traditional beliefs on her body map (writing 'Ancestors' down one arm, and 'God' down the other), and only one participant took a photograph of a *sangoma* (traditional healer), many others mentioned their beliefs in the discussions. The rural homes, to which traditional beliefs tend to be strongly linked, were prominently represented on most of the body maps, and were described by all as places where the pressures of life in the city fall away. The quality of life may have been poorer there for some – especially those who now live in the formal areas of Khayelitsha – but rural homes were perceived to be safer, greener, and calmer; places where participants felt a greater peace of mind and a 'sense of belonging'.

Stress and depression, mainly related to fear of crime and lawlessness, and to a general sense of hopelessness about the state of deprivation that participants found themselves in, had a major impact on their mental health and wellbeing. Fear of crime permeated the lives of all of the respondents, especially in Taiwan and Site B. For example, Anele noted, 'I feel angry when houses are broken into', and Mandisa described 'always feeling scared' and 'not trusting anyone'. Respondents said that they generally stay home at night, plan their routes to avoid open spaces, and avoid walking through residential areas other than their own. In the older, more formal areas, such as Section A, participants said they felt safe inside their houses, with their strong walls, doors and burglar bars. However, in Taiwan, the weakness of the physical structures meant that respondents felt they could not protect themselves, even inside their houses. One young man said that he hides under his bed when he hears gunshots nearby, as bullets could go straight through his walls.

In addition to crime-related stress, many young people also expressed

---

[4]   All names used in this chapter are pseudonyms.

a sense of hopelessness, of not being able to get a job and of not knowing how to get help to realize their dreams and ambitions. For example, Ayanda, a young woman, said 'Life is just terrible, as there is nothing for me to do.' Sometimes, she said, she just sleeps until the day has passed.

Access to shelter and services
Physical living conditions vary considerably between the three areas we worked in. In Section A, people have formal houses with running water, flush toilets and electricity. The streets are relatively wide and well maintained, garbage is collected regularly, and many houses have well-kept gardens with walls around them. Participants living here told us that their ward councillor lives around the corner, so if something is broken, they go and find him and things get fixed. Mandisa said that in contrast to the informal settlement where she used to live, 'life is better now, there is running water, electricity'.

In Taiwan, however, participants lived in shacks without access to services. Residents there described their built environment and houses as severely deficient, and unable to protect them from illness, crime or weather (heat, rain, floods). They have strategies to safeguard their goods when the rains come, such as digging drains in and around their shacks, and putting plastic sheeting on top of their roofs. Rats obtain entry into the houses through the floors, and bite through the buckets in which residents keep their food. Some participants from Taiwan told us that 'the rats are as big as cats', and that 'the cats are scared of them'. Some put rat poison down at night, and remove it again before the children in the house wake in the morning. The lack of electricity, and the use of paraffin stoves and candles, means that there is a constant fear of shack fires, exacerbated by the fact that emergency vehicles cannot access the narrow, sandy lanes between the shacks.

Residents of Taiwan have to share toilets with up to 20 other families. These toilets are on the edge of the settlement, and residents sometimes have to walk up to 15 minutes to get to them. Those who live closest to the toilets often put locks on them to try and claim them. Mothers pointed out that their children cannot go to the toilets alone as they would then have to ask for a key from a neighbour they do not know. The toilets are, anyway, a contested space for children as chances are high that 'they would get taken and raped'. Because of the fear of being mugged at night, residents of Site B noted that they relieve themselves in buckets inside their houses, and then empty these in the morning. Fear of violence affects health at many different levels.

Khayelitsha's many shebeens (illegal drinking places) gave rise to feelings of powerlessness among those who live close by and cannot sleep until the noise from the taverns dies down, often only early in the mornings. In Taiwan, especially, participants mentioned that they often lay awake at night, listening to make sure possible conflicts between drunken shebeen goers would not literally spill into their own houses. Some mothers were worried about the effect of shebeens on their children. For example, Mandisa said, 'I educate my children inside the house to tell them they should not drink or smoke, but there are three shebeens in our road.'

Spaces for outdoor activities

The physical environment of the formal part of Khayelitsha seems, at first sight, to be fairly conducive to outdoor physical activity. There are a number of sports facilities and parks, especially in the more formal areas. However, with the notable exception of the large Peace Park in Section A, many of these facilities are badly maintained and considered dangerous by residents. Many of the young men from Section A talked about a local park that they cannot use anymore because 'the thugs have vandalized it all; there used to be things that children could play on, but not any more'. In addition, *tik* (methamphetamine) smokers frequent such playgrounds. By contrast, the Peace Park seems to be a family place, where residents stay until quite late on weekends. In terms of respecting public spaces, the Peace Park is in very good condition, free of litter and vandalism, which might speak to its symbolic impact in the community.

The pavements in Khayelitsha are generally treeless and are thus particularly exposed to the elements (especially wind-blown sand). The area's fairly isolated location also means that Cape Town's major facilities and shopping centres can only be reached by car or public transport. Above all, walking is constrained by fear of crime. Lulama said that she used to walk at night, but 'Now I prefer to stay in my house at all times, with the door and burglar gate locked. I trust no one ... We are scared of the young ones.' The narrow winding streets of Taiwan and Site B were singled out as being particularly dangerous. Ndileka, a resident of Section A, said that she is scared to go to the informal and site-and-service areas of Khayelitsha: 'There are lots of informal shacks, it is all informal housing, no streets, just small narrow paths with lots of corners, and that is where you get attacked, or robbed, or worse.'

Mothers in Taiwan do not allow their young daughters to play on their own due to fear of rape, and insist that they play between the shacks where an eye can be kept on them. There are no parks, and young boys play on the stretch of grass between the settlement and the freeway, risking their lives whenever a soccer ball gets kicked near the road. Deep pools of stagnant water make this play area even more hazardous. Finally, although only one respondent raised this issue, the large numbers of minibus taxis can make road-crossing hazardous.

The physical urban environment and food

Apart from one person who expressed concerns about meat prepared on the roadsides, respondents raised few issues with respect to food (in terms of access, variety, affordability or quality) and health. A shopping mall, which includes a major supermarket, has been established in Khayelitsha, and respondents generally do their major (weekly or monthly) grocery shopping at this mall (or at an even larger mall in a neighbouring township). For smaller, *ad hoc* food purchases, residents use the local *spaza* shops, which are mostly run by Somali traders and which are perceived to be more expensive than supermarkets but are accessibly located, and offer convenient 'hampers' of goods. (These shops are readily identifiable by the signboards and paintings of grocery items on their walls.)

A few respondents were conscious of eating what they regarded as healthy foods. For example, Mandisa, who has heart disease, wrote her typical menu on her body map: 'Fruit, brown bread, fish, chicken with skin taken off, drink water every day.' For the most part, however, respondents were not concerned with 'healthy' eating. Some young respondents said they sometimes spent their limited money on fried hot chips, which are considerably more expensive than healthier alternatives, suggesting that for young people, choices regarding food are less about health and more about an opportunity to socialize. For example, Thabo said 'I eat a lot of junk food and I drink a lot of alcohol to socialize. That's how I live.' Although there are a range of food outlets, most respondents were from households with limited incomes and this undoubtedly had a big impact on their ability to access food. Although there are some community vegetable gardens in the area, only a few houses have vegetable patches (one of the participants took photographs of his mother's lush vegetable garden), and none of the participants mentioned using such gardens for their food supply.

Key issues emerging from the literature and the fieldwork

Participants in our research expressed ambiguous feelings about Khayelitsha. On the one hand, most expressed an allegiance to their social networks and did not want to move away. On the other hand, most respondents live in fear of crime: 'The thugs are everywhere, and even if it is busy, it is not safe, because they carry guns and knives and will just rob you if they get a chance.' Ntombi coloured her body map in red, as she associates red with violence, and she said 'Khayelitsha is a dangerous place.' The high crime levels do sometimes make people wish they could live elsewhere. For example, Lulama said that 'you wished you lived in the suburbs, because there it is quiet, you can be at ease, you can walk.'

The commonly expressed view about not wanting to move away from Khayelitsha is informed by the knowledge that there are few alternatives available to low-income households that cannot afford to access the formal housing market. In terms of lifestyle choices, although clearly there are at least some choices (as in the case of the respondent who consciously tried to eat healthy food and exercise regularly), many, particularly, younger respondents, seemed to feel constrained in terms of lifestyle by lack of income, and feel that they have few options.

Conceptions of health and wellbeing
Participants largely subscribed to the biomedical understanding of health, especially when they had been diagnosed with a severe health problem through the formal health care system. However, conceptions of human health and wellbeing were broader than those used by most quantitative measuring instruments. In particular, the spiritual and relational dimensions, as well as the importance of stress and depression were given prominence, whereas these are largely absent from official data, as well as from most government policies and strategies. The high levels of stress and depression were strongly linked to fear of crime and the perceived lack of social and economic opportunities in the area. Fear of crime is, in itself, strongly linked to the (often older generation's) perceptions of youth involvement. This, in turn, leads to a sense of community breakdown, which perpetuates feelings of hopelessness and depression.

The relationship between the urban environment and health and wellbeing
Our findings confirm a strong relationship between neighbourhood environments, and the health and wellbeing of residents, but this relationship is more complex than in conventional conceptions of the modern Western city. For example, the use of space in Khayelitsha seems to be strongly determined by fear of crime. The main implication of this additional complexity is that social issues need to be central to processes that aim to guide the creation and management of the physical urban environment. Participatory processes are essential, so that people's real needs can be adequately met.

The relationship between neighbourhood environments and the health and quality of residents' lives also varied considerably between areas. In formal housing areas, people had adequate shelter and basic services, and the focus of those participants, with regard to creating healthier urban environments, was on issues such as providing more access to green spaces and building stronger communities. In Taiwan, by contrast, where residents lack adequate shelter and basic services, the focus was on the appalling living conditions – the absence of protection from the elements, the lack of clean water and sanitation, the piles of garbage and pools of stagnant water.

Changes in Khayelitsha's physical environment aimed at making streets and public spaces safer for walking, playing and other outdoor activity, would be beneficial. Possible interventions include upgrading sidewalks and public spaces, improving street lighting (and ensuring that criminals cannot disconnect street lights as currently seems to be the case) and creating a range of appropriate and accessible public spaces for recreation. Reducing the risk of violent crime through street patterns and urban designs that facilitate the creation of 'defensible spaces' may help to address the high level of fear around violent crime (Liebermann and Landman 1999; Newman 1986). Although raised by only one respondent, the observations of the research team suggest that appropriate traffic calming measures and the provision of more appropriate pedestrian routes would help to reduce the incidence of traffic injuries (Moudon 1987).

Though most participants lived in formal houses and had access to services, those who lived in informal houses without proper access to services highlighted the importance of providing these through participatory upgrading processes that minimize the need for relocation. Thabo noted that 'good houses make good people', indicating that a change in the physical environment could facilitate a change in the social environment. Lindiwe said that 'The community of Taiwan wants to live healthy lives. We need our own toilets, water and electricity.' Improved maintenance of existing infrastructure (water, sanitation, stormwater drainage) and more frequent refuse removal are also necessary. In addition to shelter and infrastructure, more appropriate social facilities are also required.

Despite the relatively well-stocked public libraries in Khayelitsha (which featured prominently in the photographs taken by participants from the formal housing areas), many respondents expressed problems accessing information about resources and programmes, as well as other opportunities for growth and advancement. Community centres or cultural centres, where various services to residents could be clustered, would help. These could take the form of the 'Lighthouses of Knowledge', such as those built in Curitiba, Brazil, which provide access to books and the internet for residents, and 'Citizenship Streets', which, located next to transportation nodes, provide access to a range of local government services (Gamble and Weil 2010).

Although some respondents perceived parts of Khayelitsha as already having adequate green spaces, improving the access of all residents to safe green space can have a beneficial impact on mental health and social wellbeing (Evans 2003; Kuo 2002; Mitchell and Popham 2008). This was borne out by Vusi, who lives next to a park: 'The breeze in the morning makes me feel fresh.' Many respondents from Taiwan in particular highlighted the need for spaces for children to play in. For example, Nomsa wished for 'open fields for my child to play.'

Food outlets in the area provide a range of options. However, the lack of local food production and the unsuitable nature of the spaces where street food is cooked and prepared is evident. A number of possible interventions could improve the access of poor urban residents to healthy food. These include:

- Redesigning local markets to provide greater availability of foodstuffs, and to be more welcoming and accessible to residents (Dixon et al. 2007);
- Using spatial plans and land-use zoning to ensure space for urban agriculture, either communally or on individual plots (Turner 1980); and
- Designing suitable spaces, and providing appropriate infrastructure, for the cooking and selling of street food, which offers an important source of food security for the poor (Atkinson 1995).

The issue of choice
The findings of our fieldwork confirm that residents are often constrained in their choices by factors largely beyond their control. Despite this, most of the respondents said that they did not want to leave Khayelitsha. This may be due, in part, to the awareness of the severe lack of alternative residential options; in most cases the only alternative options would be overcrowded and unserviced informal settlements on the urban periphery. This seems to confirm that in such contexts as Cape Town, with high levels of poverty and inequality, socio-spatial segregation and distorted property markets, assumptions about residents' choices in terms of where to live (which much of the literature on the relationship between the physical urban environment and health and wellbeing tends to assume) do not necessarily hold. What is not clear is the extent to which residents' intentions to remain in Khayelitsha are informed by a sense of community – which could be considered either as 'communitas' (Turner 1969) or

'habitus' (Bourdieu 1998) – or by a realistic assessment of the current socioeconomic context and a recognition of the limitations of their own resources to overcome issues of social injustice.

While most residents have little real choice as to where they live, they clearly have some choices concerning their lifestyles and are able to choose between various options. However, the physical urban environment can make these choices more difficult. For example, only certain routes and areas are safe for walking, and accessing certain healthy foods might require taking public transport to the larger supermarkets. Thus, health-promotion programmes that attempt to change the lifestyles of residents, implemented in many cities of the global North (via, for example, physical activity and diet), may be less effective in cities of the global South.

Given the constraints on freedom of choice in many cities of the global South, physical interventions such as creating safer streets and public spaces, as well as healthier food markets or suitable spaces for urban agriculture, seem to be essential preconditions for health-promotion programmes. In turn, health-promotion programmes need to take greater cognisance of African conceptions of health and well-being, particularly the importance of relational and spiritual aspects of life (Omonzejele 2008). In addition, the state should provide space and support for community initiatives aimed at improving living environments, through for example, encouraging food co-operatives and neighbourhood watches.

Conclusion

Northern urban-planning approaches and Southern urban realities do not make a perfect match. Where conceptions of health and wellbeing go beyond the biomedical and into the realms of the spiritual and emotional, it is important to take account of this in planning healthy urban environments. Thus, to enhance the health and wellbeing of residents in a multifaceted way, a variety of indoor and outdoor spaces are required to cater for the full range of social, economic, cultural and spiritual needs of local residents, including social interaction and interaction with the natural environment. Furthermore, although the physical urban environment has a significant impact on health and wellbeing (as summed up by Thabo's comment that 'good houses make good people'), the way people interact with the physical urban environment is also strongly mediated by social factors (which suggests that good houses may not necessarily make good people). Nevertheless, where the use of space is strongly influenced by fear of violence, care must be taken to ensure that newly created spaces are safe, usable, and accessible.

Researchers, planners and residents need to co-produce and implement knowledge about healthy urban environments. There is a vast gap in perspectives between planners and residents, and it is essential that processes be put in place to develop transversal hybrids of the dominant 'formal' system and local informal practices and perspectives (Harrison 2006). Methodologies such as body mapping are helpful. The existing literature on the relationship between the physical urban environment and health and wellbeing, and case studies of isolated projects, also offer some ingredients for healthier urban environments, but participatory processes are required to assemble these ingredients into a well-functioning, sustainable, and contextually relevant whole. Although good houses may not always make good people, planners and residents working together can potentially make physical urban environments that can help residents lead healthier, happier lives.

References

Atkinson Sarah J. (1995) 'Approaches and actors in urban food security in developing countries', *Habitat International*, 19 (2): 151-163.

Barton, Hugh and Catherine Tsourou (2000) *Healthy Urban Planning: A WHO Guide to Planning for People*, London: E & FN Spon.

Boarnet, Marlon G. (2006) 'Planning's role in building healthy cities', *Journal of the American Planning Association*, 72 (1): 6-9.

Bourdieu, Pierre (1998) *Practical Reason: On the Theory of Action*, Stanford CA: Stanford University Press.

Bradshaw, Debbie and Krisela Steyn (2001) *Poverty and Chronic Diseases in South Africa*, Cape Town: Medical Research Council/ WHO Collaborating Centre.

City of Cape Town (2005) *A Population Profile of Khayelitsha: Socio-economic Information from the 2001 Census*, Cape Town.

City of Cape Town (2011) Urbanisation and Poverty in Cape Town. Working document.

Commission on Social Determinants of Health (2008) *Closing the Gap in a Generation: Health Equity through Action on the Social Determinants of Health*, Geneva: World Health Organization.

Cook, G.P. (1986) 'Khayelitsha: Policy change or crisis response?' *Transactions of the Institute of British Geographers, New Series*, 11 (1): 57-66.

Diez Roux, Ana V. (2003) 'Residential environments and cardiovascular risk' *Journal of Urban Health*, 80 (4): 569-589.

Dixon, Jane, Abuid M. Omwega, Sharon Friel, Cate Burns Kelly Donati and Rachel Carlisle. (2007) 'The health equity dimensions of urban food systems', *Journal of Urban Health*, 84 (Supplement 1): 118-129.

Evans, Gary W. (2003) 'The built environment and mental health' *Journal of Urban Health*, 80 (4): 536-555.

Freund, Bill (2007) *The African City: A History*, Cambridge: Cambridge University Press.

Galea, Sandro and David Vlahov (2005) 'Urban health: Evidence, challenges, and directions', *Annual Review of Public Health*, 26: 341-65.

Gamble, Dorothy N. and Marie Weil (2010) *Community Practice Skills: Local to Global Perspectives*, New York: Columbia University Press.

Groenewald, Pam, Debbie Bradshaw, Johann Daniels, Richard Matzopoulos, David Bourne, David Blease, Nesbert Zinyakatira and Tracey Naledi (2008) *Cause of Death and Premature Mortality in Cape Town, 2001–2006: Key Findings*, Cape Town: South African Medical Research Council.

Groenewald, Pam, Debbie Bradshaw, Johann Daniels, Nesbert Zinyakatira, Richard Matzopoulos, David Bourne, Najma Shaikh abd Tracey Naledi (2010) 'Local-level mortality surveillance in resource-limited settings: A case study of Cape Town highlights disparities in health', *Bulletin of the World Health Organization*, 88: 444-51.

Hamilton, Richard P. (2010) 'The concept of health: Beyond normativism and naturalism' *Journal of Evaluation in Clinical Practice*, 16 (2): 323-329.

Harrison, Phillip (2006) 'On the edge of reason: Planning and urban futures in Africa', *Urban Studies*, 43 (2): 319-335.

Hofmann, Bjørn (2001) 'The technological invention of disease', *Medical Humanities*, 27 (1): 10-19.

Kuo, Frances E. (2003) 'The role of arboriculture in a healthy social ecology', *Journal of Arboriculture*, 29 (3): 148-155.

Landman Karina and Susan Liebermann (1999) Designing Safer Living Environments: Support for Local Government. Paper presented at 8th International Seminar on Environmental Criminology and Crime Analysis (ECCA), Pretoria, South Africa, 20-23 June 1999.

Mchiza, Zandile J., Julia H. Goedecke and Estelle V. Lambert (2011) 'Intra-familial and ethnic effects on attitudinal and perceptual body image: a cohort of South African mother–daughter dyads', *BMC Public Health*, 11: 433.

Mitchell, Richard and Frank Popham (2008) 'Effect of exposure to natural environment on health inequalities: an observational population study', *The Lancet*, 372: 1655-1660.

Moudon, Anne Vernez (ed.) (1987) *Public Streets for Public Use*, New York: Van Nostrand Reinhold.

Muzigaba M. and T. Puoane (2011) 'Perceived and actual cost of healthier foods versus their less healthy alternatives: A case study in a predominantly black urban township in South Africa', *East African Journal of Public Health*, 8 (4): 278-285.

Myers, Garth (2011) *African Cities: Alternative Visions of Urban Theory and Practice*, London: Zed Books.

Newman, Oscar (1986) *Defensible Space: Crime Prevention Through Urban Design*, New York: Macmillan.

New York City Department of Health and Mental Hygiene (2010) *Survey of Vital Statistics 2009*, New York.

Okpako, David T. (1999) 'Traditional African medicine: Theory and pharmacology explored', *Trends in Pharmacological Sciences*, 20 (12): 482-485.

Omonzejele, P.F. (2008) 'African concepts of health, disease, and treatment: An ethical inquiry', *Explore: the Journal of Science and Healing*, 4 (2): 120-126.

Peer N., K. Steyn, C. Lombard, E.V. Lambert, B. Vythilingum and N.S. Levitt (2012) 'Rising diabetes prevalence among urban-dwelling black South Africans', *PLoS One*, 7 (9):. e43336.

Karl Peltzer, Karl, Sharon Kleintjes, Brian Van Wyk, Elaine Thompson and Teresa-Ann Mashego (2008) 'Correlates of suicide risk among secondary school students in Cape Town', *Social Behavior and Personality*, 36 (4): 493-502.

Puoane, T., K. Steyn, D. Bradshaw, et al. (2002) 'Obesity in South Africa: The South African demographic and health survey', *Obesity Research*, 10 (10): 1038-1048.

Puoane, T., L. Tsolekile and N. Steyn (2010) 'Perceptions about body image and sizes among black African girls living in Cape Town' *Ethnicity and Disease*, 20: 29-34.

Robinson, Jennifer (2002) 'Global and world cities: a view from off the map' *International Journal of Urban and Regional Research*, 26 (3): 531-554.

Sarli, Leopoldo, Marta Scotti, Ketty Bulgarelli, Giuliana Masera, Emile Enongene and Annavittoria Sarli (2012) 'Concepts of health, disease, and treatment in a rural village of Senegal' *Journal of Medicine and the Person*, 10 (2): 68-76.

Seedat, S., C. Nyamai, F. Njenga, et al. (2004) 'Trauma exposure and post-traumatic stress symptoms in urban African schools', *British Journal of Psychiatry*, 184 (2): 169-175.

Simone, T. Abdoumaliq (1999) 'Thinking about African urban management in an era of globalisation', *African Sociological Review*, 3 (2): 69-98.

Simone, T. Abdoumaliq (2000) *On Informality and Considerations for Policy*, Dark Roast Occasional Paper Series No. 9. Cape Town: Isandla Institute.

Slater, David (2004) *Geopolitics and the Post-colonial: Rethinking North–South Relations*, Oxford: Blackwell.

Smit, Warren. (2004) 'The urban development imagination and *realpolitik*', *Development Update* 5 (1): 53-80.

Smit, Warren (2006) 'Understanding the complexities of informal settlements: insights from Cape Town', in Marie Huchzermeyer and Aly Karam (eds) *Informal Settlements: A Perpetual Challenge?* Cape Town: Juta.

Smit, Warren, Trevor Hancock, Jacob Kumaresen, Carlos Santos-Burgoa, Raúl Sánchez-Kobashi Meneses and Sharon Friel (2011) 'Towards a research and action agenda on urban planning/ design and health equity in cities in low and middle-income countries', *Journal of Urban Health*, 88 (5): 875-885.

Spiegel, Andrew, Vanessa Watson and Peter Wilkinson (1996) 'Domestic diversity and fluidity among some African households in Greater Cape Town', *Social Dynamics*, 21 (2): 7-30.

Turner, Alan (1980) *The Cities of the Poor: Settlement Planning in Developing Countries*, London: Croom Helm.

Turner, Victor (1969) *The Ritual Process: Structure and Anti-Structure*, New York: Aldine de Gruyter.

UN-Habitat (2010) *State of the World's Cities 2010/2011: Cities for All, Bridging the Urban Divide*, London: Earthscan.

Vlahov, David, Nicholas Freudenberg, Fernando Proietti, Danielle Ompad, Andrew Quinn, Vijay Nandi, Sandro Galea (2007) 'Urban as a determinant of health', *Journal of Urban Health*, 84 (1): i16-i26.

Vlahov, David and Sandro Galea (2002) 'Urbanization, urbanicity, and health', *Journal of Urban Health*, 79 (4, Supplement 1), S1-S12.

Watson, Vanessa (2003) 'Conflicting rationalities: implications for planning theory and ethics', *Planning Theory and Practice*, 4 (4): 395-408.

WHO (World Health Organization) (1948) *Constitution of the World Health Organization*, Geneva.

WHO (World Health Organization) (2006) *Constitution of the World Health Organization: Basic Documents*, (45th edition, supplement, October). Geneva.

10 Men of God & Gendered Knowledge

Akosua Adomako Ampofo
& Michael PK Okyerefo

Despite important strides brought about by legislation and civil-society advocacy, contemporary Ghanaian society remains unequal, and women continue to be largely confined to subordinate roles. In this chapter,[1] we examine the ways in which some of the key leaders within Ghana's Pentecostal and charismatic churches speak to this gendered context, and aim to assess whether they contribute to gender equality or inequality. We also consider whether their writings reveal evidence of a new and emerging African knowledge. We focus on Christian churches because, according to Ghana's 2010 population census, 71.2 per cent of the country's population profess their belief in the Christian faith. Christianity is also the dominant religion in all but one region. According to the census, more females (73.4 per cent) than males (68.8 per cent) consider themselves Christian (Ghana Statistical Services 2012: 6). The Pentecostal or Charismatic groups with their 6.9 million adherents form 28.3 per cent of the population (Ghana Statistical Services 2012: 40) and anecdotal evidence suggests that these denominations are the fastest growing and possibly most popular and influential, even among members of other denominations.

The (independent) Pentecostal and charismatic churches (PCC) should not be confused with what the literature refers to as African independent churches or African indigenous churches.[2] According to Birgit Meyer (2004: 447) 'the adjectives "African" and "independent" were once employed as markers of authentic, indigenous interpretations of Christianity', however, such descriptions prove 'increasingly

---

[1] Earlier versions of the chapter were presented at diverse forums in 2011, and we are grateful for the feedback we received from colleagues at these meetings. We are also grateful to Kyerewaa Brobbey for research assistance.

[2] Meyer also notes that the *World Christian Encyclopedia*'s confusion about the use of categories such as African independent churches and Pentecostal-charismatic churches shows how difficult it is to adequately capture the diversity of Christianity in Africa. However, for conceptual ease of distinguishing the older from the contemporary independent churches, we opted to use these terms.

problematic to capture the rise, spread, and phenomenal appeal of PCCs in Africa'. Where the African independent churches consciously sought to infuse both the liturgy and worship with African content and praxis, PCCs seem to seek a more global appeal, including building transnational congregations (Okyerefo 2008:78). Although they may frequently dissociate or at least distinguish themselves from both the mainline Christian denominations and the African independent churches, the PCCs are very important in that they do what the missionary churches of the nineteenth century did, namely: run missionary outreach programmes, feed the hungry, heal the sick, and provide education including, in some cases, building universities (Okyerefo 2011). In addition, these churches produce television and radio programmes, as well as video, audio and printed materials, which reach a wide audience, well beyond the congregations that attend Sunday services.

The men who lead these churches (and they are dominated by men) are deeply involved in the business of knowledge production that extends beyond the religious. They (re)produce concepts and theories that resonate with a large majority of Ghanaians, to the extent that they are becoming universally accepted and form part of a popular 'meta' knowledge. The knowledge they produce differs from that produced within the mainline churches in its emphasis on personal, temporal success and wellbeing, as well as on the need for global outreach. At the same time, while PCCs disassociate themselves from traditional (read 'heathen') roots of the African independent churches, they support the traditional notion of the 'big man' (or benevolent patriarch) who provides for and controls both the household and the community, distributes largesse, and is revered by all.

Since the structural adjustment years of the 1980s, the Ghanaian state has struggled to meet the needs of its citizens, and seems unable to provide a way out of material poverty and social exclusion. In addition, the middle-class's contribution to alternative intellectual models is weak. In this context, the teachings of these new churches are potent. As shown by Mbugua wa Mungai in Chapter 6 of this volume, the disconnection between states and citizens has forced many to question the bona fides of their governments, as well as the relevance of contemporary geopolitics and its associated knowledge systems. At the same time, Africa's intellectuals are accused of not effectively challenging and subverting dominant paradigms. Hountondji, for example, argues that African intellectuals have been too extraverted in speaking to audiences in the North and adopting Northern concepts, while neglecting the interests of their local audiences. Perhaps the failure of African states to meet the needs of their citizens, combined with the failure of intellectuals to decolonize intellectual life, and speak eloquently on behalf of citizens, has created the space for alternative (popular) discourses to emerge in societies where popular culture is powerful in shaping attitudes and opinions (Adomako Ampofo and Asiedu 2012).

Contemporary gender politics pushes both the state and civil society to create greater gender equality, such that women's status is not defined by domesticity. Historically, however, constructions of gender often meant that women had available to them diverse gender scripts that were complementary to men's, playing important social roles as mothers, sisters, wives, chiefs, queens and priestesses (Adomako Ampofo, forthcoming; Aidoo 1985). As early as 1949, however, scholars of Akan society – the most populous ethnic group in Ghana – noted a 'marked jural equality, a lack of basic sex discrimination in the roots of the kinship terminology' (Fortes 1949: 93), and the fact that men and women shared similar social commitments and responsibilities (Tufuor and Donkor 1969). Research done in the 1980s with coastal Ga and Fante traders noted women's financial autonomy and clout when it came to household decision making (Hagan 1983; Robertson 1986). Colonial rule upset this gender balance. On the one hand, it provided women with access to modern education and new opportunities for autonomy. On the other hand, individually focused social arrangements removed the protections and roles that had been central to the more communal arrangements of earlier times. Although women as a group had generally not enjoyed equal status with men in pre-colonial times, colonial rule removed the traditional structures that had allowed them some autonomy, such as independent access to resources and economic ventures, as well as the mutual dependence of the sexes based on an efficient division of labour. Under colonialism, new forms of subordination emerged, based on differential access to resources in the 'modern' economy (Bortei-Doku 1992; Boserup 1970, 1990; Robertson 1986). These shifts drew partly on the European Christian cultural values championed by the missionaries.

In contemporary times, PCC leaders pronounce on many issues, particularly marriage, in ways that have a profound impact on women's 'citizenship' in the church and on their positions within marriage. Yet, although it responds to the disenchantment people feel about governance, the state, and mainline Christian denominations, discourses within the PCCs may not necessarily emancipate women. While such discourses speak to some of the challenges of contemporary gender politics such as spousal abuse and parental neglect, they also hearken back to idyllic notions of Euro-domesticity that are inimical to women's autonomy.

The analysis that follows reflects our position as Christians, academics, and individuals committed to social justice. Michael, as a Catholic priest is a member of a fraternity that can pronounce on the expected character of marriage from a position of power, the pulpit. Akosua is an occasional lay preacher in her Baptist Church and in other Christian spaces. We are both all too aware that Ephesians 5:22, 'wives, submit onto your own husbands'[3] has been employed far too often, and mostly by those who conveniently skip over Ephesians 5:21, which reads 'Submit one to another', and Ephesians 5:25 which exhorts husbands to 'love your wives, even as Christ loved the church, and gave himself for it.' Consequently, the narrow interpretation of this periscope simply glosses over the core of the passage, which exhorts men and women to defer to each other out of mutual respect.

We also acknowledge that our own denominations are not without challenges in the area of gender. Well into the 21st century, the Catholic Church still does not ordain women priests. Baptist churches, under the Ghana Baptist Convention, have permitted the ordination of women since the early 2000s, but women ministers still cannot have congregations of their own. However, few individual Catholic priests or Baptist ministers hold the elevated and influential, local and even transnational positions that the leaders of many of Ghana's PCCs do.

In this chapter, we analyse the writings of three prominent contemporary Ghanaian PCC leaders. The selected leaders, or 'men of God' as they are frequently called, are Bishop Charles Agyin-Asare, Bishop Dag Heward-Mills and Pastor Eastwood Anaba. The popularity and influence of the leaders whom we have selected is arguably on a par with popular national and international icons such as the footballers, Samuel Eto'o, Didier Drogba, and Michael Essien, or popular musicians, such as Youssou N'Dour or Kojo Antwi. They were not selected through any particularly scientific process. However, each of them belongs to the Ghana Pentecostal Council,[4] each heads a large church, with international branches; each has either a television or a radio show (or both), as well as several books, pamphlets and audio or video tapes to his name.[5]

---

[3]   Unless otherwise noted, all scripture references are taken from the New International Version.
[4]   The Ghana Pentecostal Council is an umbrella body of Pentecostal and charismatic churches in Ghana, which, as of 2011, had a membership of 230 denominational churches and ministries (http://ghanapentecostalcouncil.org/ accessed 17 January 2011). Other major Christian groupings in Ghana include the Christian Council of Ghana, the Ghana Catholic Bishops' Conference and the National Association of Charismatic Churches.
[5]   Among other influential leaders not included is Pastor Mensa Otalbil of the International

Using the lens of 'masculinity' we examine their writings as a form of gendered African knowledge, with implications for gender equality in Ghana. While much of what the 'men of God' say is not revolutionary, who is saying it, and how it is being said means that the words take on new forms, and give the discourse an elevated prominence. Lindsay and Miescher define masculinity as 'a cluster of norms, values, and behavioral patterns expressing explicit and implicit expectations of how men should act and represent themselves to others' (2003: 4). Some refer to this as hegemonic, ruling or dominant masculinity (Adomako Ampofo 1999; Lindsay and Miescher 2003; Ouzgane and Morrell 2005; Ratele 2008).

After describing the 'men of God' and their audiences in a little more detail, we review the published discourse of the three church leaders under the following themes: the nature of woman; women and sexuality; and marriage and gender roles. The publications we reviewed are: *Daughter You Can Make It* (2008), a 144-page book of 33 chapters by Dag Heward-Mills targeted at women in the church, which, according to the blurb on the back, will 'heal the hurts of the daughters', and *The Strange Woman* (2006), also by Heward-Mills; Charles Agyin-Asare's *Celebrating Marriage: How to be Friends and Passionate Lovers* (2005, co-authored with his wife Vivian)[6] and Charles Agyin-Asare's, *Till Death Do Us Part: Handling Marriage, Divorce & Remarriage* (2006), which are pamphlet-type booklets, divided into short, easy-to-read chapters; and finally, Eastwood Anaba's *Time of Love: The Marriage Covenant* (2010), which was printed in the UK, and is a more standard-format, glossy book.

(Re)creating popular knowledge (and who is listening?)

Yemisi Ogbe, a Christian woman and a former PCC member in Nigeria, explains why these 'men of God' touch a nerve for 'ordinary citizens'. In a pamphlet titled 'Men of God as Superstars' she notes, 'for as long as superstar men of God can promise us the ability to master our environment, live well, marry well, afford good health, then they would have satisfied all the parameters for our belief in them'(2005:

[contd] Central Gospel Church. However, he does not pay a great deal of attention to gender issues in his writings. Another prominent pastor is Sam Korankye Ankah whose writings we have not, for reasons of space, been able to include. Others we might have included did not have books we could find that speak to gender issues, even though their sermons are replete with the theme woman and/or wife.

6   Although a co-authored book, the chapters are written separately and we focus on those written by Charles Agyin-Asare.

25).[7] A nation of hungry people, neglected, used, and abused by both politicians and the educated middle class alike, find succour in the discourse of church leaders who promise victory and prosperity in this life. This 'popular discourse', a form of popular culture, deals with mundane, everyday issues, in a basic language that almost anyone can understand. Perhaps the gender discourse used by these leaders also promises to restore the self esteem of Ghanaian men in these uncertain economic times, when many husbands and fathers feel unable to meet the rigorous expectations of being an *opinyin* (a wise elder and a generous provider) (Miescher 2003).

Although Christianity is not monolithic and emancipatory visions should and sometimes do emanate from it, when these men of God turn to the Bible for inspiration, they may also draw on colonial and pre-colonial patriarchal legacies to shape their messages and produce ways of seeing the world. Therefore, we explore whether their 'big man' image and their privileged roles in Ghana's patriarchy, are reflected in the knowledge that emerges. Given the popularity of the PCCs as social and cultural sites, their church teachings are probably among the more popular, accessible and influential forms of popular culture in Ghana.

The trajectory of Ghana's independent churches

Missionaries sowed the seeds of Christianity on African soil south of the Sahara in the 19th century. Their messages invariably reflected their own social environments and prescribed values that were often discordant with those of their intended flock. In other words, the mission societies exported their own (European) cultural Christianity. However, although vestiges of those early messages remain, enculturation or indigenization has been so effective that Christianity in Africa must now be read as an African religion, rather than merely a European import.

Christianity is a powerful force in the global South. As Philip Jenkins notes, the 'centre of gravity in the Christian world has shifted inexorably southward, to Africa, and Latin America ...[where] the largest Christian communities on the planet are to be found' (2007: 1). In particular, pentecostalism and charismatic Christianity, have attracted huge support (Martin 2006). African churches are growing both locally and internationally, and while their followings in the

---

[7] Ogbe is a well-known Nigerian journalist and blogger. Her article was in a magazine we picked up on the streets of Accra, which appears to have been published in Nigeria. The title of the magazine and Yemsi's article are the same, and the only publication detail on the magazine is the date, 'October 2005'. We have a copy of the magazine in our possession.

industrialized North may not yet appear significant, they do, in terms of popular discourse, factor into people's beliefs, practices and behaviour in new and interesting ways that remain underexplored. The growth of African independent churches and 'independent' strands within the mainline churches has been phenomenal. According to the Christian Council of Ghana's website, the number of evangelical and Pentecostal-charismatic Christians in Ghana was estimated at 5.7 million people (30 per cent) of all Ghanaian Christians in 2000 (World Council of Churches). If that proportion remained valid, this figure had probably risen to about 7.4 million by 2010.

The growth of religious groups may be related to poverty, and to the fact that organized religion of the PCC variant promises that members' earthly or material needs will be met. However, this can serve as only a partial explanation because such churches are patronized by the wealthy and the middle classes as well. The communal relatedness that these churches provide, conceptions of past and present, of the living and dead (ancestors), of temporal and other-worldly rewards and retributions, as well as their articulation of the desire for a return to a more righteous society, are all at play in the growth of PCCs, and hence in the new knowledge and understandings that they create.

> The PCCs have at least two features that distinguish them from African independent churches, namely their link to transnational circuits and, for many, the emphasis on social and material prosperity. (Meyer 2004: 453)

What is distinctly new about PCCs is their propagation of the Prosperity Gospel and their strong global inclination. Their names, which often refer to the church's aspired 'international' or 'global' (out)reach, highlight PCCs' aim to develop and maintain international branches in other African countries and the West, and to deploy notions of identity and belonging that deliberately reach beyond Africa.

The PCCs meet the temporal (social and economic), as well as the spiritual needs of Ghanaians, both in the diaspora and at home, in ways that neither the traditional mainstream churches, nor the state has been able to do (Okyerefo 2008). The messages they convey are down to earth, and resonate with language that shows they are attuned to people's daily realities – unlike the policy prescriptions and polemics of existing statist or market discourses. Contrary to critiques, such as that offered by Gifford, which argue that PCCs are 'resolutely opposed' to socio-economic development, Okyerefo (2011: 205) has argued that through 'the provision of social amenities, two Ghanaian Pentecostal churches – Lighthouse Chapel International and Royalhouse Chapel International – do encourage their religious community to engage public culture in Ghana in ways that defy a simple compartmentalization of religion and socio-economic development'. In addition, the PCCs provide a legitimate body of discourses in which cultural meanings for 'appropriate' gender relations are located.

As shown, the men of God have a significant influence on Ghanaians and others, and they have the potential to contribute to gender equality. We now examine whether their writings provide an opportunity to reinscribe or 'modify conventional understandings of men and masculinities by offering different images, different roles and different options for men' (Ouzgane and Morrell 2005: 10-11). We suggest that these men invoke a particular strand of masculinity that, while protective of women, also emphasizes the limitations and inequalities of women relative to men, and especially to their husbands.

On the nature of women

Writing with his wife, Charles Agyin-Asare explains God's rationale for creating males and females. 'If all we have were "macho men" there would be no "music" to the rhythm of the world. The world would have been drab with everybody having muscular features, manly faces, not much emotion and not many smiles', 'while if the world had been filled with women', he argues, 'there would have been confusion, jealousy, gossip and *you can imagine what it would have looked like*' (2005: 4, emphasis added). Thus, early in the first chapter of their book on marriage, this husband and wife team establish the physical attributes of men, and juxtapose these, not against woman's weaker physical frame, but against the negative stereotypes of women – their penchant for creating confusion, and their supposed tendencies towards jealousy and gossip.

Agyin-Asare (2006: 46-47) believes women should be protected and provided for because they are weaker vessels in terms of physical strength, and they are less able to separate emotion from logic. In his view, a woman is a life-giver, a nurturer, tender and more durable. The image of women he presents is complex, highlighting both their weakness relative to men but also their unique and vital life-giving and caring capacities. While women's strength is praised, this representation does not contest or destabilize conventional understandings of womanhood; that is, it draws on both modern and traditional discourses without creating an emancipatory path for women. Similarly, Eastwood Anaba (2010: 70-84) also believes women constitute a weaker vessel which must be loved and protected. He argues that although women are not inferior to men, their source and 'head' is the man.

Dag Heward-Mills claims that Jesus distinguished between women and daughters when referring to females. He says women are embittered by life's experiences, and are 'hardened, unforgiving and unmerciful' (Heward-Mills 2008a: 3). Daughters, on the other hand, are 'receptive', 'more open and humble', 'sweet and innocent' (2008a: 5). He argues that although females are created in 'beauty and glory' (2008a: 31), many are 'ruled by emotions'. They are associated with 'quarrels and instability' (2008a: 45). Although they are, without exception, cursed by the original sin that affected Eve (and Adam), and they are thus considered second-class citizens, there is 'promotion and betterment' (that is, 'power and wisdom') for those that are of God (2008a: 44). According to Heward-Mills, when a person becomes a Christian, the curse associated with childbirth and labour (the enmity between women and Satan) still exists: 'Christ did not come to release us from the curse of Adam, he redeemed us from the curse of the law' (2008a: 82). Thus, he argues that 'the main thing that defines the spiritual state of women is the curse that took place in the Garden of Eden' (2008a: 71), and that this leads to women seeking their own bondage. For this reason, according to Heward-Mills, women do not fight for independence from men but rather fight to 'come under the domination of a husband' (through the curse of desire) (2008a: 47, 88). Yet, he adds a spiritual note: a woman's purpose is to please God, and she must realize this if she is to overcome the curse of desire for her husband.

Other aspects of women that should be worthy of note, according to Heward-Mills, are that women are susceptible to deception, weak, and have more problems than men because they are specially targeted by evil spirits. Ultimately, his view appears to be that women are thus almost naturally consumed by three main goals: finding husbands, ensuring successful and peaceful marriages, and bearing and raising children (2008a: 68).

Women and sexuality

Are women sources of temptation to men, creatures to be viewed with caution, whose bodies need to be policed and restrained? Do women have the potential to destroy men with their sexuality? Is women's physical beauty the source of men's downfall? Should women conceal themselves to save men from lust, sin and destruction? Is the (naked) body itself a source of temptation and evil? These questions speak to

the controversies that surround some of the values that were brought
to Africa by European missionaries, and they are rife in the books we
reviewed.

Heward-Mills, for example, admonishes women to cover themselves
decently with appropriate clothing so as not to promote immorality and
licentiousness (2008a: 34). 'Strange women' he says, are particularly
to be feared as they deliberately entice men to have sexual relations with
them, and thus bring down many mighty men of God. Some women, he
notes, 'specialize in sleeping with pastors', and he narrates the fearful
story of a pastor who spoke of a lady who had slept with all the pastors
in town (Heward-Mills 1997: 29). In the light of this, in his *Ministerial
Ethics*, Heward-Mills cautions male ministers to keep their doors open
or be in the company of other ministers when executing their duties
towards women, and to resist the temptation to touch women, especially
on their buttocks and or chests (2008b: 36-37).

In a more progressive vein, Heward-Mills advocates that a woman
should not always be judged in terms of physical beauty but, above
all, in the light of her other gifts. 'It is not all about physical beauty,
it is about the tenderness in the eyes. God endows every woman with
beauty or with tender eyes' (Heward-Mills 2008a: 95). By 'tender eyes',
he explains that he means a 'friendly disposition', the 'gift of cooking
and home-making', 'enchanting sexual energy', 'financial input to the
marriage', and an 'exciting sanguine personality' (2008a: 96). He also
warns women not to believe that sex can keep men attached to them
(2008a: 21). Nonetheless, he does also contend that physical beauty,
while it does not last forever, is a good thing.

In another progressive moment, Heward-Mills goes on to argue that
women are *more* than their physical bodies, and says that that the real
reason for daughters being on earth is not to find a husband, or bring
forth children, but to serve God and do His will. Thus, Heward-Mills
appreciates women's fears around not getting married, or not having
children, but he dispels this fear as out of place. Women are more than
wives and mothers, he says, and their fear of not accomplishing these
roles is a limitation imposed by the devil that can lead them to fall prey
to temptations, such as marrying unbelievers, trusting in their beauty,
and having sex with many men before marriage.

Marriage: till death us do part?

Christian doctrine sees marriage as a central pillar of societies, and
much of the discourse from contemporary church platforms in Ghana

concerns marriage, including its breakdown.[8] The pre-colonial practice of polygyny is still widespread in Ghana, but Christian denominations discourage it, and men who are known to have more than one wife are rarely given leadership positions in their churches.

The following basic beliefs on marriage are found in all the books we reviewed: marriage was instituted by God; marriages, especially those of church leaders, are under (satanic) attack; and the best foundation for a solid marriage is the word of God. In this discourse, the authors accord different responsibilities to women and men for the welfare of marriages, and they also differentially apportion blame for failed marriages. Some of this discourse on marriage could be considered liberating for women as it calls on men to shoulder their responsibilities in ways that are very much in line with traditional notions of being an esteemed elder, or *opanyin*. Men are called upon to court and love their wives, to provide for them and their children, and to lead their families spiritually, physically and socially. Irresponsible husbands and fathers are chastised and exhorted to return to the path of true leadership. For example, Agyin-Asare holds that the onus is on the man to make the marriage work and proposes that the woman be relieved of much of the burden of securing her family's livelihood. Anaba, too, relieves women of undue responsibility for making a marriage work; this contrasts strongly with the frequent exhortations given to young women at traditional marriage ceremonies. Yet, at the same time, all three church leaders remind women that the man is the head of the family. Anaba holds that the 'woman is to be in subjection to the man and call him lord and the man is to give honour to his wife.' Further, he points out that those 'women groups who think the days of women submitting to their husbands are over' are wrong (2010: 187). Agyin-Asare demands that marriage be headed by the man in all aspects, but makes some room for mutual respect. He exhorts wives to understand that the husband must stand 'in a place of spiritual authority for your home' (2006: 17).[9]

This discourse on 'headship' cannot be separated from the concept of the spiritual protection, or 'covering', that women require. Heward-Mills notes, 'Women need a covering for their lives' (2008a: 9) to serve as a shield of protection. He goes on: '...unfortunately, there are many women who do not acknowledge this reality. *They see themselves as equal to men and as good as anyone else*' (2008a: 9; emphasis added).

---

[8]   Our visits to Christian bookshops in Accra revealed that books on marriage were highly popular, as were books on Christian leadership and inspirational texts.

[9]   This resonates with the ideas of the US-based Promise Keepers, who advocate for a new, empowered, 'real' man who is sensitive to his spouse but also 'in charge' (see Donovan 1998).

He explains that 'this covering is provided sometimes by husbands, pastors or spiritual fathers', and that a woman ministering without this covering is 'out of place' (2008a: 9). Thus, in his eyes, a woman clearly cannot function without a man. Anaba also stresses that a husband is a woman's 'cover', providing physical defence, spiritual protection and emotional fortitude, just as 'Jerusalem was clothed with broidered work' by God (2010:141) in a way that symbolizes the marriage relationship.

While Agyin-Asare acknowledges that a woman's consent is needed for marriage, he argues that once she gets married, she must abide by her husband's decisions. When it comes to a husband's unfaithfulness or abuse, Agyin-Asare seems to advocate tolerance, advising women in such situations to recognize that 'you are not the first woman to be beaten by your husband, and you will not be the last ... Rise up with the Word of God and use your spiritual weapons ... keep going to church, listen to tapes, pray, notice the blessings around you, keep your vows' (2005: 35). A woman's desire for her husband is not wrong, however, referring to Genesis 3:16, he writes: 'A woman's desire for a husband has been made into a curse because it was part of the woman's punishment for disobeying' (2005: 35).

Agyin-Asare (2005) argues that women must understand what marriage can and cannot do for them, echoing Heward-Mills's perspective that a woman can be single and be happy because her main purpose is to accomplish God's will rather than to get married. There are many exhortations and promises to women in the Agyin-Asares's book, including: women should not tire of their marital duties; a marriageable woman must be homely, involve herself in practical housework, be respectful and have good manners (in order to merit the title 'virtuous'); she must be hospitable (2005: 32-33), providing sex for her husband; if necessary she must (re)gain her husband's attention; prevent her husband from falling into sin; and preserve the marriage (2005: 105-108). The Agyin-Asares provide direct prescriptions including: 'submit to your husband. Humble yourself, obey his instructions, do not oppose him publicly, do not disgrace him' (2005: 128-129). Ultimately, they identify two options for married women: 1) that they humble themselves, obey instructions and preserve their marriages or, 2) stand up for their rights, refuse to be bullied, and lose their marriages thereby losing their 'God-given position' (2005: 128).

Like Promise Keepers in the United States, the men of God aim to provide women with responsible, caring husbands, but in so doing, they also reinforce the gender hierarchy, re-inscribing domesticity and asymmetrical relations between men and women.

Conclusions: which way forward for Ghanaian wo/men?

The three men of God that we have quoted in this chapter have (re)created and (re)packaged a powerful popular discourse. They reflect a version of masculinity that has the potential to protect women to the extent that it calls on men to eschew violence, to commit to companionship and monogamy, and to take seriously their responsibilities as husbands and fathers. All three men advocate the liberation of women as God's own creation. Here their discourse resonates with the calls of Ghanaian 'gender advocates' whose professional and civic commitments push for gender equality. At the same time, they invoke a particular brand of masculinity that emphasizes the limitations and inequalities of women relative to men, and especially their own husbands. Contradictorily, they persist in advocating the notion that women should be subject to men, thereby perpetuating gender inequality.

Traditionally, although wives were expected to see their husbands as lords, they were not limited in quite the same ways, since they simultaneously retained allegiances and responsibilities to their lineages, allegiances which could trump marital obligations. Further, in earlier times, women were subject mainly to their husbands but not to all men. Indeed, being seen to be subject to another man (such as today, a 'man of God'), could cause a woman to be suspected of adultery.

Contemporary PCC discourse is, in our view, fraught with mixed messages of liberation and subjugation, woven into a context-specific interpretation of gender that could possibly be described as a 'new' (or repackaged) conservative gender ideology. We must stress, however, the differences of emphasis among the three men whose writings we have analysed. Anaba subscribes to an 'equal but different' status for women, emphasizing their roles as people with spiritual gifts. Meanwhile Heward-Mills and Agyin-Asare underscore the hierarchical relationship between men and women, noting the 'inherent nature' of women that makes them more susceptible to deception, and thus they are in need of the leading and controlling hand of men (husbands, as well as pastors or spiritual leaders). It seems to us that the writings analysed suggest that women are not equal to men, even though scripture states clearly that both are created in the image of God – and surely God cannot have an unequal, hence schizophrenic, status. There seems to be a conflation of the different (but perhaps equal) roles that may have pertained in 'traditional' societies, with an unequal spiritual hierarchy. If a woman is subordinate in marriage and requires a 'covering', this begs the question of the status of single adult women, be they unmarried, widowed or divorced. It also begs the question of women's own responsibilities for their individual spiritual giftedness.

So, while the knowledge provided by the men of God may *seem* new and liberating to women and men who are yearning for greater conjugal togetherness (relative to traditional norms of lineage allegiance), the discourse provides little creative autonomy for women. It constructs men and masculinity as powerful and superior, albeit 'respectful' and 'responsible', with a contradictory positioning of femininity as subordinate, yet also having a degree of agency and choice. This view departs markedly from African feminists' conceptions of biblical femininity (Oduyoye 2000).

Read together as a meta-text, the framework provided by these three men of God is helpful in understanding gender relations in Ghana, as men struggle to be the *opanyin* in difficult economic times. Ghanaians' love for this image of men in society and the privileged role that it allows men to occupy in the country's patriarchy means that the knowledge that emerges is not emancipatory or egalitarian, even as it resonates with the concerns and value systems of Ghana's general populace. This form of gendered knowledge differs from other forms of popular knowledge in Ghana in that men of God, like those discussed in this chapter, are seldom interrogated by their followers. This distinguishes them from, for example, politicians, intellectuals or even icons of popular culture, such as sportsmen and women or those in the entertainment industry, who are all subjected to closer scrutiny.

References

Adomako Ampofo, Akosua (forthcoming) 'An introduction to gender in Africa' in Manuh, Takyiwaa and Esi Sutherland-Addy, eds, *Africa in Contemporary Perspective*, Accra: Sub-Saharan Publishers.

Adomako Ampofo, Akosua (2006) 'Intimate bargains: Sex workers and "free women" negotiate their sexual space', in Christine Oppong, Yaa PA Oppong and Irene Odotei, eds, *Sex and Gender in an Era of AIDS: Ghana at the Turn of the Millennium*, Accra: Sub-Saharan Publishers.

Adomako Ampofo, Akosua (1999) 'Resource contributions, gender orientation, and reproductive decision making in Ghana: The case of urban couples', *Research Review*, 15 (2): 93-125.

Adomako Ampofo, Akosua and Awo Asiedu (2012) 'Changing representations of women in Ghanaian popular music: Marrying research and advocacy', *Current Sociology*, 60 (2): 258-279.

Adomako Ampofo, Akosua, Michael P.K. Okyerefo and Michael Pervarah (2009) 'Phallic competence: Fatherhood and the making of men in Ghana', *Culture, Society & Masculinities*, 1(1): 59-78.

Adomako Ampofo, Akosua and John Boateng (2009) 'Socialisation of children in Ghana: Parents' teaching methods', *Research Review* 19 (Special issue on Knowledge Transmission in Ghana), 243-261.

Agyin-Asare Charles and Vivian Agyin-Asare (2005) *Celebrating Marriage: How to be Friends and Passionate Lovers*, (Vol. 2). Accra: Advocate Publishing.

Agyin-Asare, Charles (2006) *Till Death Do Us Part: Handling Marriage, Divorce & Remarriage*, (Vol. 3), n.p.

Aidoo, Agnes Akosua (1985) 'Women in the history and culture of Ghana', *Research Review*, NS 1 (1): 14-51.

Anaba, Eastwood (2010) *Time of Love: The Marriage Covenant*. Dunstable: Polestar.

Bortei-Doku, Ellen (1992) 'Theoretical directions in gender relations and the status of women in Africa' in Takyiwaa Manuh and Akosua Adomako, eds, *Gender Analysis Workshop Report*, Proceedings of the Gender Analysis Workshop, Institute of African Studies, University of Ghana, 14-16 July 1992.

Boserup, Ester (1970) *Women's Role in Economic Development*, London: George Allen & Unwin.

Donovan, Brian (1998) 'Political consequences of private authority: Promise keepers and the transformation of hegemonic masculinity' *Theory and Society*, 27 (6): 817-843.

Fortes, Meyer (1949) *The Web of Kinship Among the Tallensi*, London: Routledge.

Ghana Statistical Services (2012) *2010 Population and Housing Census: Summary Report of Final Results*, http://www.census-ghana.net/index.html. Accessed online 26 March 2013.

Gifford, Paul (1991) 'Christian fundamentalism and development', *Review of African Political Economy*, 18 (52): 9-20.

Hagan, George (1983) 'Marriage, divorce and polygyny in Winneba', in Christine Oppong, ed., *Female and Male in West Africa*, London: George Allen & Unwin.

Heward-Mills, Dag (2008a) *Daughter You Can Make It*, Wellington: Lux Verbi.

Heward-Mills, Dag (2008b) *Ministerial Ethics*, Wellington: Lux Verbi.

Heward-Mills, Dag (1997/2006) *The Strange Woman*, Accra: Parchment House.

Hountondji, Paulin J (2002) *The Struggle for Meaning: Reflections on Philosophy, Culture and Democracy in Africa*, Athens OH: Ohio University Press.

Jenkins, Philip (2007) *The Next Christendom: The Coming of Global Christianity*, Oxford: Oxford University Press.

Lindsay, Lisa and Stephan Miescher (2003) *Men and Masculinities in Modern Africa*, Portsmouth NH: Heinemann.

Martin, David (2006) *Pentecostalism: The World Their Parish*, Oxford: Blackwell Publishing.

Meyer, Birgit (2004) 'Christianity in Africa: From African independent to Pentecostal-Charismatic churches', *Annual Review of Anthropology*, 33: 447-474.

Miescher, Stephan F (2003) '(Re)making men in colonial Africa: The making of Presbyterian teachers, masculinities and programs of education in colonial Ghana' in Lisa A. Lindsay and Stephan F. Miescher, eds, *Men and Masculinities in Modern Africa*, Portsmouth NH: Heinemann.

Oduyoye, Mercy Amba (2000) *Daughters of Anowa*, Maryknoll: Orbis.

Okyerefo, Michael Perry Kweku (2011) 'The gospel of public image in Ghana', in Harri Englund, ed., *Christianity and Public Culture in Africa*, Ohio: Ohio University Press.

Okyerefo, Michael Perry Kweku (2008) '*Ausländer*! Pentecostalism as social capital network for Ghanaians in Vienna', *Ghana Studies*, 11, 77-103.

Ouzgane, Lahoucine and Robert Morrell, eds (2005) *African Masculinities: Men in Africa from the Late Nineteenth Century to the Present*, New York: Palgrave Macmillan.

Ratele, Kopano (2008) 'Ruling masculinities in post-apartheid South Africa' in Andrea Cornwall, Sonia Correa and Susie Jolly, eds, *Development With a Body: Sexuality, Human Rights and Development*, London and New York: Zed.

Robertson, Claire (1986) 'Women's education and class formation in Africa, 1950–1980', in Claire Robertson and Iris Berger, eds, *Women and Class in Africa*, London: Africana.

Tufuor, J.W. and C.E. Donkor (1969) *Ashantis of Ghana: People with a Soul*, Accra: Anawuo Educational Publications.

World Council of Churches (n.d.) 'Ghana': http://www.oikoumene.org/gr/member-churches/regions/africa/ghana.html. Accessed online 17 January 2011.

11

Retrieving Traces of Knowledge-making while Editing a Book on Postgraduate Writing

Linda Cooper & Lucia Thesen

Writing is essential to the making of new knowledge as it enables the communication of research across configurations of time and space. However, writing may also close down possibilities of making new knowledge. In this chapter, we reflect on the production of a book on postgraduate writing that we co-edited (see Thesen and Cooper 2013). The book originated within a collaborative research project established at the University of Cape Town's Centre for Higher Education Development. The Centre's role is to enhance the quality of teaching and learning in the university, and to advance the theoretical and practical understanding of these processes. The research that led to the book arose out of a concern with how postgraduate students' research-writing voices are enabled or constrained by dominant academic writing practices. We became aware that the writing-related challenges encountered by research students were not solely a legacy of South Africa's apartheid past, or an 'African' phenomenon, but were part of a broader concern. The project was, therefore, widened to include colleagues from elsewhere in Africa, and from the United Kingdom, Australia and the United States. The two of us (both based at the time at the Centre for Higher Education Development, and with our respective backgrounds in language and academic writing practices, and in adult education) took the lead in conceptualizing the framework for a book that we hoped would involve a global dialogue around postgraduate writing and pedagogy.

In this chapter we write a meta-reflection on the knowledge-making processes involved in putting the book together. We focus on how we, and the contributors, developed a novel conceptual frame with a reworked notion of *risk* at its centre, in order to understand what is at stake in the interplay between the production and reception of research writing.

The book draws on a research and development project on the barriers that writing-based practices present to the successful completion of postgraduate research and, in particular, on the struggles that students experience to find a voice in the writing of their research. All the contributors shared a common starting point: a view that was critical of the technicist 'how to' approaches to research writing. This approach, explicitly or implicitly, drew on other established conceptual resources, amongst these, the notion of academic-literacy practices (Lillis and Scott 2007), the idea of 'voice' as the capacity for 'semiotic mobility' (Blommaert 2005), and the understanding that the world's dominant epistemologies are rooted in unequal global and local power relations (Frickler 2007). While the key focus was on writing, we shared a keen interest in the implications of writing practices for knowledge making.

A common theme emerged as salient across all the chapters in the book: that for many novice researchers – particularly those writing from the geopolitical periphery – writing involves a profound sense of loss or deletion of experience. This seemed to echo the historical knowledge-making relationship between metropole and periphery that Connell (2007) speaks of. She argues that a cycle of loss, or deletion of experience, is a central feature of writing and theorizing by social scientists and intellectuals in the South, operating as they do in a global academic terrain that is dominated by 'Northern theory'.

It was this problematic – that is, accounting for the deletions and silences in postgraduate student writing and trying to understand the consequences of what is lost in this process – that led us to search for new conceptual tools through an iterative dialogue between theory and practice. The notion of 'the postgraduate condition', a term coined to describe the postgraduate writer's state of uncertainty, paradox and contradiction, emerged out of a pedagogic experiment with writer circles, a safe space where postgraduate students could rehearse their ideas before taking them in writing to more threatening audiences. It was out of this pedagogic practice that the centrality of the concept of 'risk' emerged as a means of trying to understand what happens in the interplay between the production and reception of research texts. In order to place the notion of risk at the centre of a constellation of other critical concepts, we developed new indexes of meaning, whereby risk is seen less as a way of managing danger, and more as something that is potentially generative and productive.

The geopolitics of postgraduate research education

Our book originated in the South African context but aimed to address the rapid changes that have taken place in higher education worldwide (see Boud and Lee 2009; Enders 2004). These changes centre on the development of official policies and discourses on increasing participation and widening access to higher education. In the context of globalization and lifelong learning, these changes have led to a significant growth in the number of international students and an increasing number of adult learners.

The massification and diversification of the student body impacts on postgraduate research education in fundamental ways (Enders 2004). For example, greater numbers of postgraduates are researching and writing in languages other than their home language(s). In addition to the challenges involved in writing in a second, third or fourth language, as Gee (1990) argues, one is never just reading and writing: one is always reading or writing something – namely, particular kinds of texts, which emerge from particular socio-cultural and disciplinary contexts, and encode particular values and practices. The writing competencies that students develop at institutions on the periphery, as successful graduates or professionals, may not translate successfully to well-resourced universities in the global metropoles.

This recognition of the partiality of knowledge in 'Northern' research practices is not new (see, for example, Canagarajah 2002). Scheurich (1997) also argues that this skewing of knowledge results in an often unconscious and hidden 'epistemological racism' – an argument taken up by Cadman's (2003) notion of research as realized in 'divine discourse'. The constraints on what counts as a relevant area of study, the criteria by which a thesis is assessed, and the styles that have become conventional in the globalized university, are embedded in an intellectual worldview that 'does not re-cognise, and therefore cannot know, the limitations of its own taken-for-granted, almost sacred understandings of what constitutes "knowledge" and its expression in the English language' (Cadman 2003:1). Cadman and Scheurich are concerned about how these limitations work against 'indigenous' or minority' students in 'first-world' contexts – an irony in South Africa where 'indigenous' students are in the majority.

To account for the existence of this 'epistemological partiality', we turned to a number of critical concepts in the fields of research on academic writing and sociolinguistics.

Common theoretical starting points

As co-editors, we forged an intellectual coherence in the book; rather than imposing a common theoretical framework, we started, instead, with a set of common metaphors and methodological assumptions that offered the contributors a 'way in', such as the critical view of 'generic advice books'. These offer structure and a set of processes that effectively narrow the possibilities of what may be said and how. As noted by Kamler and Thomson (2006), these seemingly benign technical approaches perpetuate a restricted and deficit model of student competence.

We sought to locate our book, instead, in the emerging field of 'academic literacies' (Lea and Street 1998; Lillis and Scott 2007; and, in South Africa, Thesen and van Pletzen 2006). The plural use of the term 'literacies' (as opposed to the singular 'literacy') denotes an interest in locating writing in wider contexts, and within ideologically inscribed contestations. Writing is not seen as simply a matter of skills, or as neutral competencies that are transferable across contexts. This field draws on the interdisciplinary tradition of New Literacy Studies (Baynham and Prinsloo 2001; Gee 1990; Street 1995), which views the conventions and traditions of academic meaning-making as contested. The field is explicitly concerned with the power differentials inherent in any literacy-related encounter, and it views meaning-making as a site of struggle, where diversity and inequality, rather than deficit, are at stake. However, most of these writers work from the 'Anglo-centre' and 'almost nothing' is known about postgraduate research practices in the 'South' (Boud and Lee 2009).

It is true that mobility is increasingly a feature of postgraduate environments as students move between the workplace and professional degrees, or cross continents, national boundaries, disciplines and languages in pursuit of postgraduate opportunities. Despite this greater mobility, power differentials between different conventions and traditions of academic meaning-making prevent student writings and academic texts on the margins from travelling well. Their 'voices' are not easily recognized or heard in the high-stakes centres of academic writing and publishing. Blommaert defines voice as the capacity for uptake in 'centering institutions': 'the capacity for semiotic mobility' which is 'intrinsically creative, [but] is also oriented towards one or several centering institutions' (2005: 77), in which meanings are organized and ranked through gatekeeping operations.

When students seek recognition for their research writing within the global university, their capacity to achieve 'semiotic mobility' depends on the degree of resonance between their research writing and the 'official archive'. In Foucault's work, the term 'archive' is used in the singular, while Bowker (2010), following Derrida, suggests that there are two kinds of archives that are interdependent, and need to be understood holistically. One is the formal, technological archive, which tells how things should be. Like writing, this archive is necessarily sequential; it is a 'legally aware ("jussive") presentation of the past from the present definition of rationality'. The other, which he calls the trace archive, is about 'habits and customs and place'. This archive is performed through lived experience, and it is the 'place for transgression against laws and current official groupthink' (Bowker 2010: 213). He argues that we need both archives, and that we need to understand the complex interplay between the two, working simultaneously with the certainties of the formal archive, and with the lived, embodied flux of the experiential one.

If both sides of the dual archive are crucial to the extension of our collective knowledge, how can we prevent the systematic loss to our knowledge archive of certain categories of human experience? Contributors to the book, as postgraduate supervisors, writing advisors and journal editors, were concerned with the cost to knowledge of empty conformity in postgraduate writing, and of the silencing of voice that occurs as students take the line of least resistance in their writing. If postgraduate students and novice researchers are to benefit from, and contribute to, knowledge-making in meaningful ways – that is, begin to argue with an informed voice – we felt we needed to 'undo the delete command' in order to understand better what is silenced in student texts, and by what processes these losses occur. We also wished to bring the agency and emergent meanings of postgraduate students as text-makers to the surface, while understanding the constraints that inhibit these voices.

Up to this point, contributions to the book had drawn on established concepts in the literature, albeit from diverse sources. By reconfiguring the relationship between these previously isolated concepts, and putting them into conversation with one another, it was possible to show the existence of multiple academic literacies. Not all voices enjoy the same degree of semiotic mobility because of global power differentials and the resulting hegemony of northern academic knowledge-making practices. As a result, certain ideas and categories of human experience – potential sources of new knowledge – cannot find expression in 'divine discourse', and are relegated to the 'trace archive', thus appearing to be deleted or silenced.

Having achieved these insights, we realized that there remained certain gaps in the explanatory narrative. Our explanations remained at the 'macro' level of global politics of knowledge production. We needed to understand what happens at the more 'micro' level of postgraduate pedagogy, where students make strategic choices as to what to include or exclude as they craft their research writing. Through an iterative process of moving between theory and practice and back again, some new conceptual tools emerged to explain how student voices get silenced in postgraduate research writing. Key among these was a reworked notion of risk and embedded in this, was the idea of the 'postgraduate condition'.

New conceptual tools: extending the meaning of risk

Our interest in the notion of risk as a potential explanatory concept originated in writer circles. Many students who attended these circles made high-stakes geographical, professional, disciplinary or linguistic crossings, and their engagement in writer circles foregrounded the contradictions that permeated their existence. Based on our experience of running the circles, we coined the phrase: 'the postgraduate condition' to describe the state of being a research student as a predicament – a pervasive state in which one lives with contradictions over time (Chihota 2007). In the postgraduate condition, we are simultaneously makers of new knowledge yet slaves to the old, anglicized yet not English, creative yet held by generic conventions, independent yet in need of supervision, assertive yet humble. The multidisciplinary writer circles acted as 'pedagogic safe houses' (Canagarajah 1997) where peers could rehearse their postgraduate identities, and weigh up what they felt they could or could not say, before taking their ideas to audiences upstream – supervisors, journal editors and peers in their disciplines.

Intuitively, we felt that the processes observed in the writer circles could best be described as a weighing up of risk against possible failure and censure. The circles were spaces for exploring the flux of risk. Students weighed up whether it was worth persevering with a line of thought, an analysis, a term, a method, or a site for research, all of which they had to communicate about in writing. In the circles, students translated 'mother-tongue' idioms into English in a bid to express precise ideas, or they found ways to appear to comply with supervisor feedback while stubbornly preserving their research trajectories, or simply listened until they were ready to commit. Risk was encountered not only in the supervisory relationship. It was located in wider audiences in the past, present and future, and in a pervasive uncertainty about whether one was 'in, out or colonized' as Gee so sharply summarizes the literacy dilemmas facing 'non-mainstream' students (1990: 155).

We gradually extended the concept of risk, and it became a holding frame for the book. In developing the concept, we began to see it as representing the relationship between text production and uptake – as a tilting point between self and other. However, it was not good enough to approach risk intuitively. It is as much about socially shaped meaning and perception as it is about reality out there.

Locating risk in historical perspective

The concept of risk has changed its meaning over time. Commentators link early meanings of the word to mid-sixteenth-century maritime endeavour in Europe, where it signified the possibility of a natural disaster or an 'act of God', something beyond human control. The argument goes that the emergence of modernity offered the possibility of taming uncertainty, fate and chaos; the Enlightenment's emphasis on objective, rational scientific knowledge promised to harness people and institutions for progress and social order. Thus, a story emerges about how the current obsession with risk originated in the modernist 'myth of calculability' (Reddy, quoted in Lupton 1999: 7).

   The end of the twentieth century saw a number of influential publications that placed a different meaning of risk at the centre of Western experience. Sociologists Beck (1992) and Giddens (1991) argue that contemporary late-modern ways of being in the world (that is, in what both have called 'the risk society') are characterized by a 'colonisation of the future'. 'The notion of risk becomes central in a society which is taking leave of the past, of traditional ways of doing things, and which is opening itself up to a problematic future.' (Giddens 1991: 111). Beck and Giddens both argue that there has been an erosion of faith in the promise of science, and that risks have become more globalized, giving less play to difference. The anthropologist, Mary Douglas (1992), while identifying similar features, is more interested in risk as a Western strategy for dealing with danger and otherness, and in why some dangers, but not others, are identified as risks.

   A second wave of writing on risk as a critical concept in the social sciences identifies various theoretical strands in the risk literature. A 'realist' position (common in 'techno-scientific' literature) holds that risk points to existing threats and dangers, but it does not ask 'how risks are constructed as social facts' (Lupton 1999: 18). The weak-constructionist position sees objective threats as inevitably mediated by socio-cultural processes. A range of positions from the 'risk society' perspective of Giddens and Beck, to Douglas's cultural/symbolic perspective, asks how risk operates to establish boundaries between self and other. The strong-constructionist position is interested in governmentality, and draws on Foucault's work to argue that there are no risks in themselves; all are produced in and through historically, socially and politically contingent ways of seeing.

Pat Caplan, on the other hand, argues for a more agentic view. She notes that while risk mainly operates as a hegemonic tool to discipline and regulate, it also involves agency at all levels from personal relationships through to manoeuvring between layers of discourse. She argues strongly for work that will surface this agency, and for ethnographic tools that engage with the specificity of contextual meanings; tools that are interested in difference and inequality rather than universality, and that consider both global and local situatedness. In her contribution to the book edited by Caplan (2000), Vera-Sanso analyses health related risk-talk among women in low-income settlements in India. Vera-Sanso strongly critiques Beck's Eurocentric generalizations that concerns with health and environmental risk will not be experienced in the same way in the 'third world', because communities here are still 'scarcity societies'. Vera-Sanso shows how risk-talk is always political, and how women manipulate risk-talk to enlarge their own spheres of influence.

These first- and second-generation texts on risk refer almost exclusively to Anglophone traditions. Nevertheless, three ideas from this literature emerged as pertinent. The first is that the notion of risk is always socio-culturally salient, whether one sees it as socially produced or socially mediated. Second, there is a gap between those who define risk in order to manage people and institutions, and those who move through institutions in less expert positions, experiencing risk as a pressure upon their lives. And third, risk often implies its other – a danger or hazard that lurks on the other side of where one is now, that brings together the past and the future in a decision in the present. As Luhmann notes, risk always 'protects a precarious normality' (2002: xxvii).

'At risk' in higher education

Risk operates in particular ways in contemporary higher education, and has significant implications for the writing of research. Erica McWilliam (2009) draws on sociological traditions to explore how the 'cold' notion of risk increasingly permeates doctoral education in the First World. In a perceptive article on doctoral education in 'risky times', she notes how the idea of risk contributes to the fraught dimensions of what we earlier called the postgraduate condition, and argues that risk is 'the condition in which we perform doctoral education, rather than the problem to be solved' (McWilliam 2009: 198). She argues further that the prevailing cold climate of risk with its negative logic of risk management – of 'what can go wrong' – is given a positive spin through being yoked to a positive logic of performance, with its elusive 'goods' of quality and excellence. This creates a dilemma, a contradiction that adds another dimension to the postgraduate condition.

Two aspects of research that receive much attention, and that may be seen as 'risk objects', are plagiarism and ethics. Both can be read as symptoms of how an awareness of risk serves the 'forensic needs' of universities in the context of the globalization of higher education. While an acknowledgement of sources lies at the heart of any research endeavour, citations are also countable, and thus lend themselves perfectly to an audit culture. Promotions and research funding are increasingly based on citation counts. An impressive body of research also shows just how sensitive citation practices are to gatekeeping (Angelil-Carter 2000; Pennycook 1996). The more social movement there is in higher education, the more citations are being drawn into policing the boundaries. Similarly, both students and supervisors may experience the current concern with ethics as expressions of 'cold' climates of risk management, rather than 'warm' contexts for trial and error, flux and creativity.

A brief look at the notion of the 'at risk student' also tells us a lot about how the term 'risk' operates discursively in universities. The term is a recent arrival, and can be seen as an index of changes in higher education that are broadly referred to as 'widening access'. In South Africa, the term appeared only after higher education institutions were opened up to black students in the mid-1980s. There are two sides to this risk. The dominant one is of risk to the institution, as the chances of these students failing are greater than for 'mainstream' students. The hidden side, that receives much less attention, is the risk to the student who risks falling short, and having to return home a failure.

Exploring the productive side of risk

The act of writing involves decisions about which representations of the research world will prevail, and which meanings will be silenced. As book editors, we came to see how the notion of risk, and its relationship to agency among young researchers and writers, as well as among ourselves as teachers, could illuminate the often hidden dimensions of decision making in relation to writing. This involved exploring the productive side of risk.

Risk is unstable and volatile as it lies on the cusp between the production and reception of the written word. Thus, it always points in (at least) two directions, both backwards to the past and forwards to potential audiences and readers. Working with this notion of risk meant actively seeking out dilemmas and being interested in how they are lived in the writing of research. Studying risk therefore always calls for thick description. It can never simply be read off texts.

It can be a space for chance, emotion and play. In Bowker's terms, risk is a classical example of the space of interplay between the jussive and the trace archives, in which new voices will emerge, and ultimately where new knowledge can be produced. But new voices need to be heard and acknowledged. In contested spaces we need to understand the agency that informs the decisions writers and gatekeepers (ourselves included) make about what will go into texts, and what styles and languages best carry intended meanings.

In the final parts of this chapter, we ask: what were the contextual conditions that allowed this perspective on risk to emerge in our work?

Risk in/from the South: the question of 'place'

In her book on 'Southern theory', Raewyn Connell argues that, historically, 'Northern theory' has always been assumed to be generalizable to the whole of humanity. She poses the question: 'Can we have social theory that does not claim universality for a metropolitan point of view, does not read from only one direction, does not exclude the experience and social thought of most of humanity, and is not constructed *terra nullius?*' (2007: 47).

Our postgraduate literacies research project brought local, regional and international perspectives on postgraduate writing into conversation with one another, and sought to build new kinds of linkages between contributors from the geopolitical peripheries and the metropoles. Our aim was to enrich understandings of postgraduate literacy practices and pedagogy in ways that might also challenge the global politics of research and knowledge making. The making of the book, implicitly and, at times, explicitly, challenged the intellectual and historical division of labour, whereby social theory has been built on a one-way flow of information, and where the metropole has examined 'other' societies through an 'imperial gaze' (Connell 2007: 12); or as Comaroff and Comaroff put it, where the 'global South' is seen as 'that half of the world about which the "global North" spins theories' (2012: 113).

The emergence of risk as a key conceptual tool for framing the book was, in part at least, shaped by our location as postgraduate students and teachers in southern Africa. Yet the evolution of the book's conceptual frame was not simply 'about Africa'. The new theoretical insights that emerged concerning postgraduate writing have a deeper value because they do not read from one direction only, but have relevance across diverse contexts.

Connell's notion of terra nullius (the silence of the land) in 'grand theory' is an argument about the absence or irrelevance of the local, of place and material context, in 'northern theory'. She argues that the best contributions to knowledge arise when we put our established theories into active relationship with locally generated data. It is necessary, therefore, to make the question of place visible in our work while, at the same time, avoiding ethnic or geographical essentialism.

The question therefore is why we, as book editors based in the geopolitical south, and in South Africa in particular, were drawn to the potentially productive qualities of the notion of risk? Was it some aspect of our local context that made this possible? Africa, and South Africa especially, are widely acknowledged as zones of intense risk – life can be seen as 'cheap', and existence in contexts of extreme poverty, violence, war, and environmental degradation is precarious for many.

However, what is less widely acknowledged or written about is the productive role that risk has played in South Africa. Taking risks was not optional in the everyday experience of black South Africans under apartheid – restrictive laws had to be transgressed or subverted in order to ensure survival. Risk also played a crucial role in bringing about the end of apartheid, when large numbers of ordinary people defied the obvious dangers of imprisonment or even death to join trade unions and other organizations, to support underground political movements, and to participate in mass protest. These 'risky' struggles facilitated the emergence of new voices, new visions of what a future South Africa might look like, and new knowledge about how diverse communities might co-exist. These experiences of the productive and generative dimension of risk are, of course, not unique to South Africa; they are a part of the history of anti-colonial and anti-imperialist struggles elsewhere in Africa, Latin America and Asia, and are illustrated dramatically in the 'Arab Spring' – the wave of revolutions that have swept through North Africa and the Middle East since late 2010.

Today, in the second decade after the end of apartheid rule, South African society and its institutions remain unsettled and volatile. Higher education institutions are under constant pressure to undergo deeper transformation than has been thus far achieved. This opens up potential spaces where some students and their supervisors are exploring creative strategies to enable new voices to emerge in research writing. This may be more possible than in the more stable 'northern' institutions where quality-assurance regimes are more deeply entrenched. In this way, and in our local context, risk has played a more complex and contradictory role than simply to signal a potential danger or loss.

Conclusion: Towards a 'post-colonial archive'

Helen Verran calls for the development of a 'postcolonial archive' – a future, ideal kind of knowledge archive 'in that it routinely celebrates the trace archive and attends explicitly to foregounding the tension between the trace archive and the jussive archive' (2010: 9). The reconceptualization of risk as a potentially productive force allows us to imagine ways in which the interplay between the 'official' and 'trace' archives of knowledge might be enhanced in academic writing, and thus contribute to the development of such a 'postcolonial archive'. In this way, our book on postgraduate writing can be seen as making a contribution to an 'African knowledge project' in the sense of a project that takes into account the 'situatedness' of knowledge making, and which aims to generate intellectual resources that are meaningful, not only in Africa, but across diverse contexts.

References

Angelil-Carter, Shelley (2000) *Stolen Language? Plagiarism in Writing*, Harlow: Pearson.

Baynham, Mike and Mastin Prinsloo (2001) 'New directions in literacy research: Policy, pedagogy, practice', *Language and Education*, 15 (2–3), 83-91.

Beck, Ulrich (1992) *Risk Society: Towards a New Modernity*, London: Sage.

Blommaert, Jan (2005) *Discourse: A Critical Introduction*, Cambridge: Cambridge University Press.

Boud, David and Alison Lee, eds (2009) *Changing Practices in Doctoral Education*, Abingdon: Routledge.

Bowker, Geoff (2010) 'The archive', *Communication and Critical/Cultural Studies*, 7 (2): 212-214.

Cadman, Kate (2003) 'Divine discourse: Plagiarism, hybridity and epistemological racism' in S. May, M. Franken and R. Barnard, eds, *Refereed Proceedings of the First International Conference on Language, Education and Diversity*, Hamilton: University of Waikato Press.

Canagarajah, Suresh (1997) 'Safe houses in the contact zone: Coping strategies of African American students in the academy', *College Composition and Communication*, 48 (2): 173-196.

Canagarajah, Suresh (2002) *A Geopolitics of Academic Writing*, Pittsburgh PA: University of Pittsburgh Press.

Caplan, Pat, ed. (2000) 'Introduction' in *Risk Revisited*, London: Pluto Press.

Chihota, Mapfumo Clement (2007) '"The games people play": Taking on postgraduate identities in the context of writer circles', *Journal of Applied Linguistics*, 4 (1): 131-136.

Comaroff, Jean and John Comaroff (2012) 'Theory from the South: Or, how Euro-America is evolving toward Africa', *Anthropological Forum: A Journal of Social Anthropology and Comparative Sociology*, 22 (2): 113–131.

Connell, Raewyn (2007) *Southern Theory: The Global Dynamics of Knowledge in the Social Sciences*, Sydney: Allen and Unwin.

Douglas, Mary (1992) *Purity and Danger: An Analysis of the Concepts of Pollution and Taboo*, London: Routledge.

Enders, Jurgen (2004) 'Research training and careers in transition: A European perspective on the many faces of the PhD', *Studies in Continuing Education*, 26 (3): 419-429.

Frickler, Miranda (2007) *Epistemic Injustice: Power and the Ethics of Knowing*, Oxford: Oxford University Press.

Gee, James Paul (1990) *Social Linguistics and Literacies: Ideology in Discourses*, London: Falmer.

Giddens, Anthony (1991) *Modernity and Self-identity: Self and Society in the Late Modern Age*, Stanford CA: Stanford University Press.

Kamler, Barbara and Pat Thomson (2006) *Helping Doctoral Students Write: Pedagogies for Supervision*, Abingdon: Routledge.

Lea, Mary and Brian Street (1998) 'Student writing in higher education: An academic literacies approach', *Studies in Higher Education*, 23 (2): 157-172.

Lillis, Theresa and Mary Scott (2007) 'Defining academic literacies research: Issues of epistemology, ideology and strategy', *Journal of Applied Linguistics*, 4 (1): 5-32.

Luhmann, Niklas (2002) *Risk: A Sociological Theory*, New Jersey: Aldine Transaction.

Lupton, Deborah (1999) *Risk*, London: Routledge.

McWilliam, Erica (2009) 'Doctoral education in risky times' in David Boud and Alison Lee eds, *Changing Practices of Doctoral Education*, Abingdon: Routledge.

Pennycook, Alistair (1996) 'Borrowing other people's words: Ownership, memory and plagiarism', *TESOL Quarterly*, 30 (2):. 201-230.

Scheurich, James (1997) *Research Method in the Postmodern*, London: Routledge Farmer.

Street, Brian (1995) *Social Literacies: Critical Approaches to Literacy in Development, Ethnography and Education*, London and New York: Longman.

Thesen, Lucia and Linda Cooper, eds (2013) *Postgraduate Writing, Risk and the Making of New Knowledge*, Bristol: Multilingual Matters.

Thesen, Lucia and Ermien van Pletzen, (2006) *Academic Literacy and the Languages of Change*, London: Continuum.

Verran, Helen (2010) Everting the archive. Unpublished.

Vera-Sanso, Penny (2000) 'Risk-talk: The politics of risk and its representation' in Pat Caplan ed., *Risk Revisited*, London: Pluto.

12 Hunhuism (Personhood) & Academic Success in a Zimbabwean Secondary School

Leadus Madzima

Explanations of 'success' or 'failure' in education are often limited by the choice of indicator and by the frame of explanation. In this chapter, I broaden the explanation of academic success to include the Shona conception of *hunhuism* (personhood). Analysing the performance of Zimbabwean learners from this perspective shows how learners understand themselves and energize their academic performance, while at the same time suggesting new theoretical approaches to questions of academic identity.

Weak academic performance among black African learners from low socio-economic backgrounds is generally put down to poverty. These learners' parents lack appropriate cultural resources. They live within economically disadvantaged family cultures, and in disadvantaged neighbourhoods that doom them to failure (Bourdieu 1993). This focus on failure prevents us from reflecting on the experiences of learners who manage to overcome the endemic negative influences in their lives to achieve academically.[1]

I focus in this chapter on a secondary school in the poverty-stricken, high-density township of Mbare in Zimbabwe's capital city, Harare. Harare is located in Mashonaland Province, in the north of the country where most people speak chiShona. I am myself a chiShona speaker; I grew up in Mbare and taught for many years in various secondary schools in Harare. The subjects of this chapter are Ordinary Level (O Level) learners. At the time of the study, most of the learners were in their late teens. They are heirs to Zimbabwe's long colonial history, which has left them both landless and 'wealthless' (Zvobgo 1994). In recent years, poverty in Zimbabwe has escalated. The combined effects of economic structural-adjustment programmes, governmental mismanagement, drought, HIV and AIDS and, in 2005,

---

[1] By academic achievement in this context, I mean those who aspire, and then strive to consistently achieve C symbols or above, thus qualifying for entry to Advanced Level (A Level) classes.

191

the dehumanizing Murambatsvina (clear the filth) campaign of mass evictions and demolitions, which left over 700,000 people homeless, all contribute to the worsening circumstances (Bond and Manyanya 2002: 34-35; Human Rights Watch 2005: 19). Illness, hunger, unemployment, as well as shortages of housing, water and electricity, prevail (Raftopoulos and Sachikonye 2001).

Guidance teachers tend to explain poor school performance by referring to erratic school attendance and poor home circumstances (UNICEF 2003). Such conditions are acute for children, and especially for girls and orphans, whose caregivers often fail to raise the necessary school fees, or keep them at home to attend to sick family members or to carry out household chores (Government of Zimbabwe and UNICEF 2001; UNDP 2003; UNICEF 2001). And yet, some learners triumph over such adversities. My central question, therefore, is: what enables successful learners to develop strong identities and powerful senses of agency?

To begin to answer this question I draw on the work of Bourdieu (1993), Butler (1997) and Giddens (1984), who individually and collectively approach an explanation without providing a full answer. Their theories shed light on structure and agency, including learners' resources, such as learning strategies, knowledge, attitudes, beliefs, motivation and practices. Yet, in relation to the learners in this study, it was the addition of the indigenous concept of *hunhuism* that provided a compelling explanation for their success. *Hunhuism* is an African Shona philosophy that encapsulates the experience of the Shona people as they have evolved over the past 35,000 years, and

> which inspires, permeates, and radiates ... high mental and moral attributes ... regulating our well-planned social and political organisations ... It sets a premium on human relations ... in a world increasingly dominated by machines and with personal relationships becoming ever more mechanical ... Kindness, courtesy, consideration and friendliness in the relationship between people; a code of behaviour, an attitude to other people and life are embodied in *hunhu*. *Hunhuism* is something more than humanness deriving from the fact that one is a human being. (Samkange 1980: 34, 39)

Theories about school failure and identity

In the field of education, French sociologist Pierre Bourdieu stresses that class relations of power and privilege are reproduced through *habitus*. Bourdieu defines *habitus* as a set of 'laws that determine the tendency of structures to reproduce themselves by producing agents endowed with the system of predispositions which at most is capable of engendering practices adapted to the structures and thereby contributing to the reproduction of structures' (1993: 72). Among classes, these dispositions structure embodied agents to reproduce family 'cultural habits'. These habits then become cultural resources or capital that incline people to feel or behave in a certain way. For Bourdieu, culture is cumulated capital. Since the bourgeoisie and middle classes have cultural dominance – superior tastes, desires and material wealth – their agents are endowed with 'cultured *habitus*' capable of translating their cultural capital into other modes of competent practice. These modes include intellectual, linguistic, social and economic networking, in so far as this facilitates their appropriation of exclusive advantages in specific fields. Middle-class *habitus*, therefore, produces competent cultural styles, including academic prowess (1993: 257). Within patriarchal families, fathers represent and possess 'the power of society' in terms of superior intellectual competence. Thus, gendered patterns of socialization result in boys (rather than girls) taking mathematics and physical science at school, while their female counterparts tend to take subjects in the arts (Bourdieu and Passeron 1997: 6).

The strength of Bourdieu's framework is evident in qualitative studies that consistently show working-class learners reproducing incompetent identities while their middle-class contemporaries emerge as winners. Since the middle classes know and satisfy the rules of the intellectual game, they inherit social (Coleman); intellectual (Willis) and linguistic (Bernstein) capital. Thus learners' identity formation and academic social practices are packaged in predetermined class binaries, underpinned by the power dynamics of family background (privileged or marginalized, white or black, female or male). Ensuing quantitative studies in Zimbabwe by Mloyi, and internationally by Bernstein confirm similar patterns. Analytically, Bourdieu's concept of social practice shows how systems of power and privilege can, on the one hand, render competent participants more or less equal as they become agents who produce cultural subgroups and products of legitimate value and, on the other, position and reduce unsuccessful ones to 'misrecognition' and, eventually, powerlessness (Bourdieu 1993: 25, 81). Bourdieu's concern with inequality, and the reproduction of power, ignores the success of marginalized learners. He is not concerned with the emergence of resilient identities.

Anthony Giddens' (1984) theory of *structuration* resonates with Bourdieu's work, in that both argue that structural properties reproduce families and systems, but Giddens differs significantly in that, for him, all actors, including learners, are reflexive. This means that they are conscious of how they can reside outside the system, and have power to choose the nature of their agency, action, and subjectivity. In time and space, and through memory traces, they can dig deep down and, from their structures, recreate their own new values, rules, norms and outcomes external to, and different from, the original structures. Actors do not necessarily emerge in binaries of subject or object; but are a 'duality of structure or social practice' – both a means and an outcome of their actions (Giddens 1984, 25-29; Karspersen 2000). Since structuration is undergirded by concepts of multiplicity, human action is free floating. Social structures and systems can be both freeing and self-limiting. Although Willis's 'lads' finally opt for disruptive and anti-school action, resulting in academic failure, Giddens views their ontologies not as predetermined by social structures, systems and or family background. His structuration theory is pertinent in that learners are granted some control through their own agency, and it is here that it is possible to insert the concept of *hunhuism*.

Judith Butler's (1997) feminist *performative* theories have the potential to take this further. She explains how power relations between women and men, and masters and servants, are made in and through acts and practices of iteration and interpellation that shape and re-signify subjectivity and agency. Anticipating critiques of voluntarism, Butler cautions that particular tasks and actions cannot guarantee particular effects, but are open to reversal and recontextualization: 'what we are and what we might become ... the very question of what it is to be a woman, and how our femininity and sexuality are defined for us ... we begin to redefine them for ourselves' (Weedon, 1). Learners are able to recognize, choose, accept, negotiate, contest, or reject power and assigned roles from among a range of possibilities as they ask, 'What makes for a liveable life?' (Lloyd: 135).

While Bourdieu's agent is called into being by power and structures, and Giddens' agent can call structures and power into being, Butler's performative agency is 'derived from precisely the power it opposes' (1997: 17). Identity and agency do not rest on familial and patriarchal background; but are dynamically positioned within a field of cultural possibilities. Courses of action are open to us, and are not entirely constrained. Like Giddens' duality of action, performativity then embodies the complex hybrid ambivalence of a subject who can take a multiplicity of positions in time and space (Hetherington 1998). Performativity, as a concept, enables one to shift from describing and explaining the conditions under which successful learners understand who they are, to analysing the actual subject power positions they inhabit in their daily lives as they produce academic behaviour. Like the acceptance of prescribed positions and roles, 'a normative conception of gender can undo one's personhood, [thus] undermining the capacity to persevere in a liveable life' (Butler 1997: 136). A woman enacts or scripts her gender to convey a particular preferred meaning and identity in time and space. Bauman aptly summarizes the process of identity-making thus:

> Identity is revealed to us only as something to be invented rather than discovered; as a target of an effort, 'an objective'; something one still needs to build from scratch or to choose from alternative efforts and then to struggle for and then protect through yet more struggle – though for the struggle to be victorious, the truth of the precarious and forever incomplete status of identity needs to be, and tends to be suppressed and laboriously covered up. (2004: 15-16)

Identity is considered an objective or aim to be accomplished, rather than a predefined factor or status. The fulcrum of identity is, as Nietzsche (1996) put it, to become what you are. Who you are, your distinctiveness, your separateness as an individual, is paradoxically rooted in a fight for continuity and an endless search to become.

Butler's theory permits a more comprehensive frame within which to understand how learners can acquire power to construct positive identities capable of transcending socio-economic, political, cultural, ethnic, class and gender boundaries. Butler invests most of the strength of resilient identities in oppositional culture. In this chapter, I propose that resilience can also be moulded from indigenous African sources.

Bourdieu, Butler and Giddens collectively do not provide tools to explain how learners from low socio-economic backgrounds construct resilient identities. Although these theorists could not really have been expected to do otherwise, the conceptual frameworks that they offer fail to offer a full repertoire of rich *local* tools available to describe and explain how, where and why some learners constitute successful identities in schools and neighbourhoods in chronic economic difficulties. However, in many cases, African scholars tend to take their theories on board fully, without transforming them through the lens of local (in this case, Zimbabwean) contexts. If identity and agency can emerge from a particular *habitus* that is deeply rooted in one's cultural histories and traditions (Bourdieu) – referred to by Giddens (1991) as *structural properties*, and by Butler (1999) as *performative* typified acts – then the missing link is the integration of an African-centred knowledge; an indigenous African perspective on identity formation (Connell 2007; Ingold 2008). If this is the case, the central question is: from which African structural properties should we draw the resources – strategies, knowledge, attitudes, beliefs, motivation and practices – to construct successful identities, especially if, as in Zimbabwe, most systems and structures have fallen apart?

In this chapter, I have selected pertinent traditional Shona concepts, related to *hunhuism* and identity formation, to provide an answer to this question in a spirit of fashioning and working within an all-inclusive contextual framework. When employed to try to understand the targeted learners in Harare, these indigenous concepts enhance, extend and transform the precision of other interpretative tools. The underlying claim of this new and sensitive contextual framework is that African subjectivity and agency cannot be adequately conceptualized through Western universalist models alone.

Hunhuism: an Africa-centred approach

Hunhuism is derived from the Shona tradition of *hunhu* (family origins), which summarizes the essence of a highly developed social system (Samkange, 1980: 39). Traditional cultures and concepts of community, family and relationality based on *hunhuism* have evolved among urban Shona families, despite their no longer being embedded in structures of traditional rural, agricultural life. The theory that follows neither idealizes nor romanticizes *hunhu* as panacea for the academic woes of disadvantaged learners (Guyer 1981, 2007; Guyer and Peters 2008). Rather, it proposes that *hunhuism* serves as a resource that inspired a group of learners to strive for academic success.

Hunhuism as a belief system is profoundly shaped by stories of origin, and is centred on the existence of spirit-gods. The Shona Great Spirit, Mwari (God), is believed to create and shape a person's mind and *hunhu* (identity) (Samkange 1980). The premised positive, viable identity imitates Mwari's *hunhu* (which includes all that is good in the accepted culture, behavioural and value systems). So, *hunhu* encapsulates a person's totality and identity (Gelfand 1977, 1985, 1981; Mbigi 1995; Samkange 1980). *Munhu* (a person) is born into a *mhuri* (family) which, in turn, socializes or inculcates knowledge, attitudes, beliefs and practices to develop the person into a complete well-rounded being. *Hunhu* also consists of one's external identity as this is linked to one's origins via one's totem and clan name. From *munhu*'s rootedness in the *hunhu* of family structures and their continuity, identity formation among successful learners is both a relational and multiple dialectic process of being structured and self-structuring. The collective has high currency. Thus, learners predispose themselves to work in solidarity with their nuclear families, their extended families, as well as friends and other groups whose members reciprocate in building pools of communal resources from which communal selves select the necessary products to create their personal or individual identities. Identity formation is an integrative process, complementing all the dialectic modes identified by Bourdieu, Giddens and Butler. *Hunhuism*, as a belief system, alerts learners to opportunities for setting up positive community-based structures that help them to create successful identities.

Learners believe that they will receive Mwari's blessings since these are bestowed on both rich and poor. Blessings are prompted by hard work. This belief finds its complement in Afro-Pentecostal exhortations, which can work together to inspire the creation of virtuous, coherent subjectivities (Guyer 2007). In a post-colonial society, where economic, cultural and political powers form intertwined structures, making upward class mobility both complicated and virtually impossible for the lower economic classes, *hunhu* inspires humility, trust and hope. It enables self-transformation, allowing learners to reach beyond the low and limiting ceiling that poverty and hardship frequently imposes. Academic failure, or failure in any other sphere of life, signifies the absence of a strong coherent subjectivity. The person is believed to have been overtaken or possessed by some demonic spirit (Gelfand 1977; Mbigi 1995; Samkange 1980). The judgment often made about an unsuccessful student –*hapana zwemunhu* (there is no moral being there) – says it all, while successful ones are seen as *mhunhu chaiye* (a person of real substance) (Shoko 2007).

Regarding motivation and competition, *hunhu* goals revolve around the concept of collectivism and strong kinship or *mhuri* (Gelfand 1981: 7). The Shona work hard to preserve the lineages of both their immediate and their extended families (Gelfand 1981; Shoko 2007). The mark of *munhu chaiye* (a person of substance) is having the moral conscience and responsibility to share one's material wealth, social wisdom, personal knowledge and fame with both young and old in one's family, village and clan (Samkange 1980). African socialization stresses the communal educating the personal in a process described by O'Donnell as 'communal phenomenology' (2008: 58). Thus, *hunhu* agency is partly collective and partly individual – 'a man can only be a man through others' (Mbigi 1995: 2). This is demonstrated in the principle of reciprocity, respect, dignity and compassion referred to as the 'collective finger theory', whereby many believe that one works so that others can enjoy the fruits of one's labour. In other words, whatever one earns is understood to be for the collective good of the community.

From the specific values by which honourable identities are formed, successful learners are expected to orientate themselves to relevant codes of behaviour and attitudes. They strategically monitor these to fulfil day-to-day work schedules, building and maintaining values that provide them with membership of their immediate and extended families and preferred groups. Since rules and values are supposed to be practised and perfected at school, these values predispose successful learners towards producing the strategic conduct and discipline required when striving for academic excellence.

The nature of the problem – that is, of framing the unusual phenomena of disadvantaged yet still successful African learners using a *hunhu*-centred approach – demanded the deployment of nuanced ethnographic research methodologies. In my research, I used a multi-level, qualitative paradigm, with multiple data-collection methods, including diaries, vignettes, and opinions on topical issues generated and written by learners, field notes, and semi-structured interviews. I did not appropriate the research space, but shared it by treating learners not as poverty-stricken victims to be researched but rather as co-authors, to be respectfully regarded as capable of articulating their phenomenal lived circumstances, and of contributing to new knowledge. Critical dialogues and narratives (first-hand, individual perspectives on their chosen *hunhu* or their own theses on identity construction) guided me towards unearthing the themes that were defining and signalling the unexpected sources of their human capacity and academic agency. More critically, I was in a privileged position: I am a black African, born and bred in the high-density suburb of Mbare. Since my mother tongue is Shona, I offered respondents the option of speaking in either English or Shona, and thus avoided losing valuable data through misinterpretation.

The learners speak

In this section, I weave in some of the learners' own words, as they describe their aspirations and goals. All learners were conscious of, and identified with, their poverty, unlike the more middle-class learners described by Mloyi (1998) who had to completely forsake their African values and language and assimilate with dominant school values in order to achieve academically. Paradoxically, for the learners in Mbare it was their very poverty that propelled them to excel academically, in order to create better *vanhu* (persons) both for themselves and for their families.

Dzama: I think it's an advantage ... to be an orphan because, whenever I lose focus, the fact that I'm an orphan always brings me into the line. It's like when I'm here at school and I've friends, if I play too much, then I would remember: no! I'm an orphan, I've got a mission to accomplish. If ... I ... lose this opportunity, then that's the end of me. I was born into a poor background ... I don't accept the fact that people believe that poor people will always remain poor. That is the most important fact that I don't accept. I believe that being poor does not mean that you die poor. Being poor is not a fact that you are disadvantaged in the community. It's only the circumstances you were born in. But the make up in me does not make me poor. It was a condition that I was born in. So, as a poor person, as they regard me as, I make sure that I should do whatever way that will make me a better person in life. In this case, I've discovered the channel of academics as one of the sources of becoming someone in life – someone who can be recognised – someone who can inspire people.[2]

Although poverty in the material conditions of their families, relentlessly and doggedly pursued each of the learners in all discursive contexts, they perceived these contexts as unfixed. The learners could cross, straddle and leap over borders and boundaries, no matter whether these were conceptual, structural, cultural, spatial or temporal. Although their early storylines were interwoven with multiple layers relating to a lack of basic resources (such as finance, food, clothing, accommodation), as well as educational and emotional resources (such as parental and family love and support), theirs were not the entirely negative stereotypical identities of homeless, hungry, overworked, tired, and academically demotivated learners. With contradictory moods vacillating between triumphalism, grief and fear (Guyer 2007), poverty challenged and motivated the learners into becoming new meaning-making agents, full of dreams and desires to attain something different and better. Their new identities were products of their family, class and economic woes, woven together with the optimism of *hunhuism*. Their community identity assisted the becoming of the personal, individual, subjective self. Their personal and social identities do not and cannot exist independently of each other; there is an inter-connectedness. Learners' identities were fluid, always crossing boundaries in their processes of becoming *vanhu chaivo* (persons of substance).

Analytically, what the learners did was to use a Giddensian process to dig deep into their cultural tool-kits to further create and reveal a variety of other *hunhu* identities and survival strategies. A central resource was the *hunhu* notion of discipline – the African morality that defines a person of substance as *kuzvibata* (having control or hold over oneself). All the learners defined *hunhu* as steering them away from negative peer pressure and towards *loving* school, their families and healthy disciplined lifestyles, as well as being polite and subdued

[2]   All the interviews were conducted in Zimbabwe by the author between February and August 2008.

in speech and dress. *Hunhu* guided them to choose friends who were also interested in schoolwork so that both at home and at school, they worked hard and excelled. Although patriarchy, political repression and extreme discipline subjugated and imprisoned their social identities, all indicated that their creative agency was able to negotiate and transcend what could cripple them.

> Nakayi: I don't roam around ...when it's not lesson time, I don't run away from lessons; because the teacher is – he wants to beat me or something; I don't make noise! ... I don't shout when the teacher is inside the class ... I'm not a mischievous girl.
>
> I like myself because – I'm obedient. I obey the rules; I put myself under everyone ... I don't usually show off. Because I can't show off if I don't have anything.

The learners realized that through developing their private, academic selves, they could liberate and distance themselves from a crippling fate. All learners recognized that educational success was an anchor for a competent identity:

> Musha: If a person is educated ... they're able to understand and negotiate socially or economically and politically with ... the community which surrounds them.
>
> Fungayi (stutters): I see it that in our country right, right now: without education you go nowhere. So with my school work, I see this as my ...employment as I gear myself up for-for-for the next generation ... As I am the first born, I also have to take care of my young ones such as my young brother and my young sister.

All learners confessed that the self-making project was tough – it involved subjecting the self to demeaning circumstances and identities in order to create the resources and opportunities that enabled one to reach the desired goal. For several days Tunga, whose home had been demolished, and who was living on a street corner, attended school without food or water to drink and was unable to wash. He felt lucky if he found some discarded fruit in the schoolyard.

> Tunga: But I would just work the normal way and pursue my dream; that's why at the end some ... some people at home thought I would fail because the things were tough.

With a shortage of congenial home and school facilities, and where even the streets were contested territory between the homeless and the police, all the students realized that hard work was needed to create spaces for genuine academic self-authoring. They altered their mental frames, freed their mental spaces, or bracketed out contesting social identities to leave adequate spaces for academic becoming. Gomo and

Tunga disciplined themselves to set aside their immediate poverty and social problems to mentally focus on schoolwork. This phenomenon echoes what Guyer interprets as 'utopian tendencies' of creating 'ontologies of the present'; a 'craving for intelligibility' and 'rationality' (2007: 415, 416). That is, learners distance themselves from the incapacitating doom of the immediate past and the near future to focus on the distant horizon in the hope that it might be better. As Kunda, Gomo and Tunga explained:

> Kunda: At school, normally I don't think about the home problems. I'll just say, 'home is for the home and school is for the school'. So I'll have to concentrate ... at school, that's where there are many students ...that can help me to achieve. So that's the time I have – I've to utilize it well...

> Gomo (stutters): There is no need to c-c-concentrate about poverty; so the best way – I ignore it; consider as if nothing is happening, concentrate on my schoolwork. That's the only way you can go through those p-p-problems: because if you think of them! ...they will affect your school work – they will affect your life.

> Tunga: I separated from them because I know if I continue in my mind, carrying the circumstances at home, I know I would have failed – because I would lose concentration.

Even at home, the learners turned night into study time. Njere did not sleep until after midnight; Gomo slept while the family made a noise between eight and ten, and then woke up to study when the rest of the household went to sleep.

> Njere: I myself will give myself a lot of time to study – I doesn't sleep like a person who doesn't know what his mission is about. In the evening, I always try to sleep around twelve or one, whilst all the time I'll be studying. And I'll wake up at around five o'clock...I will do my revision so as to get my mind into the tune of learning before I go to school.

> Gomo (stutters): Because ... I just needed a home that would give me a small sp-space so that I can c-continue with my studies. In order to study in peace in the crowded, noisy little room of four square metres ...

> I changed my s-s-sleeping time-table; I could sleep somewhere between eight and ten; then wh-when they come to bed, I could s-start on m-m-my reading.

Njere found ways of fulfilling duties assigned at home but, made sure to make up for lost academic time.

> Njere: I'm part of the children of this family ... I take responsibilities of being a child in our home. I normally help my parents during jobs that are – that give us life for tomorrow. I do gardening; I also sell things ...there ... to the people. I also – as a

family also do a business of selling sweets – outside there at the corner ... And that partly helps us to overcome many challenges of paying those bills that I'm telling you about ... I just play a role of being a child – I'm under my father and my mother.

Any space was turned into a rare opportunity to study – reading while hawking on street corners and public markets, or while standing in long queues to buy domestic utilities that were in short supply. Tunga, whose family lived on the street corner because of Murambatsvina turned the school hall into a study-cum-bedroom:

> Tunga: We would sleep on the desks. Whereby the desks are small, we would bring three of them into one row and we just sleep on them...
>   We would bring a full attire! Whereby the head – the gloves, the hats, and the jerseys – so we managed to conquer against the coldness.

Perhaps the key (and the most innovative) strategy derived from *hunhuism* is what the learners called 'groupworks'. Following the Afrocentric 'collective finger theory' described earlier, they formed efficient, self-selected study groups, where they shared knowledge and resources. Kunda: 'If someone finds a textbook, we have got to share that textbook. These friends have different friends elsewhere, so they borrow some books ... read and share ideas.'

It was the typical Shona practice of *nhimbe/mushandirapamwe* (pooling resources/ exchanging knowledge, and doing extensive reading and study) that ensured academic excellence. These groupworks were like intellectual safety nets, as explained by Dzama and Kunda:

> Dzama: When I borrow a book, I read ... I make sure that I understand ... I return the book, I make more friends – those with books will come to me and they'll want me to solve some problems in their own books ... And after solving the problem, then I'll say, 'Can you give me your book?' Because someone knows that I'm someone whom he might consult in the near future, I can easily get books.

> Kunda: Most of the time, we – me and my friends, just say, 'if someone finds a textbook, we have got to share that textbook.' These friends have different friends elsewhere, so they borrow some books – I go to Sunningdale – I will just search for the books. When we pool what we have found, we share ... the ideas. That's how we lead to success...

The strategy demonstrates how a multiplicity of academic products and knowledge were effectively created and traded between and within groups[3] so that learners ended up with a rich pool of intellectual wealth and resources:

---

[3] Groupworks were not limited to members of certain groups only; they worked at many levels. When not meeting, members could join or form other groups, thus enabling each learner to end up working in a crisscross of networks.

Nyika: Rugare is very good at geography, English and Shona; Shamiso is very good at Sciences – biology, physical science and mathematics. And then Siboniso and Ruzivo – they are very good at Arts subjects like Shona, history, geography; and then Soko is very good at accounts, maths and Shona. So everyone is very vital – in a group we combine and focus on the schoolwork, so the subjects in which we lack, the others help us so that we can put maximum to cover the gaps so that everyone in the group passes.

Faced with continuous teacher absence due to strikes, and chronic shortages of other educational resources, these successful learners creatively constructed groupworks as an ingenious study technology. No practice better demonstrates the height of academic agency than this self-motivated process of informally building and pooling resources, thus appropriating self-constructed and self-researched knowledge through self-directed learning.

Each learner performatively exhibited a range of educator roles, including teacher, mentor, researcher, examiner, marker, moderator, academic- and career-guidance counsellor, and educational psychologist. Furthermore, Gomo, and Musha recognized their own intellectual prowess:

Gomo (stutters): I was the the b-best student, most st-students wanted t-t-to r-read with me ... I was, eh, solving their problems, I also learned some other things; and they also contributed some other ideas that I didn't know.

Musha: As I told you...I have a good sense of humour; so that helps me in explaining to them. And from telling jokes, the person is able to understand while at the same time laughing. So, they will be understanding more.

In traditional Shona families, good results are seen as reinforcing strength. Similarly, each groupwork was built as a self-sufficient team, with the prerequisite academic skills to recreate in each individual the many academic identities that enabled them to excel intellectually (Kenway and Fahey 2009).

While teamwork was critical in the formation of the collective agency that ensured individual success, it is necessary to avoid the trap of homogenizing their identities. Typological approaches to theorizing – especially when related to indigenous concepts that have evolved – are inadequate and questionable, since such analysis overlooks the individual behavioural differences and processes of the protagonists. The tendency is to concentrate on social structures that test hypotheses instead of investigating individual patterns, or to try and fit the narratives into the theory instead of letting the narratives do the work without the theory imposing a totalizing effect (Guyer 2007; Guyer and Peters 2008).

Conclusion

The evidence presented in this chapter shows how recognizing the presence of an African resource (*hunhuism*) in the identities of learners, and understanding the epistemological implications of an ontology centred on *hunhuism*, can provide a richer understanding of the processes by which identities are formed.

The subjects are vulnerable but, in their agency, they show the fundamental quality of working extraordinarily hard to overcome their circumstances. They demonstrate their capacity to think and work their way out of their challenges. It is this agency that this chapter emphasizes – an agency hemmed in by *habitus* and structure but, paradoxically, animated by these same forces as the learners rupture crippling pressures to achieve the freedom to survive.

Most importantly, advocacy of *hunhuism* is not to claim that it is 'superior to anything evolved elsewhere' (Samkange 1980: 10) or a superficial valorization of indigenous identities; it provides the '*conditions of our possibilities*' (Butler 1997: 14, emphasis in original). *Hunhu* concepts are not an ideology but have both global and universal implications. They have the power of hope and the regenerative force that the successful learners choose to embrace in order to survive as citizens of modernity. Hence, it was *hunhuism* that provided the model for identity and agency formation, and that provided structural resources and processes through which the learners achieved academic success.

References

Bauman, Zygmunt (2004) *Identity: Conversations with Benedetto*, Cambridge: Polity Press.
Bernstein, Basil (1981) 'Codes, modalities and the process of cultural reproduction: A model' *Language in Society*, 10 (3): 27-363.
Bond, Patrick and Simba Manyanya (2002) *Zimbabwe's Plunge: Exhausted Nationalism, Neoliberalism and the Search for Justice*, Pietermaritzburg: UKZN Press.
Bourdieu, Pierre (1993) *The Field of Cultural Production: Essays on Art and Literature*, London: Polity Press.
Bourdieu, Pierre and Passeron, Jean-Claude (1977) *Reproduction in Education, Society and Culture*, London: Sage.
Butler, Judith (1997) *The Psychic Life of Power: Theories in Subjection*, Stanford CA: Stanford University Press.
Butler, Judith (1999) *Performativity's Social Magic: A Critical Reader*, Oxford: Blackwell.
Coleman, James (1966) *Equality of Educational Opportunity*, Washington: Government Printing Office.
Connell, Raewyn (2007) *Globalising the Research Imagination*, London: Routledge.
Gelfand, Michael (1981) *Ukama: Reflections on Shona and Western Cultures in Zimbabwe*, Gweru: Mambo Press.
Gelfand Michael (1979) *Growing up in Shona Society*, Gweru: Mambo Press.

Gelfand, Michael (1977) *The Spiritual Beliefs of the Shona*, Gweru: Mambo Press.

Guyer, Jane (1981) 'Household and community in African studies', *African Studies Review*, 24 (2/3): 87-137.

Guyer, Jane (2007) 'Prophecy and the near future: Thoughts on macroeconomic, evangelical and punctuated time', *American Ethnologist*, 34 (3): 409-421.

Guyer, Jane and Pauline Peters (2008) 'Introduction' *Development and change*, 18 (2): 197-214.

Giddens, Anthony (1984) *The Constitution of Society: Outline of the Theory of Structuration*, Cambridge: Polity Press.

Giddens, Anthony (1991) *Modernity and Self-identity*, Oxford: Polity Press.

Government of Zimbabwe and UNICEF (2003) *Poverty Assessment Study 11: Orphans and Vulnerable Children*, Harare.

Hetherington, Kate (1998) *Expressions of Identity: Space, Performance, Politics*, London: Sage.

Human Rights Watch (2005) *'Clear the Filth': Mass Evictions and Demolitions in Zimbabwe*, Human Rights Watch Briefing Paper, 11 September, Paris.

Ingold, Tim (2008) 'Anthropology is not ethnography', *Proceedings of the British Academy*, 154: 69-92.

Karspersen, Lans (2000) *Antony Giddens: An Introduction to a Social Theorist*, Oxford: Blackwell.

Kenway, Jane and Johanna Fahey (2009). *Globalising the Research Imagination*, London: Routledge.

Lloyd, Moya (2007) *Judith Butler: From Norms to Politics*, Cambridge: Polity Press.

Mbigi, Lovemore (1995) *Ubuntu: The Spirit of African Transformation Management*, Johannesburg: Knowres.

Mloyi, Marvellous (1998) 'Identity formation and prospects: The case of Zimbabwe', *Journal of Comparative Family Studies*, 29 (2): 243-254.

Nietzshe, Friedrich Wilhelm (1996) *Beyond Good and Evil*, (trans. W. Kaufman). New York: Vintage.

O'Donnell, Carol (2008) 'Synthesis of research on the role of culture in learning among African American youth: The contributions of Asa G Hilliard III' *Review of Educational Research*, 78 (4):. 797.

Raftopoulos, Brian and Lloyd Sachikonye (2001) *Striking Back: The Labour Movement and the Post-colonial State in Zimbabwe 1980–2000*, Harare: Mazongororo Paper Convertors.

Samkange, Stanlake (1980) *Hunhuism or Ubuntuism*, Salisbury: Graham.

Shoko, Tabona (2007) *Karanga Indigenous Religion in Zimbabwe: Health and Well-being*, Aldershot: Ashgate.

UNDP (United Nations Development Programme), Poverty Reduction Forum and Institute of Development Studies (2003) 'Towards reducing vulnerability: The ultimate war for survival', in *Zimbabwe Human Development Report 2003: Redirecting our Responses to HIV and AIDS*, Harare.

UNICEF (2001) *A Situational Analysis of Orphans and Vulnerable Children in Zimbabwe: Background Papers*, New York.

Weedon, Chris (1987) *Feminist Practice and Poststructuralist Theory*, Oxford: Blackwell.

Willis, Paul (1977) *Learning to Labour: How Working-Class Kids Get Working-Class Jobs*, Farnborough: Saxon House.

Zvobgo, Rungano (1994) *Colonialism and Education in Zimbabwe*, Harare: SAPES Books.

Index